On Fire with Fergie

On Fire with Fergie

Me, My Dad and the Dons

Stuart Donald

hachette
SCOTLAND

First published in 2010 by
HACHETTE SCOTLAND, an imprint of
HACHETTE UK

1

Cataloguing in Publication Data is available from the British Library

ISBN 978 0 7553 1980 0

Typeset in Perpetua by Ellipsis Books Limited, Glasgow

Printed and bound in the UK by
CPI Mackays, Chatham ME5 8TD

Headline's policy is to use papers that are natural,
renewable and recyclable products and made from wood grown
in sustainable forests. The logging and manufacturing processes
are expected to conform to the environmental regulations
of the country of origin.

HACHETTE SCOTLAND
An Hachette UK Company
338 Euston Road
London NW1 3BH
www.hachettescotland.co.uk
www.hachette.co.uk

To the Chancellor

Contents

Acknowledgements

Firstly, I have to thank the longest suffering people in my world, my parents and my sister, for all the years of patience, understanding and unconditional love. God knows you've needed the first two in abundance!

Thanks to my fantastic wife, Catriona, for all the hours, days, months and years of discussion and debate, all the tireless editing and re-editing, and your ever-present willingness and ability to buck me up when it all seemed impossible. I think you might once have had to put up with me in a bad mood, or am I being harsh on myself? There is no way I'd have got there without you. Thanks a million babe.

I'd like also to say a massive thank you to my publisher at Hachette Scotland, Bob McDevitt, for giving me a chance in the first place way back in June 2008 and for generally being so supportive and enthusiastic about everything since. Thanks also to Wendy McCance and Rhea Halford for all your editorial advice and guidance.

A particular thanks to two of my Dad's friends, Bryan Cooney for your time and support with getting things off the ground and to Trevor Knights for all your help in the run up to launch.

Finally though, thanks to my fantastic Dad, who left us tragically in February 2009, for all the hours of fun, all the tickets and programmes, the pennants and scarves, but most of all, for all the memories.

Chapter 1

Allosaurus

Around 11.00 p.m. on Wednesday night, 27 October 1976, I lie motionless in bed, having just been woken up by an enormous, terrifying roar. My heart pounding, I instinctively stay as silent as possible to avoid any chance of alerting whatever had made it. As I lie, gulping in silence, I know it can only be one thing. The one thing I'd been worried about every night since the dinosaur poster went up: the allosaurus in the Jurassic section had come alive! I hear a short hissing noise, followed by a thud, causing the whole house to shudder. It's coming from the lounge downstairs. I feel a wave of relief coming over me that if it is the allosaurus at least it's not in my room. I dart a glance to the wall, and right enough, it is still there ... but what's downstairs? A robber! I gulp anxiously. Maybe the robber's hurting my dad! Ten minutes later, I finally pluck up the courage to get up, dash past the poster without looking at it, out into the landing and down the stairs ...

My continual bubbling is abruptly halted as I creep to the last step by another thunderous roar reverberating through the house ... At least now I know it is definitely coming from my dad. But I am still trembling with fear, so unusual, all these noises, all this charge and emotion ... I push the lounge door gently ... I peak round into the room; I see the back of my mum's sleepy head resting against the side wing of her armchair (fat lot of good she'd have been if there had been an allosaurus in my room). And there is my dad with his back to me, on his knees in front of the TV. His hair is all over the place (and there's a lot of it, this is 1976), his shirt is out and tie tossed on the couch opposite, he's clutching a half empty pint glass in his left hand. There's something on the TV, and the volume is up unusually loud. All of a sudden, another huge cry, his arms raised in the air, punching repeatedly machine like, his tousled hair flying left and right as he shakes his head, shouting, swearing again and again. Still confused by all this, I instinctively know by this point that whatever had happened was a good thing. Although by now all my fear has lapsed, just seeing this sort of happy anger makes me wary ... wary enough to keep my arrival in the lounge behind them a secret for the time being. Then, all of a sudden, Dad makes a single punch in the air, and men on the TV are doing the same thing back to him. When he turns to Mum, he notices me out of the corner of his eye, and runs over to sweep me up in the air for a huge hug – the only time my breaching of the bedtime curfew would be treated with such celebration. That moment was when it all really started.

Dad had just watched something remarkable. He'd just seen the highlights of a football match. He was a teacher and had returned from work that Wednesday night with some homework to correct. He'd have known the game was on the radio, but deliberately avoided it, giving the marking his full attention. So, when he eventually sat down in front of the TV, he watched the game unfold as if it was live. Judging by the noise he made, he seemed to think that he was actually there. And no wonder, this match saw Aberdeen, my dad's team, win the semi-final of the Scottish League Cup. We had reached the Final for the first time in over 20 years. Not only this, we had won by the unbelievable margin of 5-1.

After all the initial trauma, all it really meant to me at the time was a rare, late-night chance to bounce about the lounge in my pyjamas and to be a five-year-old. But that's not how I remember it now. This is my earliest memory of football and its ability to turn my gentle dad into a raging animal. But maybe I don't even remember that. Maybe the reason I think I remember it is because in the not too distant future it was going to have a similar effect on me too. Things were going to get a lot more animated than just a couple of roars in the lounge. Little did I know, by the time I was old enough to go to games, I would have already become a part of European football's most unlikely fairytale. I would be taken all over Scotland to watch our Aberdeen side transformed from provincial no-hopers into Scotland's dominant force and ultimately Europe's official number one team. This is our story as I saw it, growing up in Scotland as an Aberdeen supporter with my fantastic big pal, my dad, in a football dream world. It was to be the dream world that my dad had hoped for all his life, and so tonight there was more reason than ever to believe that the reality might start now. But there was one reason more than any other behind this belief.

My dad's shouts and roars that night were not just about a crushing 5-1 victory in a high profile semi-final. It was much, much more than that. The side we beat was none other than the almighty Glasgow Rangers. For as long as Dad could remember, Aberdeen, along with most of the rest of Scotland, had lived in the shadow of this crowd and their nemesis Glasgow Celtic – together, the all powerful, all conquering, Old Firm. This emphatic victory was as serious a defiance of Scottish football's ruling class, as my dad or anyone else had ever seen. That night, his emotional eruptions were about an outpouring, a release of years and years of frustration. That night, he was savouring a long awaited revenge, revenge he never expected to see taken so emphatically, so dramatically. But much more importantly, it meant hope. Greater hope than ever that now Aberdeen could mount the challenge against them that he'd so longed for.

But, before the new challenge would start, Dad had a date with some pals at the Grampian Hotel the following night. And he couldn't wait for that. Since they'd met two or three years ago, their occasional midweek sessions had been dominated by one theme, lamenting and bemoaning the scourge of the Old Firm. So they'd surely be as thrilled as Dad at what all this might mean for the Scottish game. But, much to his surprise and annoyance, instead of revelry, his evening of indulging the dreams and hopes he thought they all held, would be drowned in cold water.

Chapter 2

Dr Harry's Rant

Gordon closed the last of the dark blue A5 jotters, squared them into a neat pile and pushed them to the edge of his large oak desk, ready for tomorrow's second-year class to pick up. Marking homework was never the easiest thing to do due to the sheer repetitiveness of it all, but tonight it had been an enormous struggle, and he'd felt guilty about how often he seemed to lose his concentration. As he stood up, giving the room a final once over, he knew it was probably that extra beer he'd squeezed in last night that was behind the nagging sore head he'd had all day and his recurrent concentration lapses. But surely anyone would have done that, he thought to himself. We won 5-1 against Rangers, the team that won the Treble last year. Whoever beat the Old Firm sides by that scoreline nowadays? And to have it all unfold, sitting there, watching the highlights as if it was live. It was as close as he'd come to feeling like he was there again, at a game in Aberdeen. Like he'd been most Saturdays in his life before moving to Perth five years ago. But deep down, he knew there was more than just a hangover preying on his mind. By the time he got onto the A85 to drive home from Crieff, he'd faced up to the real issue. He was homesick. Again! On the way home, he was obsessing about it.

That was all it would take. Any reminder of the things they used to do when they lived in Aberdeen was enough,

like the dreams he'd held for Aberdeen FC all his life, victories over the Old Firm (and the 5-1 against Rangers was the
most sensational he could remember). That was it, he
decided. Not the hangover at all. It was the longing to go
home. He realised he must subconsciously think about it
every day, and right now it was full on. But it just didn't
make any sense. Everything was great now in Perth, he was
already a Principal Teacher at Crieff High at the age of 32,
Elaine was settled in her teaching job and the kids (Stuart
[that's me] and Lynne) were happy here too. He realised that
it must be the same for his pal, Derek, although it was not
the sort of thing that ever seemed to come up in conversation. But then again, maybe it was different for him, Derek
being from Falkirk, a Falkirk supporter. His home town was
much nearer to Perth than Aberdeen, half the distance. That
meant that he was able to go back to see his folks and his
team fairly frequently. That's what made being an Aberdonian
in Perth different, much like being an Englishman, or even
a continental European.

By the time he was approaching home, he'd got himself
together again. The fact that he had pals who were fellow
exiles, was a blessing in itself, even though he only ever saw
them occasionally and all they ever spoke about was football.
And the anticipation of what should be the best Grampian
Hotel session ever in the wake of the Rangers match, had
taken over his thoughts and had him feeling much better about
everything. It was going to be full on in all senses, and he
reckoned Derek and the other guys in the bar would be as
excited as he was at what it might mean for Aberdeen. He
parked the car in the driveway, went to the front door to
give my mum a kiss, and then set off on the walk down to
the Grampian Hotel. Ten minutes later as he pulled the door
open, he caught a glimpse of Derek through the crowded bar
room, taking off his jacket at a table by the back window.

Next to him was sitting Dr Harry Carter, a Hearts fan and a regular in the bar who Derek and Gordon both knew. Excellent.

'Here's the boy! Look at him! Look at him!' says a beaming Derek, rubbing his hands enthusiastically as Gordon takes his pew. Harry on the other hand says nothing, sat back in his chair, arms folded, deliberately blanking Gordon, looking out of the window to his left. Gordon immediately picked up that something might be afoot.

'What can I get ye Gordon to celebrate the start of a new era, bottle of champagne?' asks Derek, on his feet and already on his way to the bar.

'Oh, no, a pint of 80'll do, cheers.'

'Well, well, well, young man,' pronounces Harry, breaking his silence with his avuncular air. They had all met through the table tennis club they were members of. Dr Harry Carter (his title coming from his much trumpeted PhD in classics from St Andrews), was a lawyer working in Dundee. Gordon and Derek were teachers, Derek still in an assistant post at Perth Academy, unlike 'career man' Gordon who'd gone to take the role of Principal Teacher of Geography at Crieff High in August that year. Perth Academy was a much bigger concern than Crieff High and so to get ahead you were going to have to be patient. But when they met up, none of this mattered. Gordon believed that Harry and he had more in common than simply their mutual exile in Perth. They were united in the honourable struggle against the Old Firm in a different way from Derek, a Falkirk supporter (although his secondary sympathies were with Aberdeen), and supporters of other smaller teams. Harry and Gordon's teams were two of a handful of so-called 'bigger clubs' in the struggle against the Old Firm. Harry could be aloof and patronising and his stories could go on for hours but the flip side was that Harry brought special qualities to any football discussion that really appealed to him. Harry was the walking personification of that outrageous arrogance that Edinburgh people often possessed, an edge that the stand against the Old Firm really needed. And he truly was a monument to Heart of Midlothian FC, a season ticket holder since he was a teenager (so he said) and was, as he'd documented every single time they'd met, the personal friend of most of the great Hearts team of the 1950s – the last side to have mounted a proper challenge against the Old Firm. But little did Dad know that tonight, Aberdeen's sensational League Cup semi result was to bring out an altogether different side of Harry. Dad's inkling that something was afoot was spot on. And what was said, or more accurately what Gordon would learn, would resonate with him for years to come (not that he would ever admit it).

'Five-one? Against Rangers in a semi-final?' snorts Harry. 'You'll no be used to that!' Gordon immediately senses that there really is something up with Harry as he laughs it off, nodding in agreement. They sit in an awkward silence waiting for Derek to come back, and Gordon realises there's definitely something wrong. It can't be though? Could he be annoyed that Aberdeen had hammered Rangers? Gordon would be happy if it had been Hearts who had done that to Rangers, he certainly wouldn't be off about it.

'So, is this it?' asks the beaming Derek, arriving back at the table with three pints in a precarious triangular clutch that causes his whole frame to descend in slow motion in order to land them safely on the table. 'Is this the beginning, the smashing of the Old Firm, the provincial challenge we've all been waiting for?'

'How many times have I told you pair about that word?' mutters Harry, pulling them up as usual for using the 'provincial' label for even the most indirect reference to the capital city or its football clubs.

'With a result like that, you have to believe, don't ye? It's all doun to Ally MacLeod; we've never hid a manager like it. I reckon he can do it, I really do,' chirps Gordon. 'Ah mean, in all the years that I can mine, right back to 1956 when I started goin' to games, I dinna think I've ever seen a side that wis able to beat Rangers or Celtic like 'at. It's all aboot confidence, and MacLeod jist oozes it, ken?' Derek nods away. 'So why can we nae ging on and win the League Cup and maybe mair?' says Gordon shrugging his shoulders, opening the floor for debate and taking another long satisfied glug from his pint.

'Maybe the Treble!' adds Derek. 'And then who knows? Maybe in five to ten years you'll be running the show! I can just hear Davie Francy now, "And here at Hampden it's finished Aberdeen 3 Celtic 0, sealing a second Treble in three years for this remarkable Aberdeen side, surely now the undisputed, dominant force in the Scottish game!" he commentates, holding an imaginary mike to his mouth for his renowned Davie Francy impression.

'Or what about " ... Jarvie beats Greig, beats Jardine, beats Johnstone, crosses and the diving header from Scott almost bursts the net!" roars Gordon, with no attempt to sound like anyone other than himself as commentator. " ...That's it! That's it! Aberdeen 5 Rangers 0 at Pittodrie, what a way to retain the Scottish Premier League title for the fifth year on the trot!! What a way to ..."'

'Not a hope in hell!' scoffs Harry from behind his cigar. Taken aback by Harry's interruption, Gordon slowly drops his hands from his commentator and mic mime. There was no doubt about it now in Gordon's mind. Harry was in one of those moods.

'No one, or certainly no football team, can *dominate* the Old Firm,' asserts Harry. 'For that, you'll need some Prussian warlords or dictators and another world war ...' Harry takes another couple of long drags on his cigar, assessing whether Gordon and Derek have grasped the meaning of his departure into German history. They hadn't, he concluded from the two dumbfounded faces in front of him. '... In other words, the only things known to mankind to have successfully stopped Rangers and Celtic winning trophies over any period of time.'

'What's up with the old Jambo tonight?' asks Derek to Gordon. Gordon glances once towards Harry who he found staring back at him seriously. There could be only one thing behind this. Harry was envious.

'What's up?' barks Harry. 'Listen to all this shite I'm being subjected too.'

'What do you mean Harry?' asks Derek.

'Two Trebles in three years? Five league titles on the trot? Listen to yourselves, you're in cloud cuckoo land!' Gordon takes a weary sip of his pint before sighing deeply to himself in silence. Not only is Harry envious, but he's also turning this into one of his high and mighty lectures, this time on a subject that Gordon fancied he knew at least as much about as Harry. He is not going to get his own way on this, especially not tonight, Gordon vows to himself.

'"Domination", boys, is winning three-quarters of everything all the time. "Domination" is winning one, normally two trophies a year, every year, in an unbroken continuum going all the way back to the beginning of the twentieth century. That's "domination" for you.'

'What? One of the Old Firm has won a trophy every single year for 75 years?' asks Derek.

'At least one!'

'No way, min!' rebuffs Gordon, shaking his head. 'At canna be right Harry, not every single season?'

'Every single season bar two: 1952 Hibs won the league, Motherwell and Dundee won the cups, then 1955 Aberdeen won the league, Clyde and Hearts the cups. And that's discounting the eight seasons that were never contested during the First and Second World Wars ...' adds Harry. '... That's where your Prussians and fascists come in.'

Gordon knew that the Old Firm had won a large share of trophies, but three-quarters of everything since before the First World War! He and Derek stared at each other both desperately trying to come up with another year that disproved Harry's seemingly impossible statement.

'Two seasons, two measly seasons boys,' summarises Harry, with a couple of blasé puffs from his cigar, his eyes flitting furtively between the window and the faces of his two pals, revelling in the enlightenment he knew he was shedding on them, making Gordon even more determined to find a season that proved it all wrong.

'And you can forget any ideas about winning the league – no one gets close to doing that, not with Jock Stein in charge at Celtic nowadays,' asserts Harry. 'You boys need to get real and settle for challenging in the cups, beating the Old Firm in the one-off games. And even doing that is a minor miracle.' Harry's puffing reverts to a more moderate pace, sensing he's put a lid back on the explosion of enthusiasm that had got him so charged up in the first place.

'What d'you mean "a miracle" Harry?' asks Derek frowning, looking confused, Gordon still lost in a world of stats, staring out of the window.

'Cup finals are like home games for the Old Firm boys, you know that. There are always three times as many of their fans than there are of yours and there will be pockets of drunk and dangerous ones in your own end to boot. If it makes us Hearts fans feel like country bumpkins – and it does – then God knows what it's like for you lot – the real "provincials".' Harry raises his right index finger lazily from the table to waggle generally in the direction of Derek and Gordon. 'You've been there, you know you've lost the game before it even starts.'

'But hold on Harry, that's only cup finals against the Old Firm,' says Derek. 'A strong Hearts or Aberdeen side could surely dominate in the cups if they got a run against non-Old Firm opposition.' Derek looks smugly towards Gordon who nods back in endorsement of Derek's excellent point.

'Oh really Derek?' responds Harry. 'Let me ask you a different question. Which part of Hampden do you normally go to for Scotland games?'

'The Rangers end,' answers Derek. Harry raises his eyebrows towards Gordon as a prompt.

'Normally the Celtic end,' adds Gordon.

'Celtic end for me too,' confirms Harry. 'But what sort of names are these for parts of Hampden, our national stadium, our neutral venue for cup finals?' Derek and Gordon say nothing, still not clear where this is going. 'I mean why on earth would we, as Hearts, Aberdeen and Falkirk supporters expect to be subjected to the "Rangers end" or the "Celtic end" of anywhere?' Derek and Gordon nod, still not entirely clear on where this was going. 'It's a fucking disgrace!' underlines Harry.

'Yeah, I suppose it is,' agrees Derek, smiling, 'but what has this got to do with your point though Harry?' asks Derek.

'The point is, Hampden has a Rangers end and a Celtic end because, quite simply, on cup final day in Scotland, one of the bastards is always there! Every single season bar one since the war!'

'Go on then Harry,' groans Gordon, reluctantly joining the conversation having been unable to come up with any stats that challenged Harry's initial 'two seasons' claim.

'It was 1959: Aberdeen v St Mirren in the Cup, Hearts v Partick Thistle in the League Cup,' states Harry, making a meal of his effortless recall again, Gordon thought. 'And it's being there every year that gives them another massive advantage over the other teams.' Gordon looks away as if to pretend he doesn't need to hear this, but listens keenly from one ear, waiting for Harry to elaborate. 'As soon as the match starts, you immediately realise how familiar it is for them, how used they all are to cup finals. And then in turn, you see how intimidated your lads are, many of whom have never played there, never won or lost big-time cup final matches, shell-shocked, just like their fans, overpowered by the bellowing, thundering Old Firm hordes and the sense that you've turned up in their backyard. And no wonder, it *is* their fucking backyard!'

Harry stops for a second to down some of his pint, seeming to have drawn both Gordon and Derek into his sermon, both sitting back now, arms folded, listening obediently. 'So that's it boys. We can't compete in the league, we can barely compete in the cups, and what's even worse is that we'll never be able to compete with them on the terraces either, even if you could "dominate" for a season or two.'

'What on earth are you on about now?' asks an ever more confused looking Derek.

'Take the case of wee Barry Stephenson who joined the Table Tennis club two years ago. A nice lad, family all Perth people. He's been a Saints supporter all his days and then one day last year, he goes with his new hard mates that he's met in third year at school on the Rangers bus to a game in Dundee or Edinburgh or somewhere. And within a couple of weeks, wee Barry had kissed goodbye to Perth Saints, and is a regular on the Rangers bus that leaves from the St Leonards Bar every Saturday, where he meets dozens of other wee Perth Barries of various ages who've joined up when they were in the third and fourth year too, to go and join thousands of wee Barries from all across Scotland. Come on guys, you've been ranting about this going on in your own class-rooms every other time we've been out.'

Gordon and Derek exchanged a look of resignation. There was no denying this. But Gordon had a different view.

'All you are describing Harry is glory hunting,' asserts Gordon. 'There would be thoosans a' lads queuing up to come and watch a Hibs or a Hearts or a Dundee from all across Scotland if they could challenge the Old Firm for silverware. It's jist success Harry. It's no more complicated than that.'

'Oh yes it most certainly is Gordon,' objects Harry author-itatively. 'You are not trying to tell me that you think any of our supporters could ever create an atmosphere, a product, a buzz like them? You've got to be honest with yourself Gordon, wherever and whomever they play, the atmosphere their pres-ence creates is not of this earth.' Harry pauses, as Gordon frowns and tuts disapprovingly. 'It's true. No other club anywhere in Scotland or Britain or possibly even the world for that matter can offer anything like it. And it makes the wee Barries around Scotland feel like they're the hardest wee laddies on the planet, harder than they will ever feel anywhere else in their lives.'

'I don't think I've heard so much rubbish in all my life Harry,' spits Gordon, the gloves now well and truly off. 'In fact, I reckon it would be much easier than you think, there must be thousands of Old Firm "wee Barries" who're bored out of their nuts with how predictable it all is, who'd imme-diately be attracted to a new challenger, a Hearts, a Hibs, an Aberdeen.'

'That's not how it works though, is it Gordon?' asserts Harry pompously. 'No Celtic or Rangers fan ever gets bored. Can you not see that they are not competing with anyone else, only each other? All that matters is the intensity, the bitterness, the hatred of their own rivalry. That itself keeps them from getting bored with winning everything all the time. Every success one half has is something the other doesn't. It's what guarantees to attract them, and thousands and thousands and thousands of other new wee Barries, back every other week, month and year for cause and team, every time they play. I've tried all that reconversion stuff on any turncoats I came across at table tennis and anywhere else for that matter boys, you'll get nowhere.'

'Really?' asks Derek. Harry nods. 'I'd remind them of what the great Roman poet, Marcus Valerius, once said, "There is no glory in outstripping donkeys,"' says Harry, holding the left rim of his half-moon glasses as he did so and peering over the top of them intellectually, 'but I stopped all that years ago when I realised it was hopeless. The whole thing for them has nothing really to do with our "donkey" teams at all. It's all about them, and their Old Firm cause.'

'Weel, for us "donkeys", the Aberdeen ones at least, that's what makes the dream, the challenge, so much mair exciting. The sheer "impossibleness" of it all. This is oor cause, Harry, the ultimate cause surely for all other teams in Scotland. And we should never lose sight of that,' argues Gordon forcefully, prodding his finger into the table in support of his point.

'Come on Harry, that's right,' adds Derek. 'And right now, it's Aberdeen who happen to be leading the charge. No wonder Gordon is sitting here, bouncing off his seat, more bullish than ever, he's never had more reason to be.'

'You'll never do it.'

'Come on Harry, we'd be right behind Hibs or Hearts or Dundee too if they were ever to raise a challenge?'

'What do you mean "*were ever to raise a challenge*"?', says Harry, taking his glasses off, now exasperated by his pal's refusal to listen to sense. 'Look, can you not see that Hibs have just been those donkeys? Can you not see how ridiculous all this is?' he raves, holding his hands out for some reaction. 'Have you simply not noticed that Hibs have just come through one of the longest periods of "serious" challenge ever made against the Old Firm? And look what happened to them? Their best side for decades finishing second one year, third the following year, poor bastards thinking they'd a chance of the title maybe next year, or the year after, hoping, believing that they can break through, knowing they've a side that have the measure of Old Firm? And what do they have to show for it?' Harry paused again, waiting for a response. 'One League Cup.' Harry does a nod with each word. 'A single, shitey, pishy, League Cup. When people look back in years to come, this will be the only trace of their effort over the decade. And then they'll notice that Partick Thistle, Glasgow's joke team, won the same trophy the year before them. And what will they think then? A great challenge? Somehow I doubt it.'

'Och come on Harry, their challenge was more than just that though, they got to other cup finals as well, did they not?' asks Gordon.

'Yes they did. And that illustrates my point better than anything else: 1968/69 League Cup Final, Celtic 6 Hibs 2 … 1971/72 Scottish Cup Final, Celtic 6 Hibs 1 … 1974/75 League Cup Final, Celtic 6 Hibs 3 …'

'Sounds more like Connors v Borg!' remarks Derek. 'Or should I say Borg v Connors?' asks Derek, noting that if anyone would be billed as Bjorn Borg, it should be Jock Stein's Celtic.

'Indeed,' pronounced Harry emphatically, welcoming the fact that Derek now seemed finally on his wavelength. 'Never before had a donkey brayed so hopelessly, only to be punished so mercilessly,' summarises Harry. Gordon shakes his head and

stares at Harry for a second. Harry smirked back, still enjoying
no doubt his clever off-the-cuff turn-of-phrase that served to
rubbish his Edinburgh rivals to boot. This was certainly not
what Gordon had had in mind for tonight. Sometimes Harry
really pissed him off.

'Look, sorry to depress you all boys, but that's just the way
it is,' says Harry standing up and downing the remaining third
of his pint. 'Right you pair a' hopeless dreamers. I'm away
home,' he blurts from the corner of his mouth, placing his
empty pint glass firmly on the wooden table, picking up his
jacket and shuffling to the door.

'Nother pint?' says Derek after a couple of minutes.

'OK,' says Gordon eventually, still in the grips of Harry's
sermon. Eventually, Derek and he started chewing the fat, as
they had originally planned to do, over what lay ahead for
Aberdeen, the dreams of insurrection against the Old Firm,
ignoring Harry's prophecy of doom as they went along. And
well they might have that night.

Aberdeen did win the League Cup, beating Celtic 2-1,
but their form soon fizzled out. The league challenge became
non-existent by early spring 1977, and they were embar-
rassingly bundled out of the Scottish Cup in the third round
by First Division Dundee. Both league and Cup went to
Celtic in 1977 and, between them, the Old Firm sides won
everything else for the remaining seasons of the decade in
spite of an ever-stronger challenge from an improving
Aberdeen side. Just exactly as Harry would have predicted.
But my dad still was not having it. Dad believed that the
only reason Aberdeen had failed to capitalise on their promise
in the late 1970s was as a result of a series of scandals and
controversies that had happened during the 1977/78 season.
Events that had got to him so badly, that he'd been in a
long-term sulk with football ever since. A sulk that, much
to my frustration, was still going strong right up until a

Saturday in early December 1979, when we went to stay with June and Arthur, Mum and Dad's friends from school. Something happened that day that looked like bringing the sulking to an end.

Chapter 3

The Great Sulk

... *Penalty for Aberdeen* ... says the Radio Scotland commentator, in a gap in my parents' chat on our journey to Kirkcaldy.

'I'd forgotten everything aboot 'at!' nods Dad emphatically, in approval of Mum's surprisingly sharp recall of events at a party somewhere in Aberdeen in 1966, '... 'n June and I hid jist finished teacher training 'at day, and that's why she wis there 'at night and met Arthur ...'

'At's right, 'at's right!' says Dad, whose whole body now nodded in agreement with Mum, '... an' Arthur wis jist back from the merchant navy. Aifter 'at party, me'n Arthur almost got batter'd outside ... fit wis it ca'ed, 'at bar in Widside?' Dad pauses for a second ...

Strachan scores! Two-nil, and that should be Aberdeen in the Final!

Dad, still pausing, maybe with one ear on the game now that we were two up, maybe to say, to say that we'd go to the Final, eventually said, '... Miller's bar! A right dive!'

Of course, Miller's bar. For a split second when he said the word 'Miller' I believed he might be talking about Aberdeen's captain, Willie Miller. Why he'd have been speaking about Willie Miller just then was not clear, but at least it seemed linked in some sort of way to the fact that Aberdeen had just scored a second goal in their League Cup semi match against Morton. By the time we'd reached the edge of Kirkcaldy, they seemed to have revisited and redocumented literally every milestone in June and Arthur's 1960s lives, a sort of June and Arthur *This is your Life* they were rehearsing to deliver once we got there. At the age of seven, it meant nothing to me, but there was something warm about their mood, and their ever so slightly richer Doric, brought on by the onset of an Aberdeen nostalgia evening with their North-East exile peers. It was almost as if we were on one of our journeys home, to Aberdeen itself. I suppose we were in a way. But I had my own, completely different reasons to be excited about June and Arthur too.

It was all to do with their 11-year-old son, Gavin – one of my lifelong heroes. Firstly, Gavin acquired natural hero status on account of the fact that he was simply older than me. I could barely remember the last time we'd been in each other's company, but I knew that today, now that I was big, I'd do a much better job of impressing him. And it was not just his age that commanded respect, but he was already a bigger and more advanced version of what I intended to become in a couple of important ways. He was a figure Panini sticker collector. He'd radioed ahead the previous week via his mum to mine to ask me to bring my figure Panini sticker doubles with me today, since he'd only three to get to complete his album. Three stickers were all he needed? That was unbelievable. Had anyone ever got that close? Certainly not in Perth. I couldn't wait to see it. He was a Dons fan too but the difference was that his dad had started taking him to games. A dad, an Aberdeen supporting dad who, unlike mine, was not in a sulk with football. And then, just as we reach the waterfront of the Forth Estuary at Kirkcaldy, we suddenly happen upon a place that I hadn't even thought about for a year and a half. Its distinctive brown and orange triangular shaped facade brings a strange barrage of memories flooding through my mind. I could clearly picture the last time we'd been here. It was in the late morning of 6 May 1978, the day of the Scottish Cup

Final, and we'd all come here, to Dodge City – a 1970s Ikea precursor in Kirkcaldy – to buy a new shelving unit for the kitchen. It was the last day before Dad's sulk started.

I lock on to the parking space we used, where I'd stood and watched my unusually edgy dad lead us through a bizarre shopping escapade that must have lasted at least half an hour, but that seemed only to last five minutes as I remember it now. Park motor, secure shopping trolley, briefly road-test trolley for rickety wheels with short backwards and forwards action, enter shop with roadworthy trolley, quickly assess shop floor layout, march to relevant aisle, locate requisite item, secure unit of item, proceed to checkout, execute purchase, exit shop, home. It had been a military operation, fuelled entirely by my dad's strange angst. Even my mum, who would normally indulge in some tireless browsing, seemed to know not to do it that day. He was desperate to get back to Perth in time to watch the match on the TV, but there seemed to be even more to it than that. When we got back and sat down to take in the traditional Cup Final preamble, there was something else going on in his mind, he was in a strange mood, nervous, agitated. He kept flitting between the lounge and the kitchen, unable to decide whether he would watch the game with me, or build his new unit in the kitchen. By kick-off, he'd decided, he'd watch the game. When Derek Johnstone put Rangers 2-0 up, with a looping header shortly after half-time, he stormed out of the lounge in a rage, cursing and swearing. He'd seen enough and retired to a 'football free' part of the house to come to terms with the disappointment and build his new Dodge City shelving unit. After the final whistle, I took the final score through to him, Rangers 2 Aberdeen 1. 'See? I telt ye, hopeless min!'

And that was it. That utterance was the last thing he said to me in anger, or in any mood, about the Dons, the last time he'd been bothered in any way about Aberdeen (other than ranting about it to Mum in the lounge). All the enthusiasm, the buzz about him on Saturdays, his endless stories about the players, the running about the house to find each other when we scored, watching 'Final Score' on the TV every Saturday. All of it disappeared as if it had never happened. As we arrive at June and Arthur's, and Arthur's big smiling face greets us in the driveway, I snap out of my soul searching about what really got to him that day. But as it happened, in a couple of hours' time, the first seeds were to be sown that would eventually bring the whole mystery to an end. Dad's great sulk looked like it might be over ...

'Got. Got. Got. Got. Got ...' Gavin hesitates, his eyes bulging from their sockets like in a cartoon, locked on to the top card in my left hand, the Nottingham Forest badge. Gavin zoomed through the sticker laden pages of his figure Panini album flashing Jimmy Rimmer (Aston Villa), then Alan Hansen (Liverpool) and over the page, in a sea of Viv Andersons, Trevor Francises and Kenny Burnses, there lay empty on the page the space for the Nottingham Forest badge.*

'Dad, Dad!' shouts an elated Gavin from his bedroom, before bounding over me and then the rest of his bed, along the landing passageway, swinging round the banister, and thumping downstairs into the lounge to show his dad what he'd found, me following in every bound, swing and thump.

'Wow! Do you know the last time we found a new sticker?' exclaims Arthur to me. 'September!' he shouts. He seems as delighted as Gavin, as if it was his own album. I stand and wallow in my brilliance for a second, smiling bashfully towards my mum. 'So fit een is Stuart getting in return for 'at?'

'Stuart's got all the ones I have,' says Gavin.

---

* The other two stickers missing from Gavin's collection were Liam Brady (Arsenal) and the Liverpool team photo. I didn't have either of those.

'D'ye wint a fitba programme instead min?' asks Arthur.

Football programmes! I knew Dad had some of these some-where in the loft, but he'd never managed to find them. As Arthur produces a wad of all sorts of programmes of different sizes and colours from a drawer in the lounge unit, my eyes light up.

'Choose ony een ye wint,' says Arthur.

'Any one I want?'

Within seconds, Gavin and I, along with the sticker album open at the Nottingham Forest page, are immersed in a programme sea in the middle of the lounge floor. Raith Rovers, Dunfermline, Aberdeen, Everton, Newcastle, Southampton and numerous others from various English seaside towns and cities where Arthur's merchant navy career had taken him. While Gavin practises making sure his new badge would go on straight before taking the plunge, my OCD side takes over, organising the programmes into piles ordered by home team so I could make an informed choice about which one I'd have. But there's one in particular that did not fit. It stands out from the rest, not only by its size, its bright yellow cover or its strange picture of Sandy Jardine and Joe Harper framed doing what looked like ballet on the front page. It was a cup final programme. But then I realise that it wasn't any old cup final, it was the Scottish Cup Final programme of 1978, the day of the Dodge City excursion.

'Dad, look at this one,' I say. Dad pretends to suffer a serious involuntary convulsion with a closed mouthful of beer when he sets eyes on it, 'Oh no! Onythin' but 'at een!' he squawks, putting his beer down and drawing his hands into his body, pretending to be terrified of even touching the programme I am holding out towards him. 'Were you at that game?' asks Dad, as Gavin and I charge through to the garage to check out his Scalextric.

'Aye, me'n Gav were there. Fit an embarrassment,' says

Arthur, rolling his eyes. 'Men against boys, min. The usual, ken? They froze; they completely bottled it. But the worst thing wis that fan the Dons pulled one back to mak it 2-1 wi' five minutes to go, you'd a thought the goal deficit wis five or six, there wis simply nae fight, ken? They seemed resigned; they seemed to know that there wis nae wey a winnin' the match.' Arthur pauses. 'Were you eens nae there min?'

'No, no. We hid to come through here, to buy a new kitchen unit,' responds Dad, nodding subtly in Mum's direction, trying to imply that it was her that had prevented us from going to the match.

'A kitchen unit! Fit kinna Dons fan are you min?' bellows Arthur jovially, to which Dad darts a 'watch it' face back, but then he decides to come clean.

'To be honest, it wis nothin' tae dee wi' 'at. I jist couldna Arthur. I couldna ging min. Nae aifter fit happened 'at year. I'd hid mair than enough.'

'Ach come on, we jist werna good enough. At the end o' the day, we lost fair and square min. Rangers won the Treble, you canna argue wi' 'at,' asserts Arthur. Dad feels the hackles on the back of his neck rising as he listens to Arthur, totally taken aback by his unnecessary need to be 'fair' about it all. What was fair about the Old Firm? When was it ever the case that losing anything at all to an Old Firm side was acceptable – let alone the Treble – Dad thought? But, as usual, there was much more to it than that.

'Fair and square?' retorts Dad assertively, 'Are we spikin' aboot the same season, 1977/78?'

'Aye,' answers Arthur. Dad looks at him askance, wondering if he was losing the plot.

'Fit aboot the Motherwell game?' asks Dad.

'Fit een?' asks Arthur shaking his head. Dad looks disbelievingly at Arthur now, was he pulling his leg? How could he not know about this? It must have been Gavin that was behind

Arthur's apparent renewed interest in football and all these games they were going to, Arthur was maybe just going along. Dad thought about returning the 'Fit kinna Dons fan are you min?' line to Arthur at this point, but on reflection there would simply be far too much truth in it to be good-natured. But in any case, Arthur needed to know about this.

'Fit happened? I'll tell fit happened,' announces dad, 'the most appalling, the most outrageous miscarriage of justice in modern world sport!' Dad switches to a strange sort of Queen's English to underline the objective seriousness of his statement.

'Really?' perks up June, intrigued by the billing Dad had given his story, June having been a keen athlete in her youth, and generally interested in 'world sport'.

'Oh, here we go', sighs Mum towards June. 'I could tell ye this story myself, I've heard it 'at mony times. He's been rantin' aboot it noo for 18 months at least!'

Dad wiggles his bum in his seat like a large bird in its nest, to get comfortable enough to deliver his story properly. 'Weel, for the first time in my memory, the Dons hid the measure of the Old Firm, and they kint it.' Dad sparks up a smoke, takes a drag before exhaling long and hard, like he meant business. 'Beatin' Rangers and then Celtic to win the League Cup in 1976, hammerin' them hame and awa' 3- and 4-0 in the league, I'd never seen onythin' like it. And then one Saturday roon aboot February 1978, Rangers were playin' Motherwell at Fir Park and we hid Hibs at home, and aifter half an hour Rangers were doun 2-0 and the Dons were up 1-0. Fan Motherwell's second goal came o'er the radio, I remember thinkin' tae masel, 'is is it min, 'is year, we're gan tae dee it, mak a proper challenge for the title. And then, enter the great god of 'Old Firm justice' once again.'

Mum rolls her eyes, knowing perfectly well what was coming next, although this was the first time she'd heard Dad tee it up as if it were some biblical fable.

'Jist aifter the second goal at Fir Park, fan Motherwell went two up, the Rangers fans started chantin', "There's gonnay be a riot, there's gonnay be a riot!"' Dad takes a large swig of beer. '... And they rioted all right – they all came streamin' on tae ...'

'Ach listen Gordon, how come it's always the Old Firm fans that get blamed?' interrupts Mum, determined that if Dad was going to subject her to this story again, he wouldn't get away with any of his ridiculous exaggerations. 'Ah mean, riotin' fitba fans is a' oor the TV? I even saw some St Johnstone fans riotin' in the middle o' Perth last wik! It's nae jist Rangers and Celtic!'

'Aye, bit hold on! I'm talkin' aboot a riot in the middle o' a game, actually on the pitch! Motherwell's pitch, a game that's supposed to be a hame game at Motherwell!' raves Dad, desperate to make sure the outrage is understood.

'At's right enough,' adds Arthur, grateful for a chance to pitch in and shore up his embarrassment at being in the dark about this incident. 'You say a hame game for Motherwell, Gordon, bit we a' ken fine that fan the Old Firm come to town, especially doun here in touns in Glasgow's backyard like Motherwell, it's anything but!'

Mum nods reluctantly, not prepared to attack Arthur's views with the same vigour as Dad's.

'At's absolutely right,' adds Dad, moving smoothly on from Arthur's point. 'And 'at day, there were 15 thoosan Rangers fans fae a total o' 20 thoosan inside Fir Park, kin ye imagine? At yer ain grun'.' Dad pauses, June raises her head pretending that the light has just gone on but, of course, it hasn't. '... And it wis far fae a couple a wee laddies spillin' oor the front wa', this wis twa or three thoosan o' them, all streaming onto the pitch from all parts of the ground, all sweeping across the field, an' all still carryin' their poly bags wi' their cairry oots.'

Dad makes sure he depicts the rioting Rangers fans in the

worst possible light by doing an impression of someone struggling across the pitch, laden with a full week's worth of shopping. 'Of course at 'is point, I'm thinking it's gettin' better
and better, ken? Rangers droppin' two points, fans on the
pitch, there would surely be hell to pay for a' that! And then
fan the ref took the players from the field, suddenly I realised
fit wis gan tae happen …' Dad looks round the room at them
all, expecting to see some sign that they'd got there before
him. 'When the players came back oot and the match started
again, Rangers wiped the bloody fleer wi'thum, winnin' the
match 5-3 in the end! And 'at wis it.'

'And we all knew about it at the time, didn't we Gordon?'
remarks Mum ironically, raising her eyebrows towards Dad,
who immediately blushes and chuckles. He'd been listening
to the match while changing spark plugs in the garage, but by
the end of it, it sounded like he was driving rivets into the
side of a ship. It led to him picking up a memorable bollocking
from Mum, concerned that if we (that was her, me and my
grandparents, who had come down especially for my birthday)
could hear him shouting 'dirty cheatin' bastards!' from inside
the house, then no doubt so could half of Perth.

'So fit happened?' asks Arthur.

'Rangers got fined two grand.'

'Two grand!' splutters Arthur. 'Nae replay? Nae even ony
points deduction?'

'Nae, nothin' min. A grand per point. That was the response
from the Scottish Football League. The actions of the Rangers
fans had been sanctioned.' Dad stubs out his cigarette, tossing
his tab end symbolically into the ashtray, before sitting back
with his arms folded, staring expressionlessly at Arthur. 'They
could decide fan defeat for their side was acceptable and fan
it wisna.'

Meanwhile, June, trying to mask her amusement at how
underwhelmed she already is by Dad's story of 'injustice',

turns to my mum, hoping for a change in conversation. Arthur on the other hand stares back at Dad, clearly taken aback, trying to work out how all of this had completely passed him by. He was thinking twice now about his smartarse remark to Dad about what sort of Dons he fan he was.

'And so fan the last game of the season came round, and Rangers were only one point ahead of Aberdeen, even a draw fae 'at day in February would hae pit us in pole position. And, of course, Rangers won the league that day, beatin' Motherwell ironically. So, for me, even if we'd won the Scottish Cup the wik aifter, it still wouldna hae avenged this. It jist didna matter.' Dad stops for a second, taking another gulp of beer. Arthur now understood why there had been so much swearing and ranting about cheats, as he and Gavin had left Hampden that day, right enough.

'And then fit happens?' asks Dad, leaning forward. 'Twa days later McNeill announces he's awa' back to Parkheid. Cheerio, ken?' Dad does a heartless, cruel sort of hand wave towards Arthur. 'And fa div we get to replace him? Alex Ferguson? Ex-Rangers hacker, it couldna be worse! So fan Rangers come calling in a couple of years, fit's gan tae happen? He'll be awa' like a shot jist like McNeill.' Dad pauses to spark up yet another cigarette, shaking his head ever more profusely. 'So there you go min. At's why I've shut the door on fitba completely. I jist thought, fit's the point?'

'Oh behave yersel Gordon. You should be happy you get to cup finals at all, 'at's surely better than nothing?' interjects Mum.

'Fit's the point in gettin' tae cup finals, challengin' for the league wi' a side that is clearly the measure o' them on the park if ye ken fine that the Old Firm and their fans can move the goalposts?' raves Dad, holding both his arms out. 'Or, if they're nae cheatin' on the pitch, they're steelin' yer managers and players. Look, there's jist nae wey roon' it, ye canna compete fair and square wi' the Old Firm, so I jist dinna wint tae ken. I'm absolutely sick tae the back teeth wi' the hale thing.'

'I ken fit ye mean, Gordon,' nods Arthur supportively, locking on to Dad's gaze and then winking supportively. Dad wasn't too sure about the wink, but he sensed that Arthur *did* know where he was coming from. 'Right min, let's nae get all depressed, are you wintin' anither beer?'

'Aye, go on then.'

As Arthur stands up, he sighs deeply before disappearing through to the garage and then reappears followed by Gavin and me. 'Right then loons, go on, spit it oot!' urges Arthur towards Gavin as he cracks off the bottle caps and tops up Dad's glass.

'You know how we beat Morton 2-1 in the League Cup semi today?' asks Gavin.

'Yes,' says Dad assertively; although I was fairly sure he wouldn't know for a fact that that's how the game had finished.

'Well, can you and Stuart come with us to the League Cup Final against Dundee United next week?'

Dad looks at me; I look back with bated breath, and then to Mum. Mum shrugs her shoulders as if to say why not.

'Come on min!' bellows Arthur. 'At's exactly fit you need, an Old Firm-free cup final!'

'D'ye wint to ging?' Dad asks me.

'YES!'

And that was it. Not only did it look like the sulk might be over, but we were going to our first game! Fantastic.

'Have you ever seen the Dons actually win a trophy afore min?' asks Arthur, homing in on a free crash barrier in the middle of the northern section of the Mount Florida End of Hampden (the 'Rangers end'), half an hour before the start of the 1979/80 League Cup Final.

'Never. The closest I've come was at the Scottish Cup Final in 1967 fan we lost 2-0 to Celtic, and a Celtic fan pished in my jacket pocket doun there at the front someway.' Dad points towards the front wall, where Gavin and I were swinging from unoccupied crash barriers. '... And then fan they finally won the Scottish Cup in 1970, I managed to be in the back o' beyond, on a university field trip in Germany. Fan the Germans working in the hotel telt us that Aberdeen hid won 3-1, we started takin' the piss oot a'thum assuming they'd got the score the wrang wey roon'! They werna happy!' Dad and Arthur burst into a yet another fit of laughter. The entire journey had been like this all the way from Kirkcaldy, one story after another, all on the same Scottish football rough justice theme that had rebonded them as mates last week. The difference was that today, there was an underlying, smug confidence. Today, against Dundee United, they would finally be rewarded.

'Weel, the closest I came wis at the League Cup Final last year. Naeb'dy pished in my pocket, but they might as well have! We wis robbed min, totally robbed,' says Arthur shaking his head.

'Fit d'ye mean?' asks Dad. He knew it had finished 2-1 to Rangers, but he had not heard that there had been any controversy. He'd been burning the hundred-year-old bramble jungle that was his Auntie Helen's back garden that day and hadn't bothered to find out anything about the game when he heard we'd lost.

'Weel, we were clingin' on to our 1-0 lead, right up to the last ten minutes. An' then all hell broke loose. Some Rangers hacker tries to kill Bobby Clark, breakin' his arm [this was a slight exaggeration] and before the physio could get on the pitch tae see tae him, Rangers scored through a deflected free-kick that Clark would hae saved if he'd been a'right ...'

'You're jokin'!' remarks Dad.

'... And then Derek Johnstone's play-actin' got oor Doug Rougvie sent aff and aifter six minutes of injury time Rangers snatch the winner. And fa scores the second goal? Colin Jackson, who just had to be an Aiberdonian!'

'Is he fae Aiberdeen?'

'Aye, Sunnybank!' Arthur now starts barking in ironic laughter, expecting Dad to join in. But even now, this long after an event he didn't even know about, Dad is jolted momentarily out of his upbeat frame of mind. It was almost as if there really *was* an Old Firm god of rough justice, he thought. How could they contrive otherwise to make us suffer so much apparent cheating, unfairness and foul play on almost every possible occasion? There was simply nothing to say. But he realised in a bizarre sort of way that having shut everything to do with football out that day had protected him from it, something that would have wound him up big time.

'But thinkin' back, you couldna see how we could win, even fan we were 1-0 up. We a'ready kint we were beat afore the game started, ken?'

'No, what d'ye mean?'

'Ye jist sensed it, ken? We were totally overawed by Rangers.'

As Dad nods, he remembers Harry Carter had gone on about this, a psychological barrier you faced when you met the Old Firm at Hampden, and how the bumpkins from outside Glasgow had already lost any cup final before it started. Maybe the old Jambo was right after all, he thought.

'Aye, well 'at's nae very likely the day!' remarks Dad nodding in the direction of the miserably thin scattering of Dundee United fans at the other end of the ground. How things had changed since he'd come here first, way back in 1962, when he'd stood with 132,000 to watch Scotland beat England. Ten minutes before kick-off and the place is still empty, the

Aberdeen end is not much better. He knew crowd sizes had been declining, even when one of the Old Firm *were* there, but this was supposed to be a League Cup Final. Still, it'd be different when the game starts ... but it wasn't.

By the time the game got underway, the only time to date that Aberdeen and Dundee United would ever meet in a cup final, only 21,000 had turned up – the lowest ever League Cup Final crowd it would transpire.* All I really remember was playing hide and seek around the sparsely manned crash barriers with Gavin and getting bollocked by the adult Dons fans we were irritating. Fans who might have been less irritable had the game itself not been a casualty of the atmosphere vacuum and the dank weather. The waterlogged pitch prevented the only real scoring chance that either side created when a Willie Garner header stopped in the mud on its way into the net. The final score was 0-0. But no one would remember this incident. Nor would anyone remember this match, the official League Cup Final 1979/80. It all happened instead at the replay.

All my dad's lamenting and ranting in various front rooms around Scotland about the litany of Old Firm injustices we'd suffered in the late 1970s was put into perspective on the night of the replay that took place four days later, Wednesday 12 December 1979. Dundee United tanked us 3-0 at Dens Park, opening a new world of hopelessness for my dad. This time there were no excuses. This time there was no Old Firm injustice to blame. He sat slumped in his armchair, more pished

---

* It is true to say that in general football crowds all around the world had started to dwindle in the 1970s due to the fact that by then everyone had televisions. But finals in Scotland were normally still attracting upwards of 60,000 people. And, of course, there was a simple explanation for this. The Old Firm *were* always there. Not today though.

than I think I ever saw him on a school night. It was his full-
on 'fields of Flodden' body language that we'd all joked about
since we first discovered it during the World Cup in 1978.
There was no joking tonight though. And it could only mean
one thing: the great sulk would be resumed. Only this time
it was moodier, deeper and even quieter than before.

Chapter 4

The Triumph of Hope over Experience

'Dad!' I shout, running round the back of the house to the garage in the late morning of Saturday 3 May 1980, just after 'Football Focus'. 'They're saying we're going to do it today!' I rave. I still didn't really know what 'do it' meant, although I knew it was the league and not the cup this time. According to what I'd seen on 'Football Focus', if we beat Hibs today and Celtic drew with St Mirren, we'd win the Scottish Premier League. There were some other goal difference complications, which meant that the following week, even though Celtic had no more games to play, they could still win the league if we lost by five goals or something to Partick Thistle. The bit I didn't get was that there was nothing in it for Hibs, St Mirren or Partick Thistle. Cup finals were so much easier to grasp. But Dad was still in the grip of his long-term, ultra-sulk that had kicked in following the League Cup Final defeat against Dundee United four months before. He had said next to nothing about anything to do with Aberdeen since that December night. Needless to say, we went to no more matches and had still to see Arthur and Gavin again. And, as usual, right now Dad was saying nothing. As he lay on his back with his feet sticking out from under the car, fitting a new exhaust, I prepare again to coax him into confirmation.

'Dad? If we win the next two games, Hibs and Partick Thistle, that's it?' I ask tentatively. It was a statement of fact, but I still somehow needed him onside. There was always the outside chance in the back of my mind that Dad's moods and indifference were actually because he knew something that I didn't. That there was something else I was missing that Dad could veto.

'Maybe min, maybe,' he concedes.

'But they've just been saying on TV that Hibs and Partick Thistle are rubbish teams.' Dad lets out a single burst of laughter that he disguises as part of his struggle with the exhaust fitting exercise that had taken him all morning so far. 'Aye, 'at's fit they said about Dundee United in December too,' he grumbles. 'Kin ye see a 14-millimetre ring spanner onywey, min?'

I sigh and then pause before bending down to start my search. It was a typical Saturday morning. I'd come to see him with news or hopes about the Dons, only to end up raking about in the several toolboxes that sat around our garage to find a 14-millimetre ring spanner. On Saturday afternoons I'd maybe go next door to see Martin or down the road to see Neil, and we'd watch the full-time results on *Grandstand*, but they were Celtic fans. Dad was still the only Dons fan I knew and I still remembered how energised he used to get about the team.

But if I was unhappy with my Saturdays in the early days of 1980, my Sundays were off the scale in terms of misery. On Sundays I'd be dispatched to Sunday school, where I was subjected to the literally unbelievable Jesus stories. I'd often find myself in trouble with my Granda when I was heard to ask too many questions about their validity. The real complaint though was that this seemed like school proper, and I was not happy about my Sunday mornings being interrupted, especially since this was at the expense of watching the *Lone*

Ranger or *Bod* or killing my sister, who was normally prepared
(and at other times coerced) into being our house's Red Indian
when I turned into Buck from *The High Chaparral*. And just
in case I wasn't getting enough religious education from Sunday
school, I'd be packed off on Thursday nights to march around
and recite Bible text to win badges at the Boys' Brigade, a
'little army for God'.

Back at school through the week, playing football had become
a much more serious affair. This was because of two things.
Now in Primary 4, we were officially allowed to use the big-
time football arena of the main concrete playground, the exclusive reserve of the Primary 4 to 7s. And some time in spring
that year, Gordon Moir, our class's top man (in all senses –
football, schoolwork, behaviour) made a remark that would
have the biggest single influence on my football-playing career.
He said, 'You should run with the ball more often, you're
good at dribbling.' I was good at dribbling? It was a remark
that subsequently fuelled a lifetime of hogging the ball in any
game I played.

In spite of these distractions and my dad's gloom, by April
that year there was no ignoring what was happening to the
Dons. Everyone was talking about it, at school and on the TV.
Even the hyper-strict, Bible-bashing Mr Sharples of the BB
had found time during Thursday night's session to tell everyone
how good it would be for the game if Aberdeen could clinch
the title from Celtic that weekend. Two sensational victories
over Celtic at Parkhead in the last two weeks (one of which
was a rearranged game from December) had put us in pole
position to win the league, causing the rest of the world to
sit up. The rest of the world, that was, apart from Dad. Or
so it had seemed until now.

'At's it, finished now,' announces Dad. We tidy up the garage
and head to the kitchen where an enormous wholesale tub
of Swarfega that any MOT garage would have been proud of

emerges from the cupboard under the sink for stage one in the post-car-maintenance clean-up process. Stage two was the Fairy Liquid wash, which results as usual in an argument with Mum about why we always have to grease-up the taps. I get a particular bollocking today when I decide for some reason that it would be a good idea to recycle my Granda's line that women should be thankful that they'd men folk who could do these sorts of jobs around the house, and greased-up taps was a small price to pay. We eventually set the table for lunch.

'Fit are ye dein' this aifternein?' asks Mum, perusing the fridge with her back to Dad sat at the table. Dad says nothing, concentrating on slowly cutting some fine slivers of cheese. My sister and I watch his delicate sandwich construction oper-ation as we munch through our own sandwiches, waiting for an answer.

'Gordon?' prompts Mum.

'Washin' the car,' says Dad eventually. Mum finally comes to the table, sits down, staring at him.

'I thought you did that jist a couple a' wiks ago.'

'Aye. Bit it's needin' done again,' Dad says unconvinc-ingly, still focusing on his intensely crafted sandwich. Looking back on it all, that was the moment, that was the signal that Dad was back. As he delicately slices up toma-toes, the pieces of which he surveys for evenness, incising with his knife every now and then to deal with any outsized rogues, the Dons fan he buried in his subconscious two years ago has reawakened and is now organising his day. Mum looks at him, trying hard to fathom out why on earth he would impose this task on himself so soon after having done it. Unbeknown to Mum, me and even Dad himself – still in denial – he was once again at the mercy of the triumph of hope over experience. Aberdeen's electric late surge in the league *had* brought him under the Aberdeen spell again and washing the car was the one sure way of making sure he'd get unbroken access to the football on the radio. I should have recognised the mood by the way he cleared the table and did the dishes. He was in that same bizarre trance I'd encountered before the Scottish Cup Final back in May 1978. And with about an hour to go before the game, Dad had said his last words that were not in response to a question.

'Ging and fill up the bucket wi' hot water min,' instructs Dad. It was to be the most organised car-washing experience of my life. Laid out on the workbench in the garage was an almost shop-like display of chamois, sponges, cloths for wiping, other cloths for drying. At the foot of the bench stood a bucket for soapy water (the one I'd been instructed to fill) next to a bucket full of cold clean water. And finally, the hosepipe was located, unrolled and then plugged into the water tap in the garage. Just as Dad and I had conducted a brief user acceptance test, Mum appears from the back door, her curiosity about Dad getting the better of her again, 'Look, fit on earth are you doing this for?' she asks.

'I'm washin' the car,' pleads Dad, holding his hands out as if to say, 'What's the big deal?' Mum stares at Dad's car-washing preparations, all laid out like a Halfords' promotion for car hygiene. Irritated, she gives Dad a puzzled frown, and goes back into the house.

'Are we going to listen to the football Dad?' I ask.

'Might as well,' responds Dad, now checking his watch incessantly as we get the car wash underway. He starts on the left-side front wing, while I start on the number plate and then, as Dad moves to the passenger's side door, I take on the left-side headlight ... 20 minutes on the clock, 0-0 at Easter Road, 0-0 at Love Street, Dad's hands circle at a steady pace, water streaming from the large yellow sponge that he regularly dips into the bucket and slaps back on the body of the car, in a manner that implied it was a time-invested skill he'd acquired. I was impressed.

'Is this how you do it Dad?' I ask, focusing more on trying to recreate the large streams of water flowing from my sponge than actually washing the car.

'Aye,' responds Dad without even looking at what I was doing.

'Look Dad, do it this way.' I show him a new technique I invented on the spot, a backwards and forwards motion rather than a circular one ...

'YES!' yelps Dad, the shock causing me to stand up abruptly.

... Steve Archibald scores for Aberdeen, 1-0!

Dad's listening to the game! I immediately drop my off-the-cuff alternative washing techniques just in case they might distract him and start washing like him, following his circular motions. Maybe he was out of his sulk!

... the ball runs free at the back post, Watson must score ...
and he does!

There's another stifled yelp from Dad as Aberdeen go two up. Still the washing continues in silence, only now at a faster pace. Still Aberdeen lead Hibs 2-0, St Mirren and Celtic are level at 0-0. Half-time comes just as we finish the soapy wash. We head to the kitchen for a cup of coffee. Before the kettle was even switched on, Dad puts on the radio, another positive sign that he was back. Wary of knocking him off course, I say nothing, hoping that, like me, that he was absorbing the stream of forecasting, conjecturing and statistical analysis coming from the radio.

... 45 minutes away from becoming the first side outside the Old Firm to win the League championship in 15 years ... the Dons on the brink of a first league championship in 25 years ... a historic second league championship in Aberdeen's 77 year history ...

By the time the second half starts, we are both on our way around the car again, cleaning the wheels, wheel arches, wipers and even the aerial ... Aberdeen score again in 67 minutes, causing Dad now to react with a fist in the air. I was sure of it now, he must be back; I hadn't seen him like this for years. At 3-0, the radio declares that the only thing that mattered was the result at Love Street ... with 15 minutes to go, sponges, hoses, soapy bubbles, cloths everywhere, Dad had stopped washing, resorting to pacing and smoking nervously round and round inside the garage, still clutching his clean water sponge ... then all of a sudden, with ten minutes to go, drama in Paisley ...

... penalty for Celtic!

'I knew it. I jist knew it!' bleats Dad, swinging round and launching his clean water sponge into the bucket of soapy water, muttering and swearing under his breath. He stands for a couple of seconds in the middle of the garage with his hands on his hips looking out the back window before shaking his head slowly, and then, just as he makes for the radio to switch it off, there's another twist ...

... it seems that the linesman has sensationally overruled the penalty decision! It's a free-kick at the edge of the box instead. The Celtic players are furious!

Dad draws his hand back from the switch, looking extremely serious, waiting for the free-kick to be taken.

... Provan strikes ... and it hits the wall, and is now launched back up field to safety ... it really does look now like the title is on its way to the North-East ...

'Well, well, who would a believed it, eh?' says Dad, trying hard to force a huge smile off his face. Five minutes later it's all over. Down at Easter Road, Fergie is exploding with his now legendry 'man possessed' performance, running, leaping and hugging everyone all over the pitch. Likewise, I run around the tree in the middle of our front lawn for a couple of minutes, hoping that Dad would eventually join in. But he doesn't. Instead, he remains silent, clearing away the mountains of washing equipment and cloths we'd used for the car and listening to the radio as it went on and on about how amazing it was. But I know he is elated inside, I just know. Soon, we're back inside for dinner.

Differently from the Dad I'd seen winning and losing in cup football, his delight was calm, reserved and thoughtful. He didn't stop talking about it. In the days and weeks immediately afterwards, the years of anguish, anger and injustices during the late 1970s had been well and truly washed away. Likewise, my extended Aberdonian family were surprisingly interested in it all too, all of them, even the women. My first ever visit to Pittodrie was for the unfurling of the league flag a few weeks later. The ground seemed like it was half-full with Aberdonian children, mums, grannies and aunties, giving Pittodrie a gentle face. And there was football tat everywhere, overpriced and badly printed commemorative flags and scarves, badges, pennants; it was a dreamland of football paraphernalia and the stuff bought for me hung on my walls for years (and is still readily accessible in a box in the attic). Well into the summer, the historical stocktaking and perspective of it all continued to consume my dad. But soon I started to realise that this was all very well. Dad's impassioned talk was great and it was clear now that the great sulk was well and truly over. But what I really wanted to know was would we be going to games again. 'We'll see min, we'll see,' was as much as he'd been prepared to say until one sunny day in mid-August, out of the blue, it happened. Dad announced that we were going to a home game, against Celtic in September 1980, the first of the Old Firm visits to Pittodrie that season.

I'm in the back of the car on a busy King Street in Aberdeen. By the time we get 100 yards down Pittodrie Street, Mum has to stop since the entire road and pavement is awash with hundreds of men all marching with urgency, at the same pace, towards the ground. Driving is pointless and dangerous now, so Dad and I get out to join ranks with the other Aberdonians and march the remaining 500 yards. This does not seem like a place for my mum anyway, even inside the car. As soon as I hit the pavement, I sense there is something about the purpose of these thronging men; they seem hungry, alert and unstable. My excitement quickly turns to trepidation when the threatening roar of thousands of chanting men is carried up the street. This is coming from inside the ground that we cannot yet see. I wasn't expecting this. I'm no longer sure I want to be here. We pass through the turnstiles and into the ground, the singing from the stands is deafening, my heart is racing as we run up the stairwell to the inside of the ground. It's ten to three on Saturday afternoon 27 September 1980.

The four stands of Pittodrie and the pitch open up to me as I reach the top of the stairs. The ground is alive, buzzing, a cauldron of energy, no more so than in the stand on the right. That's the away end – the Celtic end today. That one stand – the King Street End – the smallest of the four, is already packed with 4,000 Celtic fans. That was what I'd heard on the way to the ground. This was maybe behind the urgency of the Aberdonians I'd seen going to the game. They knew their home was being invaded by Celtic supporters.

Festooned in a sea of green, white and yellow, the noise coming from them is electrifying. All standing up, they sing, gesticulate, clap, chant and stamp in unison. Somehow, they all know the words, actions and routines to what seems to be an endless list of songs, all heartily delivered with a hostile passion. When they start a new song they homogenise into an enormous bouncing army, all professional soldiers of their cause. The Dons fans aren't doing this though; are they here for the same event? The Celtic fans have travelled 140 miles from Glasgow, and they are outnumbered inside the ground by a factor of four to one by the Aberdeen supporters. But they give the impression that they are at home; there is no sense among them that they are on away turf. There is no suggestion of deference or respect for the fact that they are in someone else's backyard; they are totally defiant. I wondered what it would be like at Ibrox or Parkhead, where the crowd would be at least ten times bigger than this one? This is one half of the Old Firm, live! And this is just their fans!

Dad decided that since I was still nine, it would be safer for us to get tickets in the Main Stand. The Main Stand usually attracted the more retiring and genteel supporters, so it was an appropriate location for my inaugural home match. But since Celtic would normally be able to attract twice as many fans than those permitted by their ticket allocation, there would always be some overspill to other parts of the ground. Somehow, I knew that these Celts were very different from the home fans in the Main Stand. They were mostly regular foot soldiers of the mainstream Celtic army, who had failed to get tickets for the King Street End. I could see this because they were joining in with the ritualistic stamping, chanting and singing of the King Street contingent, in spite of being surrounded by a majority of disapproving Dons toffs. Disturbingly, three

of them are sitting right in front of us, and they're half cut.
I had butterflies in my stomach and so did my dad (he admitted
to me many years later). There was something terrifyingly
unstable about the mood that surrounded me; surely the Dons
fans were not going to put up with this.

It's not until the teams trot out onto the pitch that the local
fans make their presence felt as a huge cheer greets Fergie's
champions. But Celtic go two up after 19 minutes, with Charlie
Nicholas on fire. If I'd been impressed with the Celtic fans
before the match, now I was totally in awe. I hadn't even had
time to recognise that my team were losing for the sheer spec-
tacle created by the audacious, single-minded adulation of their
fans. It was off the scale in every sense I'd come to know, in
particular the three Celts in front of me. Their drunken celebration had them spilling over the seats in their group hug,
falling into my lap on each occasion and leaving me with
bruises all over my legs. I'd already noted an unnerving looking
protective eye on my dad's face, and had, for the first time
and certainly not the last, acted to calm him. All I wanted to
do was hide behind him, but my instinct was telling me to
pretend the buffeting and bashing I was taking from the Celts
in front wasn't happening. 'Referee, get that fuckin' Hun off
the park!' shouts the middle Celt following a late tackle by
McLeish. I sit petrified as I see my dad's temples pulsing, planning a response, 'Never a foul, referee!' shouts Dad between
the two heads of the Celts in front of us, now standing up.
'Great pass Roy Aitken!' the one on the left shouts as Celtic
mount another attack. 'You couldna lace Willie Miller's boots
Aitken!' roars Dad ... please stop Dad, please stop, I pray to
myself. Half-time comes round, and the three Celts head off
into the stand, the leader giving my dad a cheeky wink on
their way. 'Dad I want to go.' 'You want to go?' Dad sits and
stares at me for a minute. Meanwhile, the three Celts return
to their seats with pies and drinks. Then, before we'd decided

what we were doing, the inevitable confrontation I'd feared happens. One of them turns round to my Dad.

'Hey pal!' says the one on the left towards Dad. I see Dad's face suddenly lose all its colour. He says nothing. 'Your wee boy wantin' this carton ay orange? I cannay drink it, it's goat a blue straw!'

In other words, it's a 'Rangers straw'. Dad, relieved, welcomes the offer and thanks the Celt and I am given the juice (it does not occur to me at nine years of age that, if the blue straw is a Rangers straw, it is equally as inappropriate for me as a Dons fan). We relax, realising that these guys, although half cut, are not as dangerous as they might have seemed. This moment became legendary for us as we'd laugh about it regularly for years and years after.

In the second half, the Dons players are transformed, so are the fans. All the bravado, and posturing of the visiting Celts is dwarfed when the Dons fans eventually become animated. When Aberdeen pull one back within ten minutes of the restart, the enormous eruption of the 19,000 or so Aberdeen supporters heralds a change in the balance and mood of the game. The Dons fans now break out of their reserve, including my dad, who is now behaving like a Celtic fan. The whole ground is charged with the Dons fans in full swing, now muting the ever-vocal Celtic supporters. So when we score again to pull the match level, the place goes ballistic. My dad lifts me off my feet with an enormous bear hug, like he'd done that night in the lounge when I was five, but this time, it was louder, wilder, scarier but somehow much more fun. All the emotions of those two hours and seeing my dad so elated have me momentarily in tears. We miss a number of chances that should have won us the match, which finishes 2-2. At the end of the game, my dad chats with the three friendly Celtic fans on the way out of the ground, each acknowledging the efforts of the other's side, with polite clichés, game of two halves, and all that.

What a match, what a day, what a way for me to get blooded. The manner of the recovery in the tense atmosphere, that I would come to realise only occurred against Old Firm sides, had me feeling like we'd carried off a victory. But the match was also the first of three events that would fully rehabilitate Dad from his sulk. The second was a home match that December against Rangers, the biggest of all Dad's enemies, which we won 2-0. It was the first time I saw the Dons win. The third thing was the most amazing, a thunderous annihilation of Celtic for their second visit to Pittodrie just after Christmas, a match that finished 4-1. A result that saw Aberdeen, reigning champions of Scotland, back at the top of the league, three points clear with a game in hand. Few Dons fans had probably ever lived to see a series of Old Firm matches like that, certainly not my dad. Anyone experiencing it would be hooked on the game for a lifetime. And those late months in 1980 gave Dad something else too. They brought him closer to Aberdeen; they gave him a real link with the city again.

And it was just as well, because within three days of the 4-1 game against Celtic everything started falling apart. We lost Gordon Strachan for the rest of the season when he picked up a leg injury against Dundee United. Then we lost to Morton and St Mirren, got knocked out of the cup and by Easter our title challenge had petered out. By mid-April, Celtic had already won the league and in May Rangers won the cup. Then, in the following season, stuttering and stammering, we were already out of the title race by January. It really did look like our moment had come ... and gone. The old order was back in place. This would have pushed a pre-rehab Dad back into a sulk, maybe for ever. Instead, we were going to more and more games. Even when we watched Celtic play us off the park, hammering us 3-1 at Pittodrie, the second time they'd done so that season, Dad was able to be quite philosophical about it. 'Nine points adrift now, forget it. Celtic will win the league again, it's all going back to the same old story, same Old Firm story.' Dad chuckles ironically at the turn of phrase he'd stumbled over with this gloomy conclusion, as we swing right, out of the old Bridge of Dee onto the old A92 on our way south. 'We'll look back in years and say that 'at Hibs match in 1980, fan we were washin' the old A60, was our glory moment, our peak. D'ye mine 'at day?' I nod. 'An' we should all think oorsels lucky we won the league at all. We never ever thought we'd even see 'at day again in the first place. That old rascal Harry was right after all.'

'Who's Harry?' I ask. Dad looks at me, realising he'd inadvertently spoken his mind.

'Disna matter,' answers Dad, after a lengthy pause. 'But let's nae write aff the season yet,' he says. 'If we can jist somehow beat Celtic in three wiks in the Scottish Cup,' Dad reflects, before running out of steam. He knew just as well as me that parking our hopes in the 'somehow' word was an extremely tall order. Still, we were going to the game and this was the only sensible way we could look at it. As it happened, that Saturday, 13 February 1982, would be the pivotal moment for the fate of Aberdeen over the whole era. It was to change football for ever for me too. I was to come face to face with one of Scottish football's most terrifying realities, one from which I had somehow been shielded so far. From that day over the course of the rest of the season, we were all going to grow up. Dad's dream, our dream, was about to start becoming reality.

Chapter 5

Coming of Age

I watch as half the entire flock of North Sea seagulls swarm and circle like vultures over the nearly empty Pittodrie stadium, preparing to dive bomb the junk food bonanza strewn along the terraces before the stewards clear it all away. We've waited behind to catch up with Eddie, my second cousin, who we'd stumbled across through a chance encounter at half-time. Dad takes a final, triumphant drag on his tab as he nods profusely, endorsing Eddie's latest glowing reflection about Hewitt's sensational Brazilian-style overhead kick, before exhaling satisfied, long and hard, with a column of smoke funnelling up towards the roof of the Beach End. Against all the odds, we had somehow snubbed out and tamed Burns, McStay, McCluskey and McGarvey – who'd run rings round us three weeks ago – and clung on to win a pulsating Scottish Cup fourth round match against Celtic, 1-0. We are all on cloud nine and now I know the chances of Dad returning to the days of sulking are more or less nil. Still conferring enthusiastically, we finally start to climb up the steps of the empty Beach End, and the panorama behind the ground gradually starts to fill our view. Firstly the blue of the North Sea, then the end of the Main Stand to our left, across the golf course to the seafront and down to the sand dune known as the 'broad hill' on our right. During the next 20 minutes this scene would become the stage for a drama that would change football matches for the rest of my life. Little did I know that the result of the match we had just watched, the event we would now witness and the remainder of the season was all about a coming of age – for me, for Dad, for the Dons, for Aberdeen.

As soon as we pass through the doorway onto the open tarmac behind the Beach End, a few dozen young guys can be seen running down the bottom of Pittodrie Street. They keep on coming, now spilling across the road, still running at full pelt. My heart rate picks up, something tells me that they are not arsing around or running to get a bus. I had a fair idea what might be happening. But by the time we and the last few stewards reach the landing on our way down to the exit, the sheer volume of people making for this end of town means that whatever is happening outside the Main Stand is much more serious than it first seemed. Within seconds, half of the entire city of Aberdeen seems to be scrambling frantically down Pittodrie Street in waves, then fanning out mostly onto the golf course and along the pavements on the Golf Road. With a restraining hand on Dad's arm, I make sure that we are going nowhere for the time being. Dad and Eddie's glory forecasting is brought to a close.

Although there's clearly a mood of alarm down on the street, there's something comical about it all, like a scene from a 1940s monster movie. Hundreds of running frames with arms stretched out in front of them with heads turned looking back through bulging eyes at Godzilla about to appear from the edge of the Main Stand, with a couple of badly animated, wriggling legs protruding from its closed jaws. Then all of a sudden, no more Aberdonians … a gap … a roaring crescendo … we stand in silence, gripped by the uncertainty. Then it finally appears … much worse than a dinosaur … certainly much more dangerous – it is the entire contents of the King Street End, 3,500 raging Celtic fans.

Ten metres or so behind the last line of Dons fans, the

frontrunners charge round the corner, shouting, roaring, running at lightning speed taking up the full breadth of the road. Even though I could see the terror they were causing below me, it was electrifying, their fearlessness, their rabid hunger, the 'square-go' gestures everywhere, then punching, head-butting, everywhere I look, their concerted, collective anger, every bit as intimidating and fearsome as their bravado inside the ground had always implied. Within no time though, there is too much action to take in as dozens of them overwhelm the sluggish Dons fans, causing running skirmishes to break out everywhere. Less than 50 yards in front of me Aberdeen supporters are pulled to the ground, and then kicked, and kicked and kicked again. I can hear their yelps as well as the thud of the adult feet thumping into their prostrate ribs and faces. I think I'm going to be sick. And when I see a battered policeman's hat getting kicked out onto Golf Road, I take the biggest gulp of my life …

Surely it was a toy police hat, one that had simply been whipped up and booted out of someone's garden as the Celtic fan tsunami had flooded Pittodrie Street sweeping everything down towards Golf Road. Surely the police are not at the mercy of this too … and then I got the answer I feared. Three policemen come tearing round the corner running for their lives, with a division of Celtic's finest right behind them, lunging voraciously at their heels to try to trip them up. Two with hats, one without … To my disbelief, they keep going and going, it seems with one thing in mind, to save their own skins, running and running till they are out of sight. That is it. We are all on our own, and the Celtic people seem to know it. The constant hail of missiles raining down on the retreating Dons fans intensifies … half bricks, stones, bottles, an orange crate and even a ten-foot long piece of scaffolding, launched 20 yards, clatters and rings as it hits the ground in a pool of tarmac created just in time by the Dons fans scrambling frantically out of its way. The pace and the pressure of the thousands of Celtic fans expose the fully open back gate of the Beach End … Jesus, they can get at us now if they want … and then it happens, a group of three men suddenly see our huddle on the Beach End steps. I turn and run back up the steps, just like in a dream, I feel like I'm running through treacle … I get to the gate at the top, look round and to my relief a steward has appeared to shut the gate just in time … my legs turned to jelly, I skip back down and stand behind Dad, trembling, heart racing. Now the lightning advance of the Celtic fans outside the closed back gate traps a pocket of Dons fans in the inset between the Beach End and South Stand turnstiles. There must be a hundred or so, although out of our sight, we can hear them, 'Leave him! Please leave him!' Bottles smashing, screaming women … I clench my teeth, shut my eyes, trying to fend off my imagination as it runs wild …

'They're nae happy!' laughs the steward, hands in pockets, chuckling as he wheels round to Dad and Eddie with a bob of his head. Not happy? Does he think this is pantomime? This was not the time for any humour. How on earth could it occur to him to arse around at this moment? Has he not just seen what I'd seen – had anything like this ever happened before, anywhere? And look at the sea of terrified Grandpas, dads, teenagers, boys my age, now stranded on the golf course before us, some in tears, others holding smacked jaws or ribs, all of them in shock at the scale of the riot they've somehow survived. How could anyone laugh just now, when we – that was Dad, Eddie, me, the Aberdeen fans, the Aberdeen police and the whole of the city of Aberdeen – were helpless, totally helpless. All this because Celtic lost 1-0?

Eventually the flow of Celtic fans from Pittodrie Street slows and the front line gradually retire towards their buses, now singing about the IRA, still foaming at the mouth, still looking pent up, still seemingly unfulfilled about the result.

The Dons fans below us gradually appear from their ordeal, police vans and ambulances now speed up and down Golf Road, going through the motions of appearing urgent, screeching to a halt, taking off with sirens blaring, but those of us who've been present for the last ten minutes know that it's too late for that. As soon as the last Celtic fan was a hundred yards or so up the broad hill, Dad decided it was safe enough to go, a full 15 minutes after we'd tried to leave the ground, a full 30 minutes after the end of the game.

'Where on earth have you been?' asks an anxious Mum at the wheel of the car, parked up on King Street, as we opened the door. Dad says nothing. 'So!' she says the moment we'd pulled off, expecting at least one of us to be enthusing about the match. 'Fit a great result!'

'Aye, great,' responds Dad after a considered delay. Mum looked round from the driver's seat to me, anticipating a bit more of a reaction.

'Yeah. Good,' I nod. She stared and frowned at me for a second, sensing something was afoot.

'Have you two fallen out or something?'

'No no,' says Dad. Dad and I catch each other's eye in the car mirror, sussing the other out about what we should say, whether to tell Mum about the riot we'd almost got caught up in. For a split second he thought about it. 'Oh, we bumped into Eddie in the Beach End, that's why we were late,' Dad plays it safe, and diverts Mum on to a safe course.

'Oh, foo's he?'

It works. I knew what he must have been thinking. If we'd told her about what we had seen, if we even explained half of what we saw, there would be serious trouble. I could imagine what she'd say, the foot would be going down, and he'd get pulled up for not being responsible enough since I was still only ten. And she'd be right. In short, there was no way we'd be allowed back. Right at that moment, I wasn't sure if I wanted to come back at all anyway. The more I thought about it on the way down the road, the more unlikely our escape seemed.

For a start, if we'd watched the game from the Main Stand that day, as we had every other Old Firm encounter I'd witnessed, we would definitely have been injured or killed in the riot. At the very least, we'd have been among the monster movie fans we'd seen fleeing onto the golf course. The only reason we had not was because Dad had finally yielded to my pleading to get tickets for the Beach End. I had had enough of the geriatric old codgers of the Main Stand with their sheepskin jackets and boring chat. I suspected that the more down-to-earth Beach End would suit my dad on the swearing front too (his passionate, expletive-ridden tirades – normally towards the ref – seemed often to attract a disapproving eye from the toffs sitting around us). It was home to the only Aberdeen fans who behaved remotely like the Old Firm fans that I'd been so overawed by. They were the 'Beach End boys', a group of maybe 500 or so teenagers and 20-somethings, who would congregate in the top back right-hand corner of the covered end. Only they would offer any sort of response to the normally more vocal away fans.

But this was only one half of the reason we'd escaped. Had we not bumped into Eddie we'd have ended up right in among them, as had hundreds of others when the Celtic fans went berserk, and what would have happened then? Could I have run fast enough? Could my dad? What would happen to my head if it had absorbed the impact of that ten-foot scaffolding pole, one of the bricks, or even the orange fizzy drinks crate? Where on earth did all that stuff come from anyway? And what would it have been like if they'd attacked Dad? I knew I could barely even now think about what it would be like just watching, as he'd cower behind a raised hand, begging for mercy, as they dragged him to the ground, kicking him,

punching him across the Golf Road, like all those dozens of
Dons fans I'd seen earlier. How easily all that could have
happened to me, to us ... Maybe this was the price we would
eventually have to pay for going to games, that sooner or later
it would be us the victims, not other people we didn't know.
It just all seemed so unpredictable, so dangerous, so unfair.
As we approached the final few Perthshire villages on our way
home, it was clear. The only course of action was to get home,
go upstairs and immerse myself in the comfort and security
of my four-gallon pail of Lego and wait for Dad to come and
tell me it would all be OK. A couple of hours later, as I'd
hoped, Dad appeared.

'Are you a'right min?' he whispered sternly at me. But
before he'd even waited for me to respond, he'd carefully but
purposefully closed the door and immediately launched into
the rant of a lifetime. 'I have never ever, ever, ever seen onythin'
like 'at!' he proclaimed, pacing nervously about my room,
stepping between the Lego piles and half-built bits of spaceship as he offloaded in his usual way, only he'd normally have
been able to do this on the way home in the car.

'It's bad enough fan the Old Firm *behave* themselves at oor
hame games, ken?' moans Dad ironically. '... Remember the
last een? When we were forced tae wait by the police; standin',
cowerin' at the door o' the Main Stand, oor ain main stand!
Jist tae let them get back tae their buses, singing a' their muck,
tauntin' and spittin' at us ...' ranted Dad, his true anger betrayed
by a single kick he gave a tennis ball that smacked off the radiator back into the main pile of Lego spares. 'This is jist totally
oot a' order!' he ranted. 'A full-scale riot? In Aberdeen? How
on earth can they be allowed tae dee 'at at an awa' match,
jist because they lost 1-0 in the cup? We a' ken they think
they've a divine right tae win everythin', but 'at's jist totally
aff the scales!' blasts Dad. 'And you shouldna hae tae see things
like 'at min,' he said looking at his feet, sighing, almost ashamed,

as if it was his fault. 'Naeb'dy should!' He went on and on as
I worked away on the Lego spaceship that I'd decided I would
call the *Parkhead Destroyer*.

'Fit kinna world do we live in if we still hiv to suffer anything
remotely like 'at in our day and age?' Dad asks. But what I
really wanted to know was what we were going to do about
it, was there anywhere else in the ground that was safer? How
was he going to make it OK next time? 'The last time onyb'dy
in Aiberdeen sa' onythin' like 'at wis fan the Vikings came
raidin' and burnin' and pillagin' awa' back in the dark ages!'
mutters Dad, and with that, a worrying truth starts to dawn
on me. I stop building my spaceship and look up at him. It
was becoming clear that other than showing me how angry
he with the Celtic fans, there was nothing else really he could
do about it.

Then, all of a sudden, there were signs that a recommen-
dation was coming. 'Well, we're jist nae havin' this min!' Who
was not having what, I thought. 'Fit I'm gan tae dee min is
write a letter, a proper een, to the Aberdeen police makin' it
clear that we canna hae 'is in the future.' I frowned at him.
Was that it? Was he telling me it was OK? A letter to the
Aberdeen police. A proper one. This was the measure, the
package of reforms that would ensure we survived Old Firm
games in the future? It was about as much use as the almost
complete *Parkhead Destroyer* in front of me. He stared blankly
back at me for a second, shrugged his shoulders, went downstairs and had some pints. I finished my spaceship, before going
to bed.

As I lay that night, turning it all over in my ten-year-old
head, it seemed there was no way round it. If what I'd seen
today was anything to go by, then there was just no way of
knowing if you were going to escape football matches against
the Old Firm in safety. I now knew that their supporters
were every bit as terrifying as I'd suspected from seeing them

on the terraces, although seeing it was to believe it. But even by Old Firm standards this riot was particularly angry, not that I was to know that at the time. When the dust eventually settled around this game over the next few months, you could be forgiven for believing that the reaction of the Celtic fans was actually a group tantrum following a mass premonition about what was to come. That day was as much about a coming of age for me, as it was for my team. In time we would come to realise that it was that slender 1-0 victory over Celtic that caused the balance of power to finally start tipping away from the Old Firm, for the first time in history. This was the day that Aberdeen's ascent to the top of the game really started.

The first signs came immediately when Aberdeen's form in the league transformed with every other match, taking Dad and me to more and more games. But the first big test for our new promise would be to reach the Scottish Cup Final. To do that, we had to win our semi against St Mirren on 3 April 1982, to be played at Parkhead of all places – the home of Celtic! And we would be going to the game, too. After what I'd come through in February, the idea of going there even for a neutral game seemed an enormous risk. It would turn out to be another eye-opening day.

'They say that it's one o' the maist dangerous places in the whole a Europe …' pronounces Uncle David sombrely, as he starts the car, reverses and then horses down our drive in his Cortina, on our way to Parkhead for the Scottish Cup semi. Everyone loved Uncle David. He was cool.* He was my mum's

---

* Not only was he cool, but I'd discover many years later he was among the first journalists to take a rollicking from the great man, Fergie, at a press conference at Love Street in the 1970s before Fergie left St Mirren. If that isn't cool, I don't know what is!

younger brother by six years but there was a youthfulness
about him that made him feel much closer to my generation
than my parents'. However cool he was, right now, this was
the last thing I needed to hear. This was exactly why Dad and
I had observed a sort of unwritten rule; that we simply did
not go to games in Glasgow. And the only reason we're going
today is because he was with us, he is our security measure.
He'd know how to get there and how to deal with any Glasgow
things that happened, having lived there for a couple of years
in the 1970s. But he clearly had no idea of just how terrified
I had become about being around the Old Firm (even if it
was just their ground).

'... and I was always told that it wisna really wise to get
oot a the car ...' continues David. Judging by the fairly wary
look my dad is giving him from the front passenger seat, his
hysteria is not far behind mine. '... Even the cats carry knives!'

Dad does a laddish sort of exaggerated laugh, as if he'd been
waiting for the punchline all the time, but I know he's really
just relieved that David was only joking. As far as I was
concerned, this was no time to joke. There was another very
good reason to be concerned that day, something that Uncle
David was probably not aware of. He maybe had proper
terracing credentials, unlike my dad, who was incapable of
even shouting in tune, but he knew next to nothing about
what had been happening over the last couple of months. For
a start, he had not witnessed the riot of the Beach End after
the Celtic game in February. The way I saw it was that we had
been warned, very clearly, outside the Beach End that day not
to upset them again. So what had we done? Almost everything
in our power to upset them even more.

Since knocking Celtic out of the cup, we witnessed arguably
the most blistering spell of league form we ever saw, hammering
Hibs, St Mirren and Airdrie, our mid-table bedfellows of earlier
in the season, with 3-0 and 4-1 victories home and away, but

more importantly beating Dundee United and Rangers too. To top it all off, our run of form had culminated the previous week with another 1-0 victory against Celtic, this time at Parkhead, narrowing the gap between them and us at the top from nine to four points. If we were due a hiding back in February, God knows what they would do to us now. Even the Scottish Football League seemed to be aware of the dangers, having rearranged a league game for Celtic along the Clyde in Greenock at the same time as our semi-final in an attempt to divert their attentions away from Aberdeen's visiting supporters. Uncle David might have been a bit less cocksure about it all if he'd been following events. But as we edged our way into Glasgow, the butterflies kicked in properly, and I started to wonder if Uncle David had been joking after all.

I'd never seen anything quite like it. Great open spaces of wasteland, interspersed with pockets of derelict and seemingly uninhabitable tenement blocks with dozens of boarded-up windows, menacing groups of locals, many of them wearing Celtic tops, hanging around on the street, staring maliciously into the cars on our route to the ground. I find myself cowering down at the window ledge. Eventually, we see the enormous curved end of Parkhead, and before it is yet another huge open expanse of wasteland that was being used as a car park. As far as I can see, it's only Aberdeen fans that are parking there, but even before I could start to relax as a result, I notice that there are dozens of little boys standing about between the cars.

It's obvious somehow that they are not with the Dons fans that are parking their Mercs, Volvos and BMWs. Their posture, clothes, facial expressions, everything makes them totally distinct. And before we've even turned the engine off, one of them is already standing outside Uncle David's driver side door. 'Watch yer motor mister!' asks the boy. I say 'asks', but you'd be forgiven for taking this as a statement. He was going to watch our motor, and it would cost Uncle David some money, judging by the open hand, unsubtly inserted into Uncle David's ajar car door, before he'd even set foot on the ground. Why would a boy of my sort of age want to watch our car? Who was going to be interested in Uncle David's relatively shit-looking Cortina here? Especially since it's surrounded by so many other, more affluent, certainly newer looking cars in the car park? And then the penny drops. They hate Aberdeen. These are the sons and wee brothers of the main Celtic army, told to go out and take our money then wreck our cars while we are at the game, the Celtic people now so sick, so fed up with us, especially after we beat them here again last week. That was surely it.

What happened next would surely guarantee my worst fears. The same boy turns to the group of Dons fans who'd parked next to us as they all emerge from their enormous Range Rover, and asks them if they want their motor watched too. While my frowning Uncle David is trying to express his dissent by making a meal out of rummaging in his trouser pocket for some change, the 20-stone Range Rover driver has an alto-gether more direct approach. 'Fuck aff ya little tink!' he bellows, bent down, shouting in the Parkhead boy's face, at the top of his voice. Jesus ... all hell is going to break loose now ... Stunned, the boy stumbles to get out of range of any violent follow up, but is already warning of the revenge that is coming as he scampers off in the direction of the tenements behind us. 'See yous aifter the match, me and ma brothers'll be back! Yous are aw deid! ... and yer fuckin' motors!' he shouts back from his crumpled hate-ridden face, clearly directing his threat to all of us. When I look round at Uncle David, I find him looking, for the first time that day, as bewildered as me. But even worse, a 10p piece is sitting in his open, outstretched hand. Jesus, he hasn't managed to pay! What are we going to do now, given that the boy had already stormed off in the

opposite direction? Run after him and apologise for forgetting and give him the money, and maybe give him our number
plate so they would know not to attack our car? Somehow, I
just couldn't see that working in practice. A payment would
surely be critical now if our car was to have any chance of
being roadworthy when we come back after what the Range
Rover guy did … But what was to stop our car being caught
up in the massive backlash of retribution caused by the Range
Rover guy anyway, given we parked right next to him? It was
as disastrous a start to our semi-final trip as you could have
hoped for.

There was surely only one thing for it. We have to go home.
We just have to go now. 'Are we just going home then?' I beg,
holding the button of the Cortina's back right passenger door
handle in. Nothing could have been worse than staying here,
if we'd broken down on the motorway we'd be stuck all right,
but there would be no danger of a band of enraged Celtic fans
appearing on the horizon. If we'd lost or forgotten the tickets
then we would just go home now. Both Uncle David and Dad
blanked me, said nothing and started making their way inde-
cisively towards the ground.

'What if they come back?' I say frantically, running round
in front of them as they walked.

'Jist you be quiet!' blasts Uncle David at me. That's it now.
My whole day is in total ruins. If there was one thing I had
been more excited about than anything else, it was going to
this game with Uncle David. Big 1970s hair, cool denim clothes,
able to sing songs heartily at football matches (I knew this for
a fact since we'd done a few verses in his lounge in Inverurie
as if we were in the Beach End), I'd been dreaming for ages
about standing with him among the real Beach End boys at
games, getting to the heart of the mental singing bit, blending
in, credible because of him. But right now, as we stand and
queue at the turnstiles, he's not only disgusted with me but

he's clearly anxious too, stretching his neck round others in our queue, looking back repeatedly towards the car, silent, sullen, reinforcing, reconfirming my conviction that we are not going to survive our Parkhead adventure. If someone came up to me and offered to teleport me back to the house in Perth as long as I never ever came back to the football, I'd jump at it. For the rest of the run-up to the game and most of the first half, none of us says a word. And in any case, the Beach End boys are nowhere to be seen (certainly not heard), as the enormous away end at Parkhead drowns the sprinkling of Dons fans in its sheer scale. The place itself was having an overall diminishing effect on the entire experience.

Initially, I am jolted out of my anxiety as the inside of the enormous Parkhead arena opens up to me. It is much bigger than I'd expected. At least twice the size of any of the East Coast grounds I'd been to and much bigger in the flesh (or concrete) than you got from the TV. I realised there and then that if it was hard to bear for the likes of us when we'd lose to Dundee United, then no wonder the Celtic people went mental when they lost to us. I then spend a good ten minutes simply in awe of the main stand. The finest piece of Scottish football ground architecture I'd seen, all seated, with the capacity of the whole of Pittodrie and a towering, modern roof dominating the rest of the arena. It had been designed to tell the world 'the home team wins European Cups'. But as the game gets underway, and the shouts of the players consistently break through the noise of the crowd, it felt like we were playing the wrong sport there. Seventeen thousand people had turned up – as healthy a crowd an Aberdeen v St Mirren game could expect to poll for any fixture – but the unavoidable emptiness of the place, the sheer inadequacy of our presence, seems to sap the occasion of its sparkle. Half-time comes and goes. Apart from a burst of drama midway through the second half, when St Mirren took the lead and then we equalised from the penalty spot almost immediately afterwards, the event was a washout. But the closer we get to the end, the more our post-match fate took over my thoughts as the sweat of my palms soaks its way through the pages of my tightly gripped programme.

I'd also realised that there was much more to worry about than just the car park attendants and their brothers. What were the chances that all the Celtic fans that usually came here had been able to get into the Morton game along at Greenock that afternoon? Would they all want to go to a crap league game like that anyway? Even if they did, I knew from my football annuals that Cappielow only held 10,000 or so and judging by the size of Parkhead, there could literally be tens of thousands of Celtic fans kicking around outside their stadium with nothing else to do but ambush us ... and why not? We beat them here yet again last week and they'll surely be incensed that we are back here today, at their direct expense, to secure our place in the Cup Final, using their home ground? They must hate us more and more ... The more all this turns over in my mind, the more I long for the game not to finish, convinced we'd walk out into a war zone of stick-wielding, bottle-hurling Celtic fans, a rerun of the riot in Aberdeen in February, only this time we'd nowhere to escape to, as our car park would surely be transformed into a scrapyard of vandalised cars ... That's what they said they'd do ... The whistle goes, final score Aberdeen 1 St Mirren 1. Gulp!

As the exodus begins, it seems that Dad is making no attempt to implement the 'stay later' policy we'd agreed sometime after the Beach End riot back in February, but somehow it seems to make sense to huddle together as we come out of the ground. As soon as a view extends across the car park, it seems to my eternal relief that no one is around, apart from us Dons fans. We don't waste any time getting to the car. David does a quick circuit, kicks the tyres; everything seems

OK. Even the Range Rover looked untouched next to us. We hastily jump in; David turns the key, ignition! Thank God! I eagerly hide the three scarves under the jackets that had been tossed into the back seat, as we drive off onto London Road. I sense Dad and Uncle David's relief as they start chatting again as if they'd been doing so unbroken throughout the game. And before we've even hit the motorway, I'm asleep like a log and remain so all the way home. Four days later, we win the replay 3-2 after extra time. Now we were going to have to go back to Glasgow for the Final. This time it's the real thing –against Rangers! Now we would face the Old Firm people, in their backyard and this time, they would all be there ...

> *We are Rangers!*
> *Super Rangers!*
> *No one likes us!*
> *We don't care!*
> *We hate Celtic!*
> *Fenian bastards!*
> *And we will fight them!*
> *Every-where!*

sing the Gers fans at the stationary traffic as they get back into their bus. We're queuing up at the bottleneck of Dunblane on the way to Glasgow for the Cup Final. Some Rangers fans had taken advantage of the jam to leave their bus and irrigate the unsuspecting farmland of Sheriffmuir with a couple of thousand gallons of pish. Once the other side of Dunblane, still behind the same bus, the Gers fans are now 'mooning' out of the window towards Dons fans they see in cars and buses. The Aberdeen fans return the compliment.

This was not really on a par with the pre-match civilisation that Dad and I had become accustomed to. The only bit of pink hide you'd see from our car window was possibly a glimpse of the wafer-thin ham slices in our sandwiches that we'd wash down with orange juice. We'd also have a ritually positioned box of tissues between the gear stick and the handbrake for mutual convenience, so we could wipe away any globules of mayo or wayward crumbs around our mouths. But the major difference today is that we are on a bus (although our dietary habits are the same). Gus Clark, one of Dad's fellow teachers (a Saints man first, Aberdeen sympathiser second), was also a piper in the Vale of Atholl Pipe Band. They were to participate in the traditional pre-match entertainment at Hampden that day and he had offered to give us a run to the game. It was all too good to be true – we were going to the biggest match ever and this time it was safe!

The pipe band bus would park within a few steps of the main stand, which meant we had only to walk a couple of hundred yards to get to the Aberdeen end. All inside the Hampden car park area, so I was told, was ultra safe. And because we were in a bus with pipers, a sort of neutral Scottish thing that everyone loved, I could take in all the antics of the football traffic and people on our way to the game, a bit like being at the safari park: you could stare as much as you like and, as long as you don't venture outside your vehicle, you're safe. And then there was the game to look forward to. We were favourites and no wonder. Although Celtic won the league again, our form had continued to improve as the season wore on, losing only once since the defeat to Celtic at home in January. It meant that we had sensationally closed a nine-point gap to two points, pushing the title campaign right to the very last game of the season. As our journey progressed, however, it became clear that there was something up with Dad. Today would not be about my Old Firm fears and worries. It was to be all about Dad's – altogether a different ball game.

When I think about it now, there must have been hundreds of Dons fans, like Dad, in buses and cars on the way to the game all sitting and looking rather vacant. Consciously or not, they were facing up to the same truth, the one that Harry Carter had forced upon Dad in the Grampian Hotel away back in 1976, that beating the Old Firm in finals at Hampden was nigh-on impossible. Haunting them right now were memories of all those recent Cup Final failures, particularly those against Rangers. They'd be recalling how hopelessly they'd coped with those defeats, like Dad during the 1978 Scottish Cup Final against Rangers, storming about the house, banging doors and swearing when Rangers went 2-0 up, before escaping and going to build his Dodge City cabinet out of earshot of the football on TV.

But, as we passed Cumbernauld on our way to Hampden, my dad's mood became even more ridiculous, when he heard the answer to a question in Gus Clarke's specially prepared Scottish Cup Final pre-match quiz that we were halfway through.

'Nineteen twenty-nine! No way!' repeats Dad disbelievingly as the answer to the question, 'In which year did Rangers last lose a Scottish Cup Final to a team other than Celtic?' is read out. 'At wis ten years afore the war even started!'

He knew that Rangers had been pretty much invincible in Cup Finals since time immemorial. But he's genuinely gobsmacked to find out it was as bad as this. The quiz rolls on, normally an occasion that Dad would have revelled in, showing off and impressing everyone with his football knowledge. Instead, he is oblivious to it all, and his communication function seems now limited to spitting out hysterical perspectives on the 1929 bombshell he'd just heard. '... Fifteen years afore I wis born!'

There was no question about it; that was some record. I'd seen him a bit like this before when we'd play the old

Firm at home in big league games. But today it makes no sense. Even if the 1929 stat was true, look at the form differences between the two sides today, we had literally been kicking Rangers' arse all over Scotland in the previous couple months: 3-1 at Ibrox in March, 3-1 at Pittodrie in April ...

'... Over half a century ago!'

... and on top of that, just last week, we meted out yet another pounding to them, this time a 4-0 demolition at Pittodrie in the last game of the league season. How could we score ten goals against them in three matches and seriously have doubts about winning today?

'I wish it was as simple as 'at min.'

I look at him as if he has two heads. If it was not as simple as 'who was the best side', then what else could it be? But he is inconsolable about 1929, so I just ignore him. Gradually, as the bus weaves its way through South Glasgow and eventually reaches the ground, the excitement starts taking over. The streets are already thronging, scarf and flag sellers everywhere, fans milling around singing, the sense of anticipation now filling the bus. And even better than I'd hoped, our bus parks in literally the very front set of spaces behind Hampden's main stand. We jump out, say bye to Gus and march round to the Aberdeen end, passing the odd Rangers fan, but none of the dangerous looking ones we'd normally see outside Pittodrie. This was what I'd always hoped it would be like: lots of excitement but no danger. Once up the steps and into the ground though, it would only get better. The enormous arena of Hampden – even bigger than Parkhead – could not have changed much since I had been there two and half years before. But, of course, today, the supporters of the sorts of team that grounds like Parkhead and Hampden were built for *are* here. All of them it seems. The six segments of the covered Mount Florida end, and four columns making up the western half of the North Stand opposite are already full. Ten neatly assembled divisions, the complete Rangers army. And gradually, they start summarily bellowing the 'formbook based' optimism out of me.

Each new song rattles at lightning speed round the cohorts who each seem to know when to start singing, each new song hits a piercing volume, each one an awesome battle cry. Initially, I find myself seduced into a smile, almost forgetting whose side I am on, in awe, in respect at their display of raw, total vocal force. Time and again in the run-up to the game, they power out songs from their now familiar list that are gradually wearing me down into submission. It is every bit as imposing, as intimidating as I had imagined. But nothing could prepare you for them in the flesh, nothing could prevent you from being cowed, diminished by their edginess, their energy, their aggression. Seconds now before kick-off, the uneasy body language, the palpable nervousness that had reeked from my dad all day and now from every other older Dons fans around me, all suddenly makes sense. We just have to pray that our players, unlike the fans, are somehow immune to all this. As we all stand serious, silent, swallowing hard, the game starts ...

The two teams dance about each other, in midfield. Every now and then I can hear the Aberdeen fans, but only the clapping hands of those in my immediate vicinity, as we win a bit of possession, then a free-kick. McLeish leaps, his header goes just over the bar. I see widespread clapping now across our fans, but still I can't hear them. And then, the hand of history falls on our shoulders ...

Rangers mount their first serious attack on goal ... the ball sweeps through midfield to Gordon Dalziel on the right wing, the Rangers crowd roar in anticipation interrupting their singing ... Dalziel crosses short to the near side of the six-yard box ... the cross is met two feet off the ground by the horizontal body of John McDonald who glances a header past the spread-eagled Jim Leighton. Hampden's awesome scale plays yet another trick on me when I see the Rangers fans leap into the air but hear no noise, and for a split second there was a hope that they'd all realised it was offside before any of them could roar in delight. But then the seismic thunder of 30,000 men reaches my ears. And their awesome clamour is gutsy, reflecting all those painful defeats against us recently, desperate to reassert their Hampden dominance over us ... The game restarts. The whole stadium suffers a series of minor earthquakes as it shudders and bounces to the rhythm of the even more thunderous choir that now seems to come from everywhere in the ground, apart from our end behind the goal. What's worse is that they sense, and so do we, that they can score again. Now, the Dons fans have visibly gone silent. Eventually I hear from close by the odd unconvincing attempt to rally, 'Come on Aberdeen!' but the stress in the Aberdeen end reveals itself when I hear tuts and mutters, minor arguments breaking out. My dad is also close to breaking too. He even bollocks another Aberdeen fan for agreeing with the ref when he gave a (justified) foul against the Dons. The doubts of the veteran Aberdeen fans are now dominating the whole mood in our end. They've been here before. It's almost as if we all have. We don't believe. We can't believe. Thirty minutes on the clock and we've already lost the game in our minds.

Two minutes later, a corner for Aberdeen ... Hewitt swings the ball in deep, which is beaten out only as far as Alex McLeish. He controls the ball, draws back a few steps as if to take a penalty in a rugby match, and sails a perfectly curled shot into the top left-hand corner of Ian Stewart's goal. The explosion of relief and elation in the Aberdeen end transports me off my feet and deposits me 15 yards away from my dad in the most enormous group huddle. We're still in there, we're still with it, we can still do it. But only just, you sense, only just.

Now pockets of singing pick up, even though from the clapping you can see there must be at least three different songs now on the go in our end. Half-time comes. Twenty thousand heads shake and shake again, even now at 1-1 the mood is all about hanging on. Have we gone back in time? Is this what it was like in 1978 and 1979? How can we be so lacking in belief after last week, when at this stage we were up 4-0? How could I have got so sucked into their lack of faith? The second half comes and goes with more of the same, lots of nervous posturing in the midfield area, lots of noise and tune from the Rangers people, thousands of pulping intestines in our end. The final whistle blows ... extra time.

Two minutes played and immediately we sense that Aberdeen are the fitter, the stronger side, there's so much space ... Strachan picks up the ball on the right ... he loops in a cross ... McGhee runs in on the blind side, a downward header on the run from ten yards, the ball powers past Stewart in goal, IT'S IN! The celebration is massive and carries on well after the restart, but there's a restraint, something kicks in as we come to our senses ... we realise this is the point we've reached so often in the past only to throw it away, and now the much more tragic, unthinkable consequences of failure seem to stare us all in the face ... 27 minutes to go ... can we hold out? We keep attacking, still by miles the fitter side, a throw-in from Simpson to McGhee, he turns and beats Alex Miller, he's now at the by-line, he crosses ... Stewart dives, two Rangers legs flail and miss the ball, it rolls perfectly to the unmarked Strachan at the back post, all he has to do is tap it in ... 3-1! A massive release of tension explodes from our end as the group hug extends and bounces its way across the terraces, constantly reconfiguring itself. Dad is delirious, I've never seen him so elated, we miss a couple of minutes of the match ... but it's almost finished now ... From now on in it's all show, as finally the Rangers people concede, the

singing stops and a mass exodus from the covered Mount
Florida end commences. 'Cheerio, Cheerio' we taunt now so
strong and confident and now so loud. Three-one would do,
3-1 was a good sound win, proper revenge for 1978 and '79
they were all starting to say, but more drama on the field was
still to come ...

Neale Cooper breaks past the Rangers last man, Jackson,
in the centre circle, who mis-hits his back-pass ... a great
whoosh rises from our end as Cooper and the Rangers goalie
Stewart suddenly start charging at each other for what has
now become a 50/50 ball ... the ball ricochets between them,
but breaks for Cooper ten yards from the empty Rangers goal
... he takes an exaggerated run up to the ball and wellies it
in the net for 4-1, before running off towards the Rangers
fans behind the goal, his arms flailing, teeth gritted, to round
off the heaviest defeat they'd ever suffer against a provincial
in a Cup Final at Hampden. We've done the unthinkable. Dad
and Uncle David are teenagers again, beaming, laughing everywhere, there's joy gushing out of every face, clapping and
shouting as usual in disorganised fashion in our end, but now,
we can hear ourselves, now everyone can hear us. Now we
had all come of age!

And so, for the first time in the modern era, the impossible was happening ... a third force was emerging in Scottish
Football, a real one, one that could beat the Old Firm when
it mattered and win trophies. The expectation levels around
Aberdeen were higher than ever. The following season,
1982/83, would certainly not disappoint, although it would
turn out to be very different from the way any of us expected.
For me personally the first part of the season was taken up
by a personal civil war that would rage on until November
with our junior 'New Firm' rivals Dundee United. And as
the promise of success mounted in the New Year, I would
find myself facing the terrifying consequences of an ever

more carried-away Dad, in a Scotland full of ever more rattled, ever more dangerous Old Firm supporters. But first, I had some serious 'unfinished business' to attend to in the very first game of the season, against Dundee United at Tannadice.

Chapter 6

I Hate Dundee United

'So are you all excited?' asks Uncle Ian, my mum's cousin, appearing in the kitchen, playfully bobbing and weaving all around me, occasionally launching a toy right hook. There were dozens of North-East relations like him, all larger than life and each with an insatiable appetite to tease, annoy and be cheery. I say nothing in an attempt to advertise to him that this was not the time for any cheer as I struggle to manage the butterflies half an hour away from the 'must-win' first match of the new 1982/83 league season.

'Fa's gan tae stop the Dons 'is year?' he says with an exaggerated clap followed by intense hand rubbing, thankfully drawing his boxing routine to a stop. I normally knew better than to get drawn into a conversation with him especially in this sort of mood, since his aim here would undoubtedly be to wind me up. But in this instance, it was difficult not to. This was more or less the same question I'd spent most of the summer contemplating and I'd had little or no opportunity to speak to anyone about it (other than Dad, who'd got bored of it months ago). I imagined it was what most of the rest of Scotland was asking itself too. I couldn't help myself.

'It depends on injuries,' I start.

'Fit d'ye mean?' Ian asks. I'd been reading and hearing about our squad's 'depth' over the summer but to be honest I neither understood this nor believed that having lots of players was good. The players who were subs were normally the inconsistent ones, that's why they were subs. If they had to play in the first team at all it weakened us, so what was the point of 'depth' if it meant crap players? As far as I could see, all we needed to do was to keep our top 13 players fit. But there was one that I knew was much more important than all the rest. 'The main thing is Strachan, if he doesn't get injured then …' I pause to find the right words.

'… the Dons'll win everything?' Uncle Ian adds, finishing my sentence. Even though I sense that Uncle Ian is once again attempting to take the piss, I shrug my shoulders, since it was difficult to see past it. Ian nods annoyingly, as if to say he'd finally been enlightened about how it all worked.

'Now, dis 'at include the Cup-Winners' Cup?'

I might have guessed it. I look at him witheringly, any faint hopes that I am, for the first time in my life, finally having a sensible grown-up conversation with him about anything, are dashed with this ridiculous suggestion. 'The important thing is to win the league,' I state indifferently, pretending to examine my nails. This was a line I'd remembered hearing Fergie say in an interview last year. It was the basic truth behind any interest in football, certainly for fans of teams that *could* win the league. If you had to choose one from the three domestic trophies, there was no question. We'd have traded it instantly for the cup-run we had the year before, in spite of how thrilling it all was. Deep down, the league was what everyone really wanted to win. And this year, 1982/83, according to all the papers, the TV, everyone you spoke to, Aberdeen were firm favourites.

'So fa's the unlucky victims the day then?' asks Ian.

'Dundee United at Tannadice,' I respond.

'United at Tannadice? A walk in the park min!' comments

Ian, chortling. Now he knew fine that games against Dundee United were anything but.

'Fit d'ye reckon, 4-0?' Ian says.

'Four-nil? At Tannadice? No way!' I snort in disgust, trying to fend off the 'fate-tempting' recklessness of even talking about such an unlikely scoreline at Tannadice.

'Come on min! Aifter the Dons haimmered Rangers in the Cup Final twa month ago?' barks Ian. 'Yer nae feart o' little Dundee United are ye?' he taunts. I tut loudly, turn and amble off towards the lounge.

'Hey min! Far are you gan?' shouts Ian now dropping any pretence at all that he wasn't amusing himself by teasing me. I ignore him and keep going. 'Gordon, 'at loon's feart! Ye canna tak him tae the fitba!'

Too bloody right I was 'feart' of Dundee United. And it was the anticipation of the struggle we knew we were going to have later that day, Scottish Cup holders or not, that had me racked with nerves and all tight inside. But there was already much more to it for me than simply playing a side we knew were a threat. Today was all about unfinished business, revenge against 'little Dundee United' for football crimes against Aberdeen last season. As we drove to Tannadice for the first time, the painful memories of the turbulent episode I'd already lived through with Dundee United came flooding back to me, something that had started in the summer of 1981.

'Stuart! Come on, we're ready to go!' shouts my mum from the kitchen window. I give my ball a final belt against the wall, before turning and leaping the two or three yards over the flowerbed to the back door of the kitchen, a jump that due to the difference in height between take off and landing, made you feel like you were in mid-air for an impossible amount of time. It was one of those novelties about a new

house* that reminded me every day about how much happier
we all were, now that we'd moved back to Perth, away from
the bleak wilderness that was the crap village of Muthill where
we had been exiled for six months since we first moved. It
meant I could play football in parks and fields with my old
pals again, and our new back garden had excellent facilities
for games of one v one, wallie or football tennis. Another
bonus was that it was 20 miles nearer Aberdeen so Dad had
promised we'd be going to more games than ever. But right
now, we're off once again to find a new dining room table.
It had already become an interminable summer-long campaign,
having kicked-off way back in June, and had taken us to literally every single town within an hour's drive or so of Perth
that had a furniture shop. That was, apart from Dundee, where
we were going today.

Initially, it had been difficult to see how I was going to cope
with the boredom of the shopping trips. But very quickly, the
whole experience would become the highlight of the summer
because of something we started doing on our way home from
these frequent excursions. As soon as Mum confirmed that
official table hunting business for the day was over, Dad was
unleashed to take all the time he needed (more or less) to
track down the local town's football stadium (or stadiums in
the case of the larger towns), either trying to trace the route
taken by the bus, if he'd been to that particular ground in the
1960s, or stopping to ask people on the street for directions.

---

* The new house was basically thanks to my mum. Although Dad was the
'Chancellor' (his family nickname for most of his life), it was my mum
who was behind the major decisions they made like buying houses, furniture, etc. She wanted the Glasgow Road house more than anyone and she
convinced Dad that although it came at a hefty price and had more space
than they could believe, it was for the long term. It was the best thing
they ever did.

Once located, we'd normally then circle the stadium, maybe park up outside the main stand, turn the engine off to pause for a moment, so we could all get a proper sense of what sort of club it was.

Dad had a 'main stand theory' that argued that you could tell a lot about a club's past from its main stand. Basically, if you'd won anything at all in Scottish football, you were likely to have a main stand that reflected this. It was true. The most successful sides had impressive main stands often with grand wooden facades (a bit like an enormous version of the front of the Waltons' house), holding up to 10,000 with an upper tier of 25 rows of seats, and normally a standing terraced area below. Mostly built before the war, they'd dominate the rest of the ground from inside but also the immediate area around the stadium. They were like great local icons, personalities from yesteryear, telling a story of lost, past greatness, of times when, according to Dad, there must have been real belief that the clubs were up there with the Old Firm. That was true for Easter Road (Hibs), Tynecastle (Hearts), East End Park (Dunfermline) and Dens Park (Dundee). But there was one glaring exception – Tannadice, home of the current holders of the League Cup, Dundee United. We all latched onto it immediately.

'Why have Dundee United got a rubbish stand like that Dad?' I ask on our way back from Dundee that day. It was true. 'Rubbish' was maybe harsh, but 'eccentric' it certainly was. It seemed as if someone had gone out of their way to build the oddest-looking main stand imaginable at Tannadice. Not only was it tiny, it had also been built in the least sensible place from which to view a match, as far as I could see. It was squashed up and wrapped in an L-shape around the south-east corner of the pitch, sticking high up above the ground like some enormous army watchtower, with a great bulge overhanging the road behind. It's capacity was only 2,500, not that much bigger than the stands at Montrose or Arbroath, and well below the capacity of those of Saints or Raith Rovers, all lower league teams. But all of those other stadiums had conventional main stands that ran the length of the pitch or were at least aligned with the middle of the playing surface – United's didn't even reach the halfway line!

'Weel, the first thing ye hiv tae understand is far Dundee United hiv come fae,' explains Dad. 'Fan I wis your age, Dundee United were nothing mair than a Stenhousemuir, a Stranraer, or an East Stirling. In ither words, a very sma' fish in a sma' pond.' It was true. Later that night, I discovered how easy it was in my Dad's United programmes from the late 1950s to find results like Dundee United 0 Greenock Morton 7 and Cowdenbeath 6 Dundee United 0.

'But at least 'at spared 'em gettin' thrashed by the Old Firm like us and a' the rest o' the First Division teams!' Dad jokes. Although why it would be better to get thrashed by one team as opposed to any other was beyond me and my mum and sister, but we laugh along with Dad anyway.

'The only thrashing United wid tak fae a side ca'ed Rangers back in the 50s wid a been Berwick Rangers!' Dad jokes.*

'But their stand looked quite new and modern though,' said Mum.

'Aye, bit 'at's jist because it's teen them sae lang to build it!' laughs Dad. 'They'd started plannin' on a new een awa' back in the 1920s, but they were sae poor, it's teen them almost 40 years tae save up the cash tae actually dee it,' Dad points out. 'At's fit it's like for the minnow clubs,' says Dad, cocking his head in the rear-view mirror to me to underline

* This was actually true; Berwick Rangers demolished Dundee United 8-2 in a home Second Division match in February 1959!

the sorry plight of ailing football clubs in Scotland. 'But 'at new stand might jist hae been fit inspired them to new levels.'

'Why's that?' Mum asks.

'Because it was jist roon aboot when it wis completed that they got promoted. And fae that time, United remained in the top flight, hackin' about in lower reaches o' the table, along wi' the other no-hopers.'

'Did they ever beat Aberdeen back then?' I ask.

'I canna really mine min, nae very often if they did. We werna a great side, but we were a good bit better than United, of course,' says Dad. Whether he meant it or not, this was absolute nonsense, the two sides were as bad as each other and beat each other regularly. But, as usual, all Dad remembered from that time were the big games against the Old Firm.

'And then, Jim "Audrey Hepburn" McLean took the reins in the 1970s ...' Dad laughs again at his own joke, the stark contrast between the actress renowned for her sparkling smile and the dour Jim McLean is also lost on me, my mum and my sister. We all laugh again anyway. '... And it wis McLean that transformed United into a consistent top four side ...' Dad paused, '... and then they won *that cup*.' Up to that point Dad's summary of Dundee United's post-war history had been delivered with, at worst, an air of affectionate ridicule. But *that cup* he was referring to, the League Cup of 1979/80, which they'd won in the replay after my first ever Aberdeen game, was certainly not a joking matter.

'They'd jist nae right to win 'at.' He mutters, now even stopping short of referring to the 'cup' itself. 'A bloody disgrace!' And he starts going on and on as he'd done regularly since it had happened, about the agony of that experience. The third Final we'd lost in 18 months, the fact that we'd felt robbed in the first match, and that we'd put out both Old Firm sides on the way to the Final while United had got there without having to play a single Premier League side. I'd remembered how devastated he'd been that night, sitting pished in his chair in the lounge, his empty pint glass abandoned between his legs. But only now, in the wake of what I'd learned that day, was it becoming clear that when he said 'disgrace' it had little to do with any of that, and everything to do with who Dundee United were in his mind. It was much more about a sense of shame, a *real* sense of disgrace; losing cup finals to the Old Firm was bad, but it was certainly a lot more dignified than losing out to our junior 'New Firm' rivals. And now I understood why my Dad would turn his nose up at this very label – 'The *New Firm indeed!*' I'd often heard him scoff disapprovingly when he'd come across it in the paper, TV or radio. This term had been coined by the press to describe the challenge Aberdeen and Dundee United were mounting against the 'Old Firm' of Rangers and Celtic. Although he never really had a bad word to say about United (any and all challenges to the Old Firm were welcome), I could now see that there was nonetheless something that just seemed wrong, some-thing demeaning about Aberdeen being thought of in the same light as Dundee United. Hibs, Hearts and maybe Dundee were what Dad considered to be Aberdeen's peers in Scotland, and as Dad had shown, they had the main stands to prove it. But not United, never Dundee United.

And that, I believe, was it. That 30-minute stint in the car between Dundee and Perth was all the propaganda that I would need to pigeonhole Dundee United in my mind as a team that would (or should) stand below us in the caste system of Scottish football. From that point on, Aberdeen *were* the New Firm in my mind, and we weren't going to need Dundee United and their crap ground to help us to dominate the Scottish game. The new season, 1981/82 would be about one thing, and one thing only – winning the league. And we'd lots of other reason to be confident.

We knew that Gordon Strachan would be back from the

injury that had kept him out of the squad since Christmas the year before. This alone had cost us the 1980/81 title we'd been on course to win at the end of December when we'd stood four points clear of Celtic. With Strachan back in the team we'd beaten Manchester United, West Ham and Southampton with some style in a pre-season knockout tournament and we'd coasted past the other teams in our League Cup section to reach the semi-finals. We seemed back to our best, bursting with confidence and ready for our first match of the new season, United at Tannadice. On 29 August 1981, the radio was blasting out from inside the garage, Dad was fixing the shed and I was on the grass, acting out the tanking we were going to give 'minnows' Dundee United later that day.

The long back wall of our garden, which in my mind was the right wing at Pittodrie, was as usual providing me with an excellent supply of crosses, and the shorter end wall was the King Street or Beach End goalmouth in front of which stood various imaginary and hapless goalkeepers. Today, I was in the middle of the lawn – now Tannadice – playing the parts in turn of Strachan or Simpson, sometimes both, setting up sweeping, devastating moves via the wall, just like the Dons were going to be doing in a little while. Up front was me again, this time McGhee or Black, finishing off the slick interplay with the wall with a variety of stylish volleys and headers past Hamish McAlpine, the United goalie. I had my new Dons strip on and was in my element, burning up the excess excitement caused by the onset of the match. But at 3.33 p.m. that day, my ball stood stationary in the middle of the imaginary Tannadice turf, and I was lying, prostrate, next to it, face down. Up in Dundee, something was going wrong.

In 33 minutes, Dundee United had already scored their third goal; they were 3-0 up. They didn't normally commentate on the first half of the 'live' game on Radio Scotland in those days, but there was such a mauling taking place at Tannadice, the other Premier League games didn't get a look in. And it had to be David Begg, with his vivid and impassioned commentary, delivering the goals over the radio. I'd already learned that this guy's electrifying description of play made you feel like you were there. But this was not the day to discover his skills since every time United got the ball in the second half, the change in his voice imparted how likely it seemed they would score. And they scored again. Final score: Dundee United 4 Aberdeen 1! This was the first time I could remember being properly 'stung' by a defeat and it left me in a daze for the rest of the weekend, searching for answers, turning over and over in my mind, trying again and again to get sense of it out of my dad. Strachan was back, wasn't he? That meant that we'd be invincible again! A 4-1 thumping though? I couldn't remember losing by such a margin.* But there was just no explaining it.

In late October we had a chance for revenge by completing a League Cup semi-final victory against them, having already won the first leg at Tannadice 1-0. But we lost again and that night, for the first time, losing a football match had me in tears, punished once more by David Begg's voice, as it rose with excitement in anticipation of Paul Sturrock's second goal and United's third, as he burst through the Aberdeen defence to lash home the killer goal. This time we were at home and defeat meant that they were in the League Cup Final at our expense. As Begg went on and on about Sturrock's goal, my anger and frustration became uncontrollable, causing me to throw my scarf across the room onto the couch. My tantrum led to me taking the mother and father of all bollockings from

---

* This would prove to be the only time that Aberdeen would concede four goals in any domestic fixture under Fergie.

my disapproving mum, even more incensed at my petulance than I was at the score, and I was sent off to bed.

I may not have realised it as I lay awake for hours, gurning and snivelling, feeling sorry for myself, but that night Dundee United had brought my childhood to an abrupt and premature end. Over the previous two-month period, Dundee United had turned me into an emotional wreck, destroyed my team's season, causing me no end of mental torture and even bollockings from my mum.

So now, eleven months later, when almost the exact same set of fixtures were produced – with the first game of the 1982/83 league season at Tannadice and then United in the quarter-finals of the League Cup – vengeance was uppermost in my mind. I had not forgotten how much I hated Dundee United.

There's only one United,
And that's the fuckin' biscuit!
There's only one United,
And that's the fuckin' biscuit!

The chant rises from the thronging corridor of Aberdeen fans, mostly in their 20s and 30s, pouring out from buses and boozers dotted along Cleppington Road as we approach our parking spot. This is too good to be true; for the first time ever our fans are looking like a proper mental support. Singing ... and we're not even inside the ground! Dad and I get out of the car, parked safely in away territory on Arklay Street behind the allotments backing on to Tannadice Park, and walk with them towards the ground for the first game of the season, 4 September 1982, and my first ever game at Tannadice.

I pick up that familiar, normally unnerving smell of second-hand booze fumes pervading the air on our way to the ground.

But right now it's turning me on, as the purpose, swagger and menace of the Dons fans around me lets everyone know that they, we, are a crew on a mission. It is exactly what is needed, another 'big club' statement to show United who they're dealing with. And there's a real cocky edge, I sense, because of our Cup Final glory the previous season. I'd never seen anything remotely like it. This was surely why there was something different about the mood of the Aberdonians, something of a more confident, adventurous character than at home. And from the chat I overhear, dozens of them, like me, remember the first game of the season last year, when United hammered us 4-1. May be that's it. We are already enjoying the revenge we know we'll get; everyone knows that a side who can beat Rangers 4-1 in the Cup Final will be too strong for United today. And, just as I'm starting to get into it, the mood suddenly changes with the appearance of a band of around 30 or 40 burly Aberdeen tounsers* in the middle of the street. Wearing tight T-shirts, some with bellies hanging out, hair-dos half evolved on their way from '70s big' into '80s mullet', they start clapping and shouting, directing their chants towards a woman digging in her front garden on Sandemans Road as we pass.

> *Yer rakin' the bucket for something to eat,*
> *You find a dead rat and you think it's a treat,*
> *In yer Dundee slums!*
> *In yer Dundee slums!*

Dundee with its council house profile was an ugly place, certainly compared with Aberdeen and its elegant, confident,

---

* Someone from the city of Aberdeen as opposed to the Aberdeenshire countryside.

granite architecture, but I'd never expected our fans to be as rude and direct about it as this, especially not to someone actually in their own garden. She stops digging and looks round, staring chillingly at us. The Aberdeen fans keep shouting obscenities, about 'Scumdee' and 'Jute bastards' and then belt out another verse of the Dundee slums song, just to let her know that they meant what they said and weren't concerned about how rude it was. Dad reverts to 'responsible Dad' mode, looking away, tutting and shaking his head. I didn't like the thought that a group of incensed Dundonians, headed by her son, might come charging around the corner on hearing this. But even then, would they mess with us in this mood? I doubt it. In time, I'd come to realise that this was all part of the Tannadice experience, the only time when the Dons fans were guaranteed to come to life. As we reach the queues for the turnstiles, the tension heightens as we hear the non-stop singing ringing out from the United fans in the ground.

Sheep shagging bastards!
You're only sheep shagging bastards!
Sheep shagging bastards!
You're only sheep shagging bastards!

It was fairly clear to me then that if I'd the choice, I'd rather shag a sheep (whatever that meant) than eat a dead rat, but then again, I was only eleven. We get through the turnstiles and run up the unbelievably steep steps to the back gate of the North Enclosure. Teams of loud Dons fans are now streaming up the steps and congregating at the congested back gate to the covered terracing. They're buzzing, already joining in with the main core of Dons fans inside the ground exchanging chants with the United fans.

Uni-Ted!!
SHITE!!
Uni-Ted!!
SHITE!!

This is fantastic. Now safe inside the ground with the rest of the family, Fergie's barmy army, I'm feeling bulletproof. And at last, I'll get a chance to sing non-stop throughout the game. Fifteen minutes before kick-off the Aberdeen end is now filling up and the singing intensifies, it seems like the whole Aberdeen support has been in training over the summer (maybe at some course for incompetent fans at Parkhead or Ibrox?). I've never seen so many of them take part in the pre-match posturing, and create such an atmosphere. And from our end, it seems like our song is dominating the rest of the ground. Dad and me are caught up in it all, we're both singing and chanting, smiling, laughing. This is amazing. With the players poised to kick off the new season, the ground now bursting with anti-cipation, an intense, prolonged roar is created by both sets of fans, for once in unison, creating a deafening stereo effect all around the ground. The whistle blows.

Immediately United are on the attack, they hit the post with a Davie Dodds header in the first minute, which is parried by Jim Leighton at full stretch. The Dons are already on the back-foot ... United take the lead, left back Maurice Malpas scoring with a clean strike from 20 yards. Midway through the first half and Aberdeen are yet to threaten, what's happening? The Dons fans are subdued and struggle to raise the vocal backing to jolt their team out of its malaise. United's pressure is relent-less. They score again, this time a Davie Dodds header with which Leighton has no chance. Into the second half, the United fans in the Shed are singing the sheep anthem again, but there's no riposte from the Dons fans. United's pressure eases off, but there's still no punch from Aberdeen. We're starting to

concentrate on our inevitable defeat. Carried away by the Cup
Final-fuelled expectations and the mood of our fans prior to
the game, Dad's putting in the performance of a lifetime. He's
even calling the referee a 'cunt', a term only normally employed
by him for uncooperative nuts and bolts on the underside of
our P6 Rover. Everyone around us drowns in the frustration,
spitting much expletive-ridden bile at everyone on the pitch.
It finishes 2-0 to United.

We sat and festered in the car on the way home, in a perfect
silence broken only by a few angry tuts and deep sighs as we
both struggled to come to terms with what we'd come through.
I'd now seen it for the first time with my own eyes. Even with
the most bullish, most intimidating atmosphere I'd ever seen
us create, even with a side that could hammer Rangers 4-1 in
the Cup Final, even when our squad was at full strength, we
still could not beat Dundee United when we needed to. Before
we got home that night, I realised the League Cup game against
them in two weeks could not come soon enough. It was time
to put the primary objective of reclaiming our Premier League
title to one side, to focus on the more urgent short-term one
– the complete and utter destruction of Dundee United.

'Three goals … three goals, at Pittodrie,' I say to Dad as we
drive to Tannadice for the second leg, still dumbfounded by
the first leg's result of two weeks ago. It had been difficult
enough to accept losing to them yet again, but the injury of
conceding three goals to them at home had not even started
to heal, leaving me still numb, flat, trying to come to terms
with it every day since. 'Did you see what Fergie had to say
about it in Saturday's programme?' Dad shakes his head. Give
United half a chance and they'll take it. 'What sort of remark
was that? Would he have dared say something like that about
getting walloped 3-1 at home by Celtic?' I moped. 'Is Ferguson
the right man for us?' Dad continues shaking his head, saying

nothing. 'So tonight, we need to pull out a blinder Dad. But it's not going to happen, is it?' Dad makes no acknowledgement at all this time, unwilling to agree, but equally unwilling to contradict me, aware that my downbeat reflections, my exaggerated gloom are all part of a pre-emptive strategy, designed as a cushion for yet more Dundee United agony. We park up, buy a programme and make our way to the ground.

As we take up what would become our normal positions on the steps of Tannadice's North Stand terracing, I ask Dad for the programme we'd bought to kill some time while we waited for our pointless game to get underway. And that just depresses me even more. I'd never seen a United programme before (we'd failed to get one last time) but I suppose I'd been expecting something like ours. Instead, it was a tawdry three-tone postage stamp of a booklet, tangerine, black and white, and it looked like it should have had '6d' written on the front of it. It's real price, 30p, was only 10p less than the Aberdeen one but it had none of its professional colour printing and photography, and even less gloss or finish. A right rip-off. No wonder the Dons fans were quick to express their ever-ready contempt and snobbery, Jute bastards right enough I thought. But it just served to underline how ridiculous it was that we should be so incapable of beating a team like this, whose programme was as crap as Perth Saints'. And it wasn't just the programme. There were other things I'd noticed inside Tannadice that showed just how two-bob Dundee United really were.

'What on earth is that? I ask Dad, pointing at a rickety, rusty old frame sticking up in the corner of the away end, again something I hadn't noticed last time due to the size of the crowd.

'United's scoreboard,' says Dad. A scoreboard? All the ones I'd seen were electronic like the one at the Bernabeu or Wembley or Easter Road. 'We hid een like 'at in the 1960s,' says Dad,

'Twa al' mannies would come oot at half-time to hoist boards up in to it, carryin' a combination of letters and numbers – A 1-0, B 1-2 – and the programme would decode the teams A, B and so on.'

'Why don't they just use their tannoy like we do nowadays?' I ask, knowing that their tannoy system was perfectly good as they used it for everything else, announcing birthdays, team sheets and so on.

'It's tae mak sure that punters buy programmes – United need every penny they can get!' says a bloke in front of me, who'd overheard our conversation.

'Just like down the road at Cowdenbeath and along the Tay at Arbroath!' says another, causing a burst of laughter around us. Jesus, I thought, swallowing hard, as yet another painful truth hit home to me. Were United so poor that they needed to do that to survive? A club, who could beat us every other time we play them, was nonetheless still as skint as teams like Cowdenbeath or Arbroath? It was just getting worse and worse.

'Or maybe they're deliberately keepin' their feet on the grun', with a reminder of fit they used to be?' shouts another smartarse cheery Dons fan from two or three rows below us.

'Maybe they're keepin' it in case they ging back?' adds another behind us, as they all cackled away even more heartily. And well they might have laughed, because poking fun at United's humble facilities would be the only source of entertainment any of us would get that night.

Despite lots of careering about, hitting the post, the bar, huff and puff, Aberdeen just couldn't score. Then, midway through the second half, United get a penalty, and it is all over. And, of course, Luggie Sturrock puts it away. Not with a subtle chip or a carefully placed strike, but an almighty batter. As if to underline our fate that night, possibly our long-term fate against United, Luggie could enjoy the luxury of a careless, directionless thunder-blaster. I watch helplessly from the other end of the ground as the ball speeds like a bullet, unchallenged under Leighton's distant mid-air frame, seemingly going through the hopeless motions of diving, diving somewhere, anywhere. All of which causes a deafening, unforgiving thunder from the United supporters, and an exultant victory display in the Shed, Tannadice's hard-core home section. At that moment, they knew they were better than us, and want us to know, so, so badly. We knew all right.

'Let's go Dad,' I say, yanking my scarf off in one violent tug. I'd absorbed enough of the elated United fans, their jubilation now pervading the whole ground. Other Aberdeen fans have the same idea, as they start leaving in their droves. 'Dad?' I plead.

'Hey min!' barks Dad, pointing his finger at me without removing his eyes from the game on the pitch, still hoping, still praying that with three or four minutes to go we could score the required three goals to take the game to extra time. I continue my protest, with my hands in my pockets, looking down at a paper coffee cup on the steps that I paw with my foot. And then things get even more ridiculous.

As the formality plays itself out, Derek Stark, United's left back, stumbles over a routine pass-back to goalie Hamish McAlpine, giving Eric Black a half-chance. In contrast to Leighton's tragic dying swan antics faced with the penalty, McAlpine comes charging out of his box, skilfully dispossesses Black, shimmies in front of Hewitt before dribbling past him, and places an excellent pass up-field, almost creating a scoring chance. Hamish's flair causes the United fans to deliver another deafening roar, as if they'd scored again.

'Come on Dad, let's go,' I plead again now with more urgency.

'Hold on min!' Dad snaps, but then says nothing. I shut up, sensing I am teetering on the brink of an unprecedented public outburst. A minute later it's all over and we plod back to the car in silence.

'Dundee United 14 Aberdeen 3,' I say.

'Fit d'ye mean?' spits Dad, irritated by my inexplicable scoreline.

'Twice they beat us in the first game of the season, and twice they've knocked us out of the League Cup. Six games in total: total goals for Dundee United 14, total for Aberdeen 3.' Dad says nothing and I continue staring at him, trying to coax some sort of response. 'I mean, are we ever going to beat Dundee United again? Is this the end of it for all for us? Halted in our tracks, not by Rangers or Celtic, but by this crowd? You'd think it was United who were favourites for the league, or who'd hammered the Old Firm to win the Scottish Cup last year, if their performances against us were anything to go by.'

'Aye, bit it's nae, is it?' says Dad rather stating the obvious. 'It's a' very weel Dundee United beatin' us in the semis and quarters, but fit's the point if they never find the bottle tae beat the Old Firm at Hampden, like the last twa years?'

'I know, I know,' I agree enthusiastically. This was absolutely right. They'd lost last year's League Cup Final to Rangers and the previous year's Scottish Cup Final to them as well.

'We'll jist hiv tae hope they can go on and beat them this time.'

'But they won't, will they? They'll crap their pants as usual.'

'Now min,' says Dad, reminding me of our unwritten rule that the swearing stops when we leave the ground. I was still only ten and he was terrified that if he allowed it in the car, it would eventually start happening at home and we'd both be in serious trouble.

'Well, they will!' I argue, defending the use of 'crap' as the only way to do justice to how 'bottle-less' they truly were. 'And losing to Rangers in cup finals, that's another thing. I mean it would be a bit different if it was Celtic, or us, but Rangers? A team we can thrash at will, home, away, at Hampden, in finals or semis? United are a waste of everyone's time Dad.'

'I ken min, I ken, it's nae right,' agrees Dad. And, not for the first or the last time, Dad and I would come to terms with disappointments against Dundee United like this, wallowing in Dundee United's routine capitulation on the big stage against the Old Firm. But when it came down to it, we both saw this totally differently. I now hated Dundee United so much, that I actually *wanted* them to lose to everyone and the more humiliating the circumstances the better. For Dad though it was a different story, as I discovered when I went to celebrate with him in the study after they lost their League Cup semi against Celtic.

'Hey min, hey min, hey min!' he shouts at me as I came into the room punching the air. 'Fit are ye dein'?' I stop and look at him, embarrassed at the rejection and at my own misjudgement.

'Never,' he says, solemnly, imparting his experience of life, 'never support the Old Firm against ony ither Scottish sides, min.' He was deadly serious.

How could he say that? After all we'd come through? I stood staring at him before turning and going up to my room, knowing that he'd start going on again about the years and decades of defeat against Rangers and Celtic. Blah, blah, blah, I thought, I've heard all this a million times, back in the 1950s and 60s and all that, yeah, yeah, all right. Disgusted, I went to bed. I'd had enough of this nonsense about the Old Firm. I didn't care, or understand. United were the problem now, how could he not see that?

It's ten to three on Saturday 6 November, the date of our fourth encounter with Dundee United since the beginning of 1982/83, the first three of which we had lost. Dad, John and

I are sitting in the South Stand at Pittodrie and I knew it was our last desperate chance for any retribution against Dundee United until the New Year. As a result, needless to say, I am absolutely shitting it.

I simply could not face another humiliation at the hands (or more likely feet) of Ralphie Milne and Luggie*. But at that moment of immediate pre-match tension, it seems so likely, so unavoidable that I can hardly contain my anxiety, biting my bottom lip, swallowing hard continuously, my right leg bouncing ever more uncontrollably. My involuntary leg spasms are irritating my dad so badly to my right that he periodically claps an ever heavier hand down on it, so that he and John Leys, his cousin-in-law, could whinge unhindered to each other about how crap their jobs were. The fact that this is all they can find to talk about is making me as irate as I am nervous. So now, I deliberately bounce my leg constantly just to piss him off.

They both deserve it. Today of all days we should be singing, creating a wall of support for our team after what we've come through against the Arabs. I'm dying to tell the United people they're Jute bastards, or that they've found a dead rat and they think it's a treat, and rightly so, after the humiliation I've suffered at their hands. So what's happening inside the ground? We're all quite happy to sit and talk rubbish, while the pathetic, thin scattering of Dundee United fans in the Beach End is allowed, uninhibited, to finish off a rendition of one of their favourite numbers about their city rivals, Dundee FC.

> *We hate Dundee and we hate Dundee,*
> *We hate Dundee and we hate Dundee,*
> *We hate Dundee and we hate Dundee,*
> *We are the Dundee ... HATERS!!!!*

* It transpired that Luggie did not play that day.

Never surely has there been such a need for revenge against anyone and we allow ourselves to be out-sung by a song like that? I say 'out-sung', but, of course, we weren't singing at all. Above the indifferent hubbub of chat in the South Stand, the only response to this I can hear are the three plonkers immediately behind me, who are discussing the technical merits of the little used word 'hater', and whether it was in fact a 'word' or not. The fact that they are even talking about something to do with what was happening inside the ground is a miracle. It is only a matter of time before they start taunting us about this with the 'Sing when you're winning, you only sing when you're winning' song. The truth was that, at home, even this was flattering, since we rarely even sang when we *were* winning and, under Fergie, that was most of the time. I mean I could live with being out-sung by the Old Firm fans who were, after all, the master-class of Scottish football's tribal rituals. But Dundee United, who'd bring no more than a handful of travelling fans? Sitting, arms folded, sinking deeper and deeper into my petulant sulk, I look around in disgust at my fellow Dons fans awaiting kick-off. It wasn't just Dad, John, the intellectuals behind me, it was the whole bloody lot of them. They had a lot to answer for.

We are all sitting in the South Stand, the biggest single enclosure inside Pittodrie, home to 10,000 when full and, outside the big Glasgow grounds, the best viewing gallery anywhere in Scotland. A pioneering cantilever stand erected in the summer of 1980, it had a great towering roof, tasteful bands of red and yellow seats that all seemed to imply that it was bigger than it really was. It gave Pittodrie a neat finish, almost like it had been built out of Lego. But more importantly, it provided bags of potential for the Dons fans to smother the ground in powerful song and lambaste any visitors with its numbers and proximity to the away end.* At any other ground in Scotland this would have been the case … to my frustration though not at Aberdeen. The bulk of the South Stand Dons fans were simply not interested or bothered by the away fans, unless it was the Old Firm, and even then they rarely sang. Most of them it seemed were in the South Stand to catch up with pals they'd bump into, and watch the game, and moan about anything and everything. Just like John and Dad. An absolute travesty, I thought. And to top things off, it wasn't just the United fans that'd shown a poor turn out. There were 3,000 less of us at the game than for the League Cup bout in September, and that was a Wednesday night. What was wrong with the Aberdeen fans? Were they all like my dad, in that the only thing that really mattered to them was beating the Old Firm? Were they not incensed at the outrages we'd suffered at the hands of United? Or were they just staying away because they knew what to expect? Nineteen minutes into the game, and it is happening again. Dundee United take the lead.

With Richard Gough's header hitting the back of the net the inevitability of it all finally starts to take its toll. My rational mind has had enough. Enough hating, fantasy, dreaming … now it's going to take control. Now my brain is to be re-configured, so that all those extreme revenge cravings, all that rabid hunger for blood and destruction are never sprung on me, ever again. I can see it now, and my unusually calm acceptance of Gough's goal is the first sign that it's happening. Soon, I'd be hardwired for ever to keep a sensible, emotional distance from all this, to prevent getting so punished again and again, like had happened to me over the last two years at the hands of Dundee United. But then, just as the rage

---

* To be fair to the casuals, they had already made one whole section of the South Stand theirs, the one nearest the Beach End. But even they were guilty of not trying properly to punish Dundee United.

and torture is being replaced with indifference and measure, just as I am yielding to the rational fold, the outrageous fantasy I'd been craving for so long, that outcome that no rational mind could ever concoct, actually bursts into life, with a vengeance ...

As a taster of what was to come, we equalise when our favourite midfield hardman – Neale Cooper – who rarely scored, drove a hostile 20-yard volley into the net. Then our 6ft 3in cult hero Doug Rougvie, who hit the net even less frequently, scores not once but twice in quick succession, the second going in off his thigh along with Narey and Hegarty, Dundee United's internationally decorated central defence, who were both bundled into the back of the net at the same time. Then a fourth goal from our much-loved young striker Eric Black seals victory midway through the second half. That would already have been more than enough, but then comes a wonder goal by Gordon Strachan to ice the cake and make the final score Aberdeen 5 Dundee United 1.

It was like a surprise birthday party. It was as if Aberdeen had simply been pulling my leg, deliberately playing hopelessly against this side, simply to egg me on. But even the home Dons fans were showing a side of themselves I'd rarely seen, upping their game like never before too. They stood for ten full minutes, giving the standing ovation of a generation, singing and clapping, well after the players had left the field of play. No wonder though. No one had seen our team produce anything approaching this. 'Happy now?' teased my Dad when we were back on our King Street bus. I simply beamed and beamed all night.

In the days and weeks following the match when we had all calmed down, I would come to realise that although an emphatic victory, this was still only one single victory. Dundee United were going to have to take a few more of these before I'd be satisfied that they were back in their place. But, when on 3 January 1983 we destroyed them 3-0 at Tannadice, it really did look like they'd learned their lesson. My early season objective, the complete and utter destruction of Dundee United, was well underway, if not almost complete. And just as I was coming to terms with Aberdeen's newest rivalry, I was about to start understanding a much older, much more bitter one. As our title challenge picked up in late January 1983, we had a home game against Rangers to take care of.

Chapter 7

Invasion

We're over 60 miles away from the rest of urban Scotland, late on Saturday morning, 22 January 1983. We've been driving for two hours through the East Coast countryside and farming settlements of Forfar, Brechin, Laurencekirk and then the fishing village of Stonehaven. With less than a mile to go, the first spires and blocks of flats at the top of Cairn Cry are visible, as we commence our final descent towards the Old Bridge of Dee, the gateway to Aberdeen. Tucked away discreetly beside the North Sea, it's an urban oasis in the middle of nowhere. It is Scotland's third most populous city, and five times the size of my home town of Perth. This is the place we should never have left. I sense it in my dad's thoughtful gaze every time we watch the silver skyline of Aberdeen expand to fill our windscreen on our arrival at its gates. This was our Aberdeen, from where we all hailed, our fortress, our home-land, our Scotland.

We head for a bungalow on Morningside Road, my dad's auntie's house in a quiet western suburb of the city. Auntie Helen is an 81-year-old spinster, and everything in her house seems at least as old as her. The old brown Bakelite power sockets, the plugs of appliances and their heavy-duty wires, the old enamel bath with its moulded dachshund feet, the musty smell of mothballs throughout. But nothing seemed to underline the time warp at Auntie Helen's more than the ancient photo of her brother Charlie on the mantelpiece. He died in the R.38 airship disaster over the Humber in 1921, only 24 years old. Memories of his tragic death were still guaranteed to bring her to tears when asked about him, something I'd discovered through a morbid fascination that I'd regularly indulged. And then there was the TV. Although the most modern piece of kit in the house by a good two decades, it still seemed like it belonged in a museum. It worked though and I'd watch *Saint and Greavsie* and 'Football Focus' and get wound up at how little time they'd devote to Scottish football.

Meanwhile, Dad would be locked in discussion with Auntie Helen. I should say 'listening' to Auntie Helen who seemed always to be trying to break the world record for the most words delivered in a single sentence, and by my memory, managed to do so on each occasion. But Dad was happy to listen, and I knew he was really fond of her. They'd spend most of this time discussing stocks and shares, and he'd sip away on a large glass of Ballantine's, Auntie Helen's special reserve for her favourite nephew. But she'd always spoil me too, with her trademark ham and mustard sandwiches for lunch. It was all part of a well-established routine that had now taken us to every single home match during the 1982/83 season, as Aberdeen's title campaign went from strength to strength.

We'd leave Auntie Helen's at around 1.30 and walk down Morningside Road to get the bus along Broomhill Road. There would usually be a few Dons scarves visible on the bus, and often another couple or so would join as it made its way towards the centre of town. No football fans of other teams, just relaxed, home-based Dons fans, going to their home games. And then we'd reach the centre of town, the main shopping thoroughfare of Union Street. Nothing underlined to me just what a big deal Aberdeen was as much as Union Street.

This was the part of the town that really told me Aberdeen was a proper city, compared to Perth or any other town outside the Central Belt. A six-lane wide, one-mile long boulevard, all of silver granite, it had been quite deliberately designed with a statement of grandeur in mind. To this day it gives Aberdeen the feeling of a much larger town than it really is. On our way to each home game we'd get a great view from our preferred upstairs seats, right down the whole mile, over the hustle and bustle of shoppers going about their regular Saturday afternoon business. But today is different and there's nothing regular about it. As our bus swings out of Holburn Street into Union Street, I've already got a knot in my stomach as I brace myself and make one final check that my Parka pocket is still firmly buttoned up and that my scarf is still securely tucked away, out of sight, just in case. One half of the Old Firm is in town and I already knew from previous experience that you just never knew what was going to happen on days like this. And today was to be a particularly memorable one.

By the time the bus is a few hundred yards along Union Street, we've already passed two or three groups of Rangers fans, on the hunt for boozers. From the bus, you could see them half a mile off, in groups of five to ten, all in Rangers tops, carrying or wearing multiple scarves and flags either being waved or fluttering above head height in the wind, each troupe it seems with at least one Union Jack. Some of them sing and clap and chant as they move along the street among the shoppers, stopping every now and then for extra loud bursts as they hail fellow troops on the other side of the road, who return the compliment. There is nothing directly aggressive about it, but I can tell that the shoppers all sense a menace. They look on warily, unnerved, giving wide berths as they pass the visitors on the pavement. Then something happened that would quell any doubt about whether this was all harmless bravado, that they were just 'gallus' Glaswegians on a day out.

My eyes almost burst out of their sockets when, along the pavement in front of our stationary bus, I see a Rangers fan tugging out an enormous floppy cock from his jeans to start pissing up a doorway. Swaying in a non-existent breeze, he seems to be totally uninhibited by the countless women and girls around who have a clear view of his knob. Then, when his compadres start singing, he joins in, releasing one hand from his cock to gesture along with the lyrics, allowing the rest of his pish to leak out in all directions. Some passers-by slow down and take in the scene momentarily, before carrying on, making a variety of attempts to hop-scotch their way across the delta of urine now running the width of the pavement. None of them dare express any complaint or disgust, it seems. Then a young couple approach, pushing a pram with an under-carriage laden with shopping bags. The dad is the first one to show any anger, snarling and muttering towards the group as he guides the pram slowly through the yellow river, anxious to minimise any splash-back on their shopping bags at wheel level. The Rangers fans respond to this by refocusing their pointing and singing towards him. When one of them rifles a badly aimed gob at him that just misses the mum's face, he shuts up and moves on hastily, well out of his depth. Our bus pulls off.

I know this stuff is hardly unique to the Old Firm, everyone has fans that pish in the street. But it's the sheer numbers of Rangers and Celtic fans that turn isolated acts of antisocial behaviour like this into something of a mass violation, an organ-ised siege on the town and its dignity. But this stuff, this behav-iour all seemed in keeping with what Rangers and Celtic fans were about, they were just like that. Surely the Aberdonians knew this; surely they knew the risks of shopping on Saturdays when the Old Firm came to town? Anyway, as long as they

were down there on the pavement and I was in the upper
deck of the bus, it was all an extension of the exhilarating,
adrenalin-filled experience of Old Firm games themselves.
Within a minute or so, my ringside view of Aberdeen's main
drag alerted me to something else that was about to happen,
something even more dramatic, something that would change
my relationship with Rangers for ever.

A hundred yards or so up the road in front of the bus, I
see a crew of teenagers taking shape on the pavement, no
scarves, nothing distinguishable, maybe other than their body
language, and the fact that they are all walking at the same
pace. It's the Aberdeen casuals and it looks like they have
an unsuspecting posse of around 20 or so Rangers fans in
their sights. My view of all this improves with every yard
we travel, as our bus slowly moves towards the targeted
group of Gers from the opposite direction. An unsettling
excitement flushes through me as the casuals launch their
attack.

At the moment of impact, three or four heads rise above
the rest, a few sporadic kicks and punches flying up and out
of the crowd, a surge of shoppers runs in our direction looking
over their shoulders, a C&A carrier bag gets knocked to the
ground in the stampede, spilling out its clothes across the pavement. And just as soon as it starts, it's all over as the casuals
tank off back up Union Street, darting between the pensioners
and pushchairs to make their escape. As our bus draws level
with the scene of the skirmish the Rangers fans are now huddled
under the bus stop, the ones I can see all panting, looking like
men possessed, like they've just seen a ghost. Two or three
scramble together an unconvincing rendition of 'you're gonnay
get yer fuckin' heads kicked in', pointing in the direction of
their now invisible assailants down Union Street. Two other
Rangers fans are at the other side of the pavement. They seem
to be casualties of the attack.

An older Ger, who looks like a fat version of the already
fat Elvis of the mid-1970s, with enormous, dark black side-
burns, is standing protectively next to a boy who must be
about 13 or 14, squatting against the wall, wearing a washed-
out 1978 Rangers top. I'm fixated by the boy as he grimaces,
eyes closed and teeth clenched, his arms crossed, clutching
his stomach that seems to be causing him a fair amount of
pain. Watching him fight back the tears that seem to be
about to break across his face, a chilling realisation grips
me for the first time. In spite of the fact he could only really
have been a couple of years older than me, the casuals still
tried to kill him. Lads his age were fair game it seemed
when the fighting kicked off. So that meant that I too was
now within range. Next time, it could be me. And there
were many more of them, the Rangers fans, than of us, and
thousands more again who were capable of this sort of
violence. Still locked on to him, as he seems to be recov-
ering, his eyes suddenly open, falling on the upper deck
windows of our bus. Not just any window, but my one.
Then, in a split second, his expression suddenly changes to
a glower … to my horror, he mouths the words 'what the
fuck are you lookin' it?' … JESUS … I slide right down
the seat; cowering below the window frame so he can't see
me … the bus has to go, now! An eternity passes and the
bus remains stationary … outside, the Rangers fans find
their voices following their attack.

> *Hello!*
> *Hello!*
> *We are the Billy Boys!!*

The bus inexplicably starts bouncing to the rhythm of their
song, stamping and clapping can now be heard from the staircase too … oh my God … they're on the bus, they're getting

on to our bus! I quickly peek out to see if the injured Ger is still on the street ... he's not there! ... Christ almighty!

Hello!
Hello!
You'll know us by our noise

My bowels turn and twist violently as the first raised arm, dancing in time with the song, rises with each step up the staircase at the front of the bus, as they reach the second deck. JESUS CHRIST!! He's coming ... I scan round to find that the only identifiable Dons fan is my Dad whose scarf is puffing out of his jacket like a pigeon's chest ... everyone else has hidden theirs surely, like me. As the Rangers fans file along the passageway, I realise I've no time to explain to him that it's probably me that has caused all this, all I can do is suggest quietly to him that he hides his scarf too.

'Hey min! This is Aiberdeen, oor toun!' he rages back at me, at the top of his voice. For crying out loud! My heart now racing like never before, I turn and look out of the window, biting my bottom lip, pretending that it hadn't happened, praying that the Rangers fans, now dancing in the passageway right next to Dad, hadn't heard him. What planet is he on ? It was the very first instance of a bizarre conflict that would occur again and again for years to come, Dad defending his martyr city by refusing to hide his enormous scarf, like he thought he was a sort of Charles de Gaulle character, and me, trying desperately to blend in with my civilian surroundings, with my scarf out of sight. But right now, I was more worried about what he might say next than anything else ...

We're up to our knees in Fenian blood
Surrender or you'll die
For we are The Brigton Derry Boys

They sing at us now bulletproof, as their brush with the casuals has them pumped up to the hilt. No sign of my new mate, thank God. All around the pensioners, old wifies, ordinary Aberdonians, are clutching their handbags and carriers, some looking petrified, some pretending it wasn't happening staring out of the window, others looking thunderous like Dad. But no one moved. No one dared say anything.

HELLO!
HELLO!

Verse two is even louder, and now, out of the corner of my eye I see a Union Jack bouncing and dangling dangerously close to Dad's head. God no. Please no. I pray it doesn't touch him, God knows what he'll do in this mood. But he just sits there, livid, looking straight ahead, taking all this on the chin. Ten minutes later and two stops before ours, now on King Street, the Union Jack brigade finally decide to leave the bus. I check as the bus bobs and bounces, as streams of Rangers fans file through the middle doors, hoping to see my new mate leaving too. Finally, his washed-out blue top jumps off the step and onto the pavement. I collapse back into my seat. All around me on the top deck, the relief is massive. Some pensioners are sitting panting, others with their mouths wide open, one or two with their hands on their cardio-stressed chests. Then the outpouring started.

Two old wifies in front of us turned to Dad, the sole representative of football on the bus (because of his scarf, no doubt). They'd missed their stop five minutes ago, too intimidated to leave the bus, apparently. Another old guy across the passageway chipped in, agreeing with them, saying it was like being on a hijacked plane, lamenting that in this day and age you could be made to feel like a hostage on your own Aberdeen buses.

They and countless others were ranting that they were definitely going to be writing to the council, to get them to put
a stop to this sort thing once and for all.

'Div oor fans behave like 'at fan they ging tae Glaisga?'

'Certainly not,' confirms Dad, adding emphatically that
he didn't travel 160 miles every weekend either to be
subjected to this in his home town (as if the Rangers fans
might have thought twice about behaving this badly if they'd
known Dad regularly made such a huge effort to come to
Aberdeen). Another guy in front of us says we should all
club together to buy an enormous pneumatic drill so that
we could physically sever Strathclyde Region from the rest
of the country and float it away for ever into the Atlantic
Ocean – no doubt ensuring that its citizens who'd just left
the bus were securely repatriated beforehand. Ten minutes
later, Dad is still shaking his head and complaining with our
fellow hostage victims as we get off the bus to walk the rest
of the way to the ground. Now finally, I thought, I understand all this. Having sat there on the bus, shitting my pants
with all the others, I now know why so many Dons fans turn
up for Old Firm games with that unnerving glint of madness
in their eyes, like the one I can see in my dad's. As we both
turn and thunder down Merkland Road with more purpose
than ever towards Pittodrie, lots of other things are becoming
clear too.

Incidents like this were surely behind all the controversial
things they said about West Coasters in Aberdeen. Things like
referring to a screwdriver as a 'Glasgow hammer' – an attack
on the underdeveloped skills of Glaswegian workmen. Now,
I could see the significance, the raw bravery in my Uncle John's
favourite Scottish Cup Final 1982 story, when a Glasgow hard
man tried to get him to give his seat in a pre-match argument
in a Glasgow pub. 'Hey big man, that's ma seat!' 'A'm fuckin'
well sittin' on it, fit are you gan tae dee aboot it?' responded

my uncle. The Glasgow hard man, or 'so-called' hard man, backed off. This was why my Aberdeenshire relations would quite forcefully rubbish my dad and his independence for Scotland ideals. They were horrified by the thought of being governed from the Central Belt, no wonder if they'd to put up with this four times a year. By the time we reach the relative safety of the back entrance to the South Stand, I had finally got it.

A chance to beat the Old Firm at home would never simply be about two points. It wasn't just avenging the decades of defeat and humiliation on the park. Now I could see that beating the Old Firm at home had long symbolised punishing them for all this, bullying us in our town, scaring our mums and grannies, people like me on our buses, expecting people to give up seats in pubs just because they were West Coasters. And as I stand, pumping myself up with all this at the turnstiles, the unusually loud bellowing from the Rangers fans already inside the ground, reminds of yet another outrage they needed to be punished for. They had been given the Beach End ... our Beach End.

Back in the summer, the club and the police had decided to switch the away supporters from the King Street End to the Beach End. This was to put an end to the flash points on Pittodrie Street after games where the home and away fans mingled as they crossed through each other. All of us agreed something needed to be done ... but surely not this. The Beach End held just over 5,000 supporters and was by a good bit the most atmospheric part of Pittodrie. With its side-walls and the support of the wind blasting in from the North Sea, the volume it could generate would dominate the rest of the ground, a much needed assist for the normally reticent home crowd. And we all knew what it would be like when the Old Firm came to Aberdeen. They did not need the superior acoustics of the Beach End to make their presence felt. But after what I'd seen today, I was now wondering how on earth could they have justified giving them the best part of our ground ... for good behaviour? As we take our seats in the South Stand, the need for a victory, to avenge all this is more crucial, more vital than ever. With the players bouncing up and down ready for kick-off, the Beach End choir reaches its pre-match climax powering up the volume to match-time levels, where it will remain for the next two hours.

In spite of the one-way pressure right from the outset, it is the Beach End that responds, provoking us, punishing us for our silence, revelling in their location inside Pittodrie. Any neutral would have thought their team was in red. You sense that they must know how unpleasant this is for us; they know we are hurting, even though their team is already on the back foot. Half an hour passes ... Each time the game stops, I am drawn to the red, white and blue bouncing mass to my right. How can they be like this? Suddenly the ball breaks to the unlikely Doug Rougvie who's unmarked, onside, at the edge of the box ... he chests it to the ground ... rifles a crisp half-volley across the face of the goal ... into the net!

We all erupt together, insatiable, but demonic, dark, not a smile in sight. We are not choosing not to smile, but the goal has reminded us how bitter we feel, how strong the need for retribution really is. And I realise that I've total got it, it was affecting me just like Dad, the others. Our celebration soon focuses entirely on the Rangers fans, screaming and shrieking as much punishment and revenge into the now still and silent Beach End as we can, before the moment passes. It's the first chance, the first opportunity of any sort all day to return fire. This is the type of revenge that really matters, this is what we and they have all come here for. Now we're winning, and now they are hurting ... what a feeling, this is what makes it all worthwhile.

Two minutes after the goal, hundreds of us are still pumping out swearword-ridden bile, shouting and pointing at the Beach End. Gradually it gives way to a ten-minute spell of 'Aberdeen, Aberdeen, Aberdeen' that soon dips under a renewed wave of Rangers songs. Towards half-time, the original balance of play and sound is restored, we pummel Rangers into the ground on the park, and they sing on and on like they are about to win the title. But no more goals ... one goal and Rangers are finished ... then we can relax, then we can come to life again and shut them up, surely for good ...

An hour passes with dozens of missed chances for Aberdeen. There are glimpses of a threat from them, there's a nasty smell of a cruel, late equaliser. Thirteen minutes to go, Weir has the ball on the left at the King Street End ... right in front of my line of vision. He swings the ball into the box ... Mark McGhee is unmarked, all of us in the South Stand rise, McGhee volleys, the ball speeds past McCloy into the back of the net. Another protracted thunder reverberates around the ground as the terminal venom cloud leaves the South Stand for the Beach End, a Beach End that finally it seems, shuts up, beaten and put to sleep. McGhee wheels away, directing his delight at Robert Prytz who he'd been having a spat with through the game. The result now confirmed, our full attention is on finishing the rout.

Now we roar and bellow; we make the dominant atmosphere inside the ground reflect what is happening on the pitch for the first time. We launch attack after attack, breaking from deep. Surely a third goal will come, our domination is worth at least three goals ... Rangers' MacDonald loses the ball to Doug Bell in midfield ... MacDonald throws a punch at Bell's face, play stops ... OFF! OFF! OFF! OFF! OFF! OFF! OFF! OFF! There's uproar in the South Stand, 10,000 arms stab and point at the accused ... MacDonald now seems to be squaring up to Bell ... they stand forehead to forehead … and then MacDonald suddenly head-butts Doug Bell! No way! Now a full-scale melee surrounds Bell and MacDonald. Incensed, we jump to our feet immediately, screaming mercilessly, demanding MacDonald's head, as if the Ger's actions had become in that split second a single metaphor for the decades of injustice, defeat, invasion. **OFF! OFF! OFF! OFF! OFF! OFF! OFF! OFF! OFF! OFF!** We chant and point remorselessly, while the ref remonstrates and lectures MacDonald, before officiously saluting the red card above his head. Another unholy clamour of bellowing and exclaiming has the whole ground shaking, as we gorge ourselves on the verdict, the justice. We follow sorry MacDonald from the field, and those nearest the players' tunnel all stay on their feet, ignoring the game for ten seconds or so, to make the most of the chance to spit as much bile as they can at the dismissed player until he is no longer visible from the pitch. Five minutes later it's all over. Invasion had been avenged, and I had played a part, a full part this time. And our performance that day saw a return to the electrifying standard of form we'd seen from Aberdeen towards the end of last season.

Four weeks later, we peaked, demolishing Celtic again at Parkhead, 3-1, Eric Black scoring a hat-trick. It was a result that saw us leapfrog Celtic to go top of the league for the first time that season and put us in pole position for the title. Now, life really was all about Saturday afternoons, whether we were at the games or not, the excitement washed everything else aside. It all finally seemed to be coming together, and this time, this season, we were hitting form at the just right time. But I'd remember the final few months of our domestic campaign in 1982/83 for different reasons. All this promise meant we'd be going to more away games, to places we hadn't dared to go so far. I was to discover that if I thought the Old Firm fans were mental when they came to Aberdeen, then I'd another think coming when we were the away fans. And I was about to discover to my horror that the same could be said about my ever more carried-away dad.

Chapter 8

Lost Sheep

'Is 'at straight min?' asks Dad, as I arrive at the top of the drive after football practice. He had just put a loud purple sticker in the middle of the top of the windscreen. It said, 'Aberdeen – Home of the Magnificent Dons'.

Dad takes a step back, admires his handiwork for a second before turning and grinning at me. 'It's great isn't it?'

'Dad!' I plead, dropping my kitbag like a stone behind me. I literally cannot believe my eyes. A sticker? An Aberdeen sticker on the bloody car windscreen? Were we on the same planet? 'Where on earth did you get that?' I ask, mindful not to reveal the full extent of my horror at what he had done.

'It came in the post the day fae Untie Frances. A'b'dy's got them in Aiberdein!' says Dad.

Everyone has them in Aberdeen? Did he not get it? These were for cars that never ventured south of Stonehaven; cars that would only ever come into contact with Aberdeenshire people, almost all Dons fans. Cars that would probably never attract the malign curiosity and the subsequent guaranteed vandalism of the ever-growing ranks of Aberdeen haters, who we knew all about given that we encountered them every other week. The only thing the enormous sticker had going for it was that it was not for some reason red, but you could still read it from surely a hundred yards at least. It was the first time I realised that Dad and I were most definitely not living in the same world. As I stared at it, I realised that I should have seen it coming.

There had been a build-up towards this over recent months, as Dad got more and more pumped up by Aberdeen, who were finally peaking at the right time. We were still in the Cup, and Europe (although no one was taking that too seriously), but more important than anything else, we were top of the league. Looking back, it all started when he bought the first of a number of lapel pins, of which he now had one for each suit or blazer he'd wear to work. He even had a rotation system for them, so he explained to me. It depended on the supporter profile in the classes he would have on a particular weekday: a 1982 Cup Winners' pin for days when his classes would have a Rangers fan bias; a League Champions 1980 pin for those with a Celtic fan bias. And then there was the scarf moment on the bus three weeks ago in Aberdeen before the Rangers game. That was really the first sign I'd picked up that Dad was starting to throw caution to the wind.

There was also the shiny metal plaque, commemorating the 1982 Scottish Cup Final hammering of Rangers that lived in the P6, wedged under the clock in the middle of the dashboard. That plaque was the object of a game we'd often play (I think he thought it was a game, but it was certainly not for me). Worried about the safety of the car whenever we were about to leave it anywhere, I'd wait a second or so until he was out and unwedge it, placing it face down on the dashboard shelf, out of sight from passers-by. But then, when he'd been in the car on his own through the week, the plaque would always be proudly resurrected under the clock. I had half been expecting for a while now to come home to find out that he was off to the scrappy to pick up a new door or window, following the inevitable assault the car would suffer while parked unattended away from the house. And now, with this loud purple sticker, shouting to the world what team the car supported, it was surely guaranteed. But what was so much more worrying right now was where the car would be going this Saturday. Another consequence of Dad's boundless enthusiasm was that he had decided that we were ready to take on Glasgow ourselves – just him, the P6 and me.

'We're going to the Partick Thistle game on Saturday, with that on the windscreen?' I ask. It had all seemed like a great and exciting new idea three or four weeks ago. We'd get to add Thistle's ground, Firhill, to our growing portfolio of stadiums visited, and it would be a 'relatively' safe game in Glasgow, a Scottish Cup game that we were guaranteed to win (Thistle were a First Division side and so it was beyond anyone's comprehension that we could lose) and no Old Firm teams, fans or even grounds in sight. But however you looked at it, we were still going to have to get to the game and that meant travelling into, and out of, Glasgow.

'Of course!' retorts Dad with disturbing conviction, underlining that he had put the sticker up just now *because* we were going to go to the Partick Thistle match, in Glasgow, at the weekend. Still staring at him, I realised that he simply could not help himself. His mad 'born-again Dons fan' side was taking over, blinding him to everything else around him. He'd willed Aberdeen for years to be great, never really expecting that they would be, and now they were the whole world needed to know.

'Dinna worry min!' laughed Dad as we headed indoors.

'I'll fuckin' pan your lights in ya sheep shaggers!' bellows the ringleader in a team of ten lads crossing the road in front of us at a zebra crossing. We both freeze like rabbits in headlights, look straight ahead, praying for the lights to change, on our way to the Scottish Cup quarter-final at Firhill on Saturday 12 March 1983. They turn green after what seems like an eternity, and just when the enormous P6 starts gliding off, just as I start to relax, something like a torpedo hits the underside of the car. 'JESUS!' shouts Dad, flicking the wipers on involuntarily and flooring the accelerator more recklessly than he'd ever allowed himself to … I look round to see a disintegrating red brick tumbling along behind us … We'd been ambushed by the 'Steps Welcoming Committee' as Dad would come to name them. Normally identifiable as a posse of Celtic fans, they would assemble along the A80 in the village of Steps on the outskirts of Glasgow to usher the football guests for the day into the city for matches with a variety of abuse, missiles and sometimes golf clubs. And right now, it could only have been that sticker that alerted them to the fact that we were sheep. Lost sheep. We soon steam past Hogganfield Loch … silent tension in the car … only a few hundred yards to the M8 … my heart is already pounding, now Dad's upset too and I can hardly speak. Our first single-handed expedition to Glasgow is already turning out to be worse than my most paranoid of nightmares.

A bead of sweat runs down the side of Dad's cheek as we approach the lights, waiting to pick up the westbound M8 that slashes its way through the heart of Glasgow. Dad looks more stressed than I've ever seen him. I know he hates this road, the real gateway to the bewildering urban sprawl that was Glasgow. Thank God I'd studied the map repeatedly before we left. I'd been clutching it in my hands since Stirling; folded at exactly the right page, ready to kick in at the moment we got to junction 16 on the M8 … That is now.

We're off, picking up the slip road that circles back to join the motorway. This is the worst bit; I've already got a tight knot in my gut. The curve on the slip road is so tight that the old P6 feels like it's going to keel over. We join the motorway. Lorries are steaming past, cars tooting, changing lanes erratically at speed, Dad's head movements are jerky, his concentration is total, he races through the gears, I'm praying it doesn't break down, especially in the middle lane … over to me now with the map, we have to find a way off this mental road … junction 16, here we come … We're on and off the M8 in a flash, both breathless, our diaphragms expanding and contracting out of sync, almost as if we'd run the distance we'd just covered on the M8. Now we need to find the ground and, more importantly, somewhere to park.

'Slow down Dad, I can't read the road signs.'

'I canna dee 'at min, ye hiv tae drive at the speed of the traffic!' Dad asserts. Oh no … Dad's so stressed he's gone into 'blend in' driving mode, a special driving technique that he would adopt in situations like this to avoid appearing out of his depth on roads in big towns. And as a result, I realise we are getting more and more lost, although Dad is so stressed I don't want to admit it in case he gets annoyed with me. Every time I look up, I pray that I set eyes on something like a known roundabout, or maybe a convoy of Dons buses and cars arriving from the North-East, like it is for matches at Dens Park or Tannadice in Dundee. Then we'd feel protected, snuggled up in the jam of Dons fan traffic, among our own flock, Dons scarves on the dashboard and hanging out of windows, so the other vehicles would know that we were brothers, in case they'd any doubts. And we'd not only know where to park, but more importantly we would have an idea where we were, too. But Glasgow seemed so big that there would never be predictable concentrations of arriving Dons fans to provide a general direction or sense of security.

Eventually, five minutes later, I finally reconcile a street name I caught a glimpse of with one on the map, but to my horror it was only a couple of centimetres away on my map from the name 'Blackhill', one that sets the alarm bells ringing even more in my head. Eddie told us about a friend of his who'd stopped there to buy chips on the way back from a game and he'd had his wheels pinched while he was in the chippy. Five minutes, five minutes was all they needed to unbolt four wheels and leave the car grounded on piles of bricks in the street and disappear. It all seemed very funny when listening to him tell his story in the Beach End ... but not now. Right enough, every street looks like a riot had either been through or could start at any moment although there was no one around.

'We're nae parkin' here!' barks Dad as we stop abruptly. He impatiently grabs the map from me and shakes it anxiously to get the folds out, looking up every now and then, trying to be professional about it. We move off again, Dad having taken control and pinpointed a street where he wanted to park. We eventually get there, Dad turns the engine off, and immediately reaches up and peels off the sticker, folding it up and then stuffing it into the glove compartment. For the first time I could remember, Dad checks that the 1982 Cup Final plaque is left face down. We get out and he drops melodramatically to the press-up position on the ground to inspect the damage the Steps Welcoming Committee's brick might have done to the underside of the car, before springing back to his feet almost immediately, startled by the appearance of a lone black Alsatian dog he'd spied while on the ground. Dad locks the car, checks again it is locked properly, pauses to look around into the windows of the houses along the street and starts walking hastily in the opposite direction from the dog, departing from our planned route to the ground before we'd even started.

'Dad, we're supposed to go ...'

'Is way min!' interrupts Dad nervously, now so spooked by everything that he's making it up as we go along. We walk a few blocks, turn left then right, and soon pick up a flow of people going to the game. As soon as the ground comes into view and a clear path to the gates is visible, I breathe a huge sigh of relief. But even secure inside the ground and 20 minutes

or so into the game, I still can't relax properly, surrounded
by an unusual Dons crowd with what seemed like more West
Coast accents than North-East ones. They all seem much angrier
that normal too, half of them are spending the whole match
barracking a Thistle player called O'Hara for being ex-Rangers,
rather than following the game. And then at half-time all hell
breaks loose a few steps in front of us, when two of the dozens
of men wandering about carrying cardboard boxes selling macaroon bars, start knocking lumps out of each other, macaroon
bars flying everywhere, police wading into the crowd to take
them away causing a minor stampede, chaos. Final score:
2-1 to Aberdeen. By five o'clock, we are already on our way
again through Steps, this time without incident, and back out
onto the open road. We'd made it.

There was just no way round it. Games in Glasgow, even
when they did not involve the Old Firm or their grounds,
were just never going to be fun. Every time we went there,
something happened. In fact, we didn't even need to be in
Glasgow for that – as long as there were Rangers or Celtic
fans around it seemed there would be hassle. But soon Dad
was all demob happy, as usual following an away win, and
started reviewing our day.

'We're gettin' good at 'is, fit d'ye think?' he says, completely
glossing over the fact that he looked like he was about to shit
his pants for most of the day. 'Ye did well min, very well,
especially on the motorway. There's nae mony loons that could
dee a' that navigatin', ye ken?' he adds. I shrug my shoulders
modestly, fairly sure this was meant by way of an apology for
getting all snippy when he thought we were getting lost before
the match. But whether I was becoming a good navigator or
not, there was one thing I absolutely needed to know.

'Dad?'

'Fit?'

'Can we please not get another sticker?' I turn and look at

him. I really wanted to add, 'And only ever come back to
Glasgow as long as we are in the Vale of Atholl Pipe Band bus,'
but I didn't want to sound ungrateful, given the time and
effort I knew he put into our trips.

'Aye, OK. On reflection, 'at maybe wisna sic a good idea,'
concedes Dad. 'It's nae fair is it?'

'What is not fair?' I ask, what on earth did he mean now?

'The Rangers and Celtic fans. It's jist nae right that they
can ging rampaging a' o'er Scotland, wi' a' the discretion o'
an enormous travellin' circus, carryin' on along Union Street
in Aberdeen, and naeb'dy, nae even the police will dare dee
onythin' aboot them,' says Dad philosophically. I nod away,
but personally, I didn't care whether it was fair or not. As far
as I could see, it was a reality of Scottish football and so there
was no point complaining about it.

'But for us on the ither hand, oor visits to Glasgow hiv to
be covert, undercover, like secret missions, if we wint tae mak
sure we get oot alive.'

I sat and frowned at him, saying nothing. Had he just realised
this now? I suppose it was better now than never. And at least
now there was some hope that he'd maybe bear this in mind in
the future. In any case, with our day of trauma behind us, Dad
making the right noises about stickers and journeys to away
games, everything seemed all right again. Dad turns the radio
up, as the Scottish Cup semi-final draw is about to be made.

Number 1, Aberdeen ...

Dad's hand hovers over the radio, in anticipation of who
we'd get – Celtic, St Mirren or Rangers ...

*Against ... number 3, Celtic ... to be played at Hampden on
16 April ...*

'Celtic at Hampden!' exclaimed Dad, his face lit up making a strange 'o' shape with his mouth, glancing between the road and me, as he started to revel in what this all meant. It would be the fixture of the domestic season – the clash of the Premier League titans, Aberdeen v Celtic in a semi-final, the biggest Celtic fixture I could remember.

'If we win that, we'll surely win the League and Cup Double!' I added.

'At's right, and we might even clinch the title the wik aifter fan we play them again at Pittodrie! On my birthday! Can ye imagine!'

'And the Aberdeen fans'll get the Rangers end!' I said, the covered end of Hampden, where the singing is the loudest, as I'd discovered last year in the Cup Final.

'Are wi gan min?' said Dad cheekily out of the corner of his mouth towards me, clearly concerned that I might not want to. Of course we were going. How could we not? I dart a face to him as if to say, 'do you really need to ask?'

And that was it. In the space of half an hour, the sense of mortal danger that had been lingering around me for days, wakening me up repeatedly through the night, the stomach cramps and the nausea that had been coming over me in waves until an hour or so ago were all forgotten, all kicked into touch, as if they had never happened. In the time it had taken us to drive half the way home, we were already signed up to go back, this time to meet one of the Old Firm – the one whose fans had shown themselves to be the more dangerous after games. At the back of my mind, I knew I'd be feeling a bit different about it all in five or six weeks time. But little did we know, this journey home was to be the last of its kind for all sorts of reasons. Everything was about to be turned on its head.

For a start, our league form was about to go into freefall, losing three times in four weeks, a spell that ultimately would see us finish the season third. Much to my disgust, after all the hammerings and humiliations they'd taken from us, Dundee United somehow managed to scrape through to the final day of the season and pip both Aberdeen and Celtic to the title. The fact that we won the Scottish Cup again the following week, beating both Celtic in the semis and Rangers in the Final, would have been little compensation for this, had it not been for something else, something much more remarkable that was about to start happening. Driving home that night from the Partick game, we knew that in four days' time, on Wednesday 16 March 1983, we were to play the second leg of our European Cup-Winners' Cup quarter-final against German giants Bayern Munich. But none of us could have anticipated that it would be the beginning of a journey that would redefine not only our season but also our lives as Dons fans. Never again that season, or for many others to come, would our focus simply be about Scottish league and cups. But it was much more than simply about Aberdeen, it was something that defied everything I had come to expect from Scottish sport for as long as I could remember. For me, this part of the story had really started on the day of the draw for the UEFA Cup way back in the summer of 1981.

Chapter 9

The English Benchmark

'Very well madam, I'll just check that we have the carvers in stock,' announces Norman, our Maples salesman, with a satisfied smile that more than advertised his confidence that the sale was a done deal. He was right. It was the day in mid-July 1981 when the interminable search for a dining room table was finally drawing to a close. It was also the day that marked the beginning of probably the most remarkable experience of my life with football. But at the moment it was Norman who was centre stage and to whom my dad was already taking an unusual, but a palpable dislike.

'Carvers! A dining room suite with carvers!' exclaimed Mum turning to Dad. 'I've always wanted carvers! It'll jist look fantastic in the house; it's exactly the right colour isn't it?' prattled Mum. 'Isn't it just perfect Gordon?' Mum pauses, exchanging a long smile with Norman. 'Gordon?'

'Aye,' grumbles Dad, as he looks loathingly at Norman with his half-moon specs and tweed jacket as he ponces around the table, continually pawing and stroking it, like he thought he was a dolly-bird showing it off on the *Generation Game*, before skipping off to answer a phone ringing over at the wall.

'My stockroom confirm that we have two carvers which will be on the shop floor in two minutes flat,' states Norman with a comedy military bow, further irritating my dad who was already blaming him for the escalation in cost. This was what was really bothering my dad. The dining room table, now complete with the carvers, was way more than the budget they'd agreed in the early summer when the campaign got underway. And had it not been for Norman, the carver idea would never have come up. But if he thought this was bad, Norman was about to take Dad to the verge of a public scene.

'... and did you gentlemen hear the great news?' Dad shakes his head and locks onto Norman for the answer. 'The Dons have drawn Ipswich Town in the UEFA Cup!'

'Oh for God's sake, nae again!' exclaims Dad, folding his arms stroppily, tutting and turning to the Union Street window.

'What do ye mean? I wasn't aware we'd played them before?' asks Norman, snapping his fingers and pointing at his stock-room colleagues to indicate exactly where the carver chairs were to be set down, to optimise my mum's view of them around the table.

'No, but it's anither English team, isn't it?' laments Dad, now turned back towards Norman, arms outstretched, beckoning him to get his point. '... And nae ony an English team. Ipswich Toun, current holders o' the UEFA Cup, runners-up in the English League. We've nae chunce min!' says Dad despairingly, dropping into a seat in front of an ornate desk. I knew exactly what Dad meant. We'd been hammered by Liverpool in the European Cup the year before, and now we'd drawn England's latest sensation. It couldn't be worse. I'd listened to both legs of their amazing UEFA Cup Final against the Dutch side, AZ 67 Alkmaar, in the bath back in May 1981, and they'd won 5-4 on aggregate.

'Come now gentlemen, let's not be as pessimistic as all that,' says Norman as he springs towards my mum to assist her with the carver she was about to test out. 'We must play the good teams at some point in the season.'

'Aye, but naeb'dy wints them in the early rounds,' says Dad, starting to wonder if Norman understood anything about foot-ball.

'Sometimes, we must show confidence in what we are brought to face in life,' utters Norman philosophically. Dad looked as if he would probably have fallen over himself at this remark had he not already been sitting down. Whether Norman understood football or not, this was not on, he thought. Here was he, about to shell out a huge amount on a dining room suite, and this bugger had the cheek to speak to him like this? But what annoyed Dad even more was the patron-ising 'confidence' remark that could well have been intended to apply not only to the Dons and their fate in Europe but also to how Dad should be coping with the ambitious finan-cial outlay he was facing for the dining room table. As Dad sat, stunned into silence, Norman went on. 'And anyway, did we not give Liverpool a good game up here last year, what was it, 1-0?'

'Listen min, 'at twa matches against Liverpool ruined us for the whole o' the rest o' the season!' rasps Dad, now jarring his finger into the leather pad on the table in front of him to let some of his indignation escape. 'We were played aff the park in baith matches, and the 4-0 annihilation we took doun at Anfield hit us so badly, that it's teen us til right now to recover!' Dad pauses. 'Aye, if wi hiv recovered!'

'Well, whatever happens sir, you'll have a spanking new dining room suite regardless, won't you?' Norman darts a false showbiz smile at Dad, before turning back to see how Mum was responding to the carvers. Although Dad's face had started to turn a light crimson colour and he was already contem-plating storming out, it was clear that Norman's salesmanship was working a treat on my mum. Now standing up after her seating trial in a carver, Dad could see that she was ever more seduced by the furniture surrounding her. 'Madam, the carvers?'

'Oh they're jist fantastic! We jist have to take them,' responds Mum assertively, turning to smile at Dad. And that was the moment we all knew it definitely was a done deal.

'Very good madam!' interjects Norman, before my bewildered looking dad had a chance to react. 'The cheque is payable to "Maples of Aberdeen Ltd", sir.'

'I'll give you sir min!' remarks Dad before locating his pen and cheque book in his jacket pocket. Ten minutes later, once Dad had been made to test out one of the carvers too and we'd sorted out delivery details, Norman escorted us to the door, still firing off superlatives towards my mum about her excellent taste and choice of furniture.

'So!' exclaims Mum once we got back into the car. 'Only two weeks to wait!' Dad says nothing, swallows hard before putting on his seat belt, looks out of the window for a second or so and starts the engine. Once ignition was engaged, and we were on our way home to Perth, that would be it. No going back.

'Gordon?' prompts Mum, looking for some sign of life.

'Aye, aye. Two wiks,' responds Dad.

'Fit on earth were you and Norman mutterin' on about in the shop?'

'I canna be dein' wi' foulk like yon,' bleats Dad. 'He wis jist spikin' rubbish! Delighted we'd drawn Ipswich in the UEFA Cup, tryin' tae mak oot that we'd run Liverpool close last year. Jist rubbish.'

'Och, he was just dein' his job, that's what they're all like, salesmen … patter-merchants.'

'Close? Close? How could an aggregate score of 0-5 be close? I've never seen the Dons so comprehensively hammered in a' ma life!' remarks Dad, as we turn out of the Old Bridge of Dee on to the beginning of the A92 dual carriageway.

'Dad's right,' I pipe up, nestled in the space between the two front seats. 'Remember Dad, remember, it was so bad we even had to turn the radio off halfway through the second leg at Anfield?' I added in support of Dad's gloom.

'Aye, 'at's right min,' nodded Dad approvingly, as if to say it was the only option available to us. I say 'us', but it had nothing really to do with me and the truth was we didn't *have* to switch the radio off. But Dad had had enough even by the time Liverpool's second of the night, their third overall, went in.

'So, fa in their right mind would wint tae subject themsels to yet mair humiliation at the hands o' an English side for them a' tae gloat over?'

'Look, jist stop bein' negative aboot a'thin!'

'I'm nae bein' negative!' pleads Dad. 'Look, I'm jist tryin' tae be realistic, I mean there's very few teams can expect tae win against English teams in Europe, it's nae jist us. And remember fit happened at the World Cup in Argentina three year ago when we a' got carried awa?'

'Fit on earth has this got tae dee wi' the World Cup?'

'We a' got pumped up wi' Ally McLeod, Scotland's Pied Piper, believing we could win it, and look fit happened?' continues Dad. '… And the English had a field day then as well.'

'The English werna even at Argentina!'

'Aye, but their bloody commentators were! And fit a laugh they a' hid! Laughin' aboot the build-up, laughin' even more fan we couldna beat Peru or even Iran.'

'So this is about English commentators?' challenges Mum, now exasperated at my Dad's lack of clarity. It was a lot more to do with English commentators than my mum realised. The real reason that Dad had petulantly switched the radio off during the Liverpool match at Anfield was as much to do with the contrasting eulogies about mighty Liverpool and the patronising pity for poor little Aberdeen that came from the English commentator, as it was to do with the score.

'Yes and no,' answers Dad after another long sigh. 'Look we a' ken that Scottish teams are never going to compete on the international stage, and 'at's jist the way it is. But I've just hid enough of it, watchin' Aberdeen, Scotland, takin' haimmerins fae English teams or makin' feils o' themsels fan their bloody commentators are a' watchin' and we hae tae listen to them as weel!' grumps Dad. 'It's always the same and I'm bloody sick, fed up o' it.'

'But hold on, hold on,' interrupts Mum. 'What about that game that Scotland won at Wembley, jist a couple of months ago? That was against England!' she said, now determined that if she's going to have the edge taken off finally finding a dining room suite, Dad was going to be made to talk sense.

'What, the Hame International?' says Dad with an air of surprise. I was surprised too. This was as incisive a football stat reflection as she'd ever made and she also had a good point as far as I could see. We'd played England off the park that day back in May, winning 1-0 through a John Robertson penalty. 'Ach, those games are jist a farce,' dismisses Dad with a wave of his left hand.

'A farce? So why on earth was there such a huge spread about it in the papers?' counters Mum.

'Well, it's niver the case tae turn yer nose up at a victory over the English right enough, even if it is jist the Hame International,' said Dad. 'Deep down though, we a' ken fine that it's nae really a competitive match, nae in the sense of World Cup games or European matches at club level.' I now found myself staring confused at Dad. I'd never ever heard him come away with this angle before. And I'd watched 'Football Focus' before the match that day back in May and I remembered that they'd even interviewed some English players, who testified how important the game was for them especially because of the cheek they claimed they had to put up with from Scots playing down south. I was with Mum on this one.

'So why did my brother travel a' the wey to London to go and watch it?'

'Ach listen, we've a' been tae the games!' I knew what was coming now. '... Me and Cooney went tae Glasgae for that fixture back in 1962 and watched it wi' 132,000,' responds Dad, reminding us for the nth time about his proud 'biggest gate' moment. 'But have you ever noticed how many a them bother comin' up for the games in Scotland?' asked Dad, leaning slightly over towards Mum, and darting an enquiring eye towards me in the mirror.

'What do you mean?' I asked.

'Put it this way, they never even get a designated part of the ground fan they play at Hampden,' added Dad, looking at us to see if the penny was starting to drop. I'd heard one explanation for this at school. We'd joked (and taunted the English kids) that this was because the England fans were all sappy poofs, all too scared to come to Glasgow, but somehow I just knew this was not what Dad had in mind right now. 'The harsh truth is that there is nothin' really in it for the English. They simply dinna care as much as we div. The rivalry only really exists in oor minds.' I sat frowning, confused, trying hard to decipher from Dad's face why on earth he would say a thing like that.

'In fact, in fact, the only time I can mine that the English really got upset about losing to us wis 'at time at Wembley back in the 1970s, an' 'at wis really all about fit the Scottish fans did aifter the game, streamin' on tae the pitch, rippin' up their turf and goalposts.' For the first and only time that day, a smile started to appear across Dad's face as he recounted this event. But by now Mum was shaking her head slowly, still staring out of the passenger window, and pretending not to listen. 'But when it comes to proper fitba, European or UEFA

Cup ties like this one against Ipswich that we're facing now, then nae prisoners are taken. No mercy is shown. Lambs to the slaughter. Scottish lambs, lambs fae …'

'Och, fit a lot a rubbish!' interrupted Mum all of a sudden, turning to stare angrily at Dad, startled into silence. 'This is all because we spent two grand on that bloody dining room suite, isn't it?'

That remark, made by Mum as we drove through Forfar, the halfway mark on the way home, was the last word on the subject and the last word for the rest of the journey. But whether it was the cost of the dining room suite or not, that conversation weighed heavily on me for the rest of the summer. Although I couldn't understand why Dad had said it, I sort of knew what he meant. We knew Scottish teams were generally crap and that when the top English teams wanted to beat Scottish teams in European football, they did (you didn't have to rake hard in the history books to confirm this).* But my hopes for our Ipswich encounter would have been fairly modest anyway, after the beginning to the season we'd had, tanked by Dundee United 4-1 on the first Saturday, then a 3-1 pounding at home the very next week against Celtic.

So gloomy were we about our form that when the first leg at Portman Road in mid-September 1981 came round, Dad and I didn't even listen to it together. In fact we only realised that the other *had* been listening to the game at all when we met on the stairs, on our way to find each other at the final whistle. And that only happened because we'd somehow managed to draw 1-1. We stood staring at each other for a

---

* From the 19 meetings between Scottish and English clubs since European football began up to 1981, the English had won 15. The last time a Scottish club had prevailed against an English side was in 1970, when Jock Stein's Lisbon Lions put out Leeds United in the European Cup quarter-final.

couple of seconds. I could tell from my dad's cartoon expression that he was asking himself the same questions as me; if we can draw away, maybe we can do it at home? We only needed one goal, a penalty, a lucky break. One thing was certain for the return leg – we'd be listening to it together, in the one room in the house where loud football commentary, in silence, was achievable ... his study. And what a night it was! It was to be the night that Fergie first arrived on the European scene with his unlikely Dons, and more than a few eyebrows were raised across the continent.

There was to be no lucky break, no luck at all, as we not only beat the UEFA Cup holders, we tore them to shreds. That night, we discovered what we had in Peter Weir, Fergie's first big signing at Aberdeen. It was difficult to believe it was my team I was listening to. Every couple of minutes, Weir broke from the halfway line, ran the length of the Ipswich half, tormenting and teasing English international Mick Mills. After only ten minutes of the second half with the score at 1-1 (2-2 on aggregate), he scored what sounded like a screamer from the edge of the box. When he scored his second (another spectacular goal, only this time scored with his right foot) half an hour later, someone slammed the study door shut from outside, as Dad and I exploded, so violently this time, we ended up damaging a floorboard, one that would creak every time someone walked on it from that day on, to remind us of this monumental second half. Final score: 3-1 (4-2 on aggregate).

We had actually broken more than just a floorboard in the study that night. We had broken an enormous psychological barrier. Our team, our Scottish Aberdeen, had beaten the UEFA Cup holders, a top English ... even a top European side. And there was no question about whether they had wanted to win. We would eventually get knocked out in the third round by Hamburg, but not before giving them a scare at

Pittodrie, winning 3-2 in a game we should have won 4-1 (we went out 4-5 on aggregate). But that didn't seem to matter, maybe we were out, but the fact that we'd scored three goals again, against another top European side, simply proved that the result against Ipswich was no fluke. For the rest of the season 1981/82, this experience fed the growing sense of anticipation, that there really was something about our team, something much bigger to come, at home and maybe beyond too. Winning the Scottish Cup in May 1982 put us into the Cup-Winners' Cup for 1982/83. Unlike the previous year, however, we failed to land any glamour ties but this meant we were able to coast past our Swiss (Sion), Albanian (Dinamo Tirana) and then Polish (Lech Poznan) opponents without any fuss at all. And before we knew it, we were already in the hat for the quarter-finals, our first European quarter-final, ever! Now, in the last eight, there could only be glamour ties.

Chapter 10

Home Game on
a Wednesday Night

Standing in the lounge bay window, making and studying a variety of shapes with my nose, mouth and breath against the central panel of glass, I'm waiting for Dad to come home. He doesn't have the car, so I'm looking out for his black shoes at the bottom of the drive. I'm hoping he doesn't know the news and I can break it to him. Earlier that Friday 10 December 1982, the draw for the quarter-finals of the European Cup-Winners' Cup had been made in Nyon, Switzerland. I was ready and prepared to roll it out to him, as follows: Paris St Germain v Waterschei; Inter Milan v Real Madrid; Austria Vienna v Barcelona and ... Bayern Munich v ABERDEEN! When he eventually arrives, I can tell as soon as his face becomes visible from the other side of the tree that he already knows the draw as he shakes his head with a huge beam across it. I run round to the front door, 'Right! we're gan tae the hame match, min, fit d'ye think?'

WHAT! I hadn't expected this. My heart rate soars to a thousand beats a second. And this was not just any old European match, this was the biggest, the most important match ever for the club. Simply arriving in the quarter-finals was a historic milestone in itself. But nothing brought this home more than the team we'd landed in the next tie. This was the same Bayern

Munich that had won three consecutive European Cups in the 1970s, and only ten months ago, they'd lost the 1982 European Cup Final to Aston Villa. I saw it on TV. The Germans had been unlucky. This was a top German side, sporting some of Germany's greatest ever stars. On their way to the quarter-finals to meet Aberdeen this season, Munich had destroyed the much trumpeted Tottenham Hotspur side of Hoddle, Ardiles, Villa and Allen, tanking them 4-1 at the Olympic Stadium. This was Bayern Munich, the heart and soul, the powerhouse of German football. But on top of all this, it meant actually going to a Wednesday night match in Aberdeen. Weekend escapades to get to matches in Aberdeen seemed to take us the whole day, and we were going to attempt all this on a school night? It was all too much to take in.

Along with my Central Belt accent, it was the inaccessibility of home European games that kept me apart from the rest of the Aberdeen world. European football was for home-based Dons fans, and not for the likes of me. No European games ever coincided with summer or Christmas holidays, and the ties seemed always to fall either side of the two-week break in October. Anyway, we'd never progressed far enough to play a European match after Christmas, let alone the Easter break. We'd listened to all the games on the radio and I'd tune into conversations I'd overhear at Pittodrie between guys who'd been to the European matches, eager to get a sense of what it was like, how it differed from domestic action. So the Bayern Munich idea was a revelation. And the result from the first leg was to make the event much more than simply an adventure. The final score in Munich on 2 March was 0-0, making the home game more of a proper football contest than we'd expected. Especially if you were my dad.

The night after the first leg, Dad was going off the scale explaining the perspective of it all as we dried the dishes. 'A' the papers, a' the English, German, even Scottish papers had us written off, min. They a' thought it would be anither Anfield, ken?' he said, pacing around the kitchen. 'It shows ye fit we've got in Miller, McLeish and Leighton if we can keep a clean sheet, away from home, against the likes of Munich. And nae Gordon Strachan on the park either?' Dad shakes his head. 'Is is the team that pit four past Spurs in the last round,' Dad pauses. 'I mean Spurs?' he uttered, holding his hands out with a plate in one and the drying towel in the other to underline just who we were rubbing shoulders with now. I could see where he was coming from. Then again, for Dad, anything Aberdeen did in those times seemed to get him totally charged up. 'Fit a chunce we've got min! And we're gan tae see it!'

For the next two weeks, the sense of anticipation kept on building. It was fantastic. Everything was ready. All I needed to do was to get out of school 40 minutes early, and the rest would fall into place. No problem.

It had been a perfectly ordinary Wednesday morning, 16 March 1983. Break-time had come and gone, 10.00 to 10.25, just enough time for a meaningful match in the playground. I say meaningful, but there were a few inconveniences we had to live with. Oakbank Primary had a concrete playground area that sloped unevenly down towards the school's main doors that we would use as a makeshift football pitch at breaks and lunchtimes. We had had to position the goals, marked out with stones or jackets, at the top of the sloping playground to keep footballs away from the school windows. Two ends and two goals, that's all we seemed to need, our imaginations did the rest. More remarkable than our lopsided, unrealistic playing area was the number of simultaneous matches we seemed able to put up with during playtimes and breaks. Each class, of which there were ten (two each of P3 to P7), would play its own match on the same pitch, all at the same time. Rain, snow, burst Mitre footballs, 'synthetic' leather balls with their glossy octagonal-shaped outer skins hanging off, tennis balls, our playground football world was fairly versatile, fifteen players or three players; two teams or eight teams, we worked it out. Today though, we'd been lucky with a five-a-side game, and everyone was up for it. Just before the bell went, we had scored a fantastic goal, and I'd played a key part.

No sooner had my cross been converted that I clicked into a discreet canter, head down, attempting to appear blasé, in a 'how-can-he-be-so-modest-after-such-a-burst-of-genius' sort of way. I certainly couldn't look at the opposition players, who I'd just skinned ruthlessly on my right-wing dash, for fear of being seen to gloat. It was easily one of the best 'run-cum-crosses' they had seen. But much more that this, it was total vindication, a moment that settled the daily arguments about when and if I, and other 'mouches',* should be passing the ball. I had secretly believed for a while that I could probably be relied upon to beat every player in the other side, including the goalie, and pass the ball into the goal – the only time it would need to leave the safety of my feet. And by my judgement, that was most of the time. Quite unsurprisingly, I sensed equally that my classmates didn't really see it like that, so I would have to dumb down the certain victory my precocious ball control guaranteed our team, by passing to less gifted players every now and then. But goals like the one I'd just 'created' gave me an extended licence to get away with trying to beat that one extra man.

When the bell went, I was nearest the grassy area next to the car park, where our stationary ball had attracted the malicious attention of some passing Perth High School second

---

* A Perth term used to describe 'greedy' players (in truth, a term used by those with little ball control to attack those who had it in abundance – people they were jealous of).

years. I'd expected to have to wait a minute or so while they indulged their rank by keeping the ball for a while before stealing it, trying to burst it or booting it as far away as possible (just as we'd do with the P5 and P6 balls that would come across our paths). I wasn't really bothered, my mind was already running riot, replay after replay of my contribution to our goal speeding through my head, with the crouched figure of Peter Weir or Mark McGhee supplanting me on the right wing at Pittodrie, in front of the South Stand, providing my run and cross that leads to the winner against mighty Bayern later tonight ... Could we do that? Against Bayern? Could we even score against them? I turn and trot off on auto-pilot, after the ball, as it is thumped as hard as possible down the particularly steep Viewlands Road that ran adjacent to Oakbank Primary ... then again, it's not St Mirren or Raith Rovers in the quarters of the Scottish Cup ... come on, get a grip ... I finally caught up with it and headed back towards the school, it's quieter than I was expecting ... if we scored just once late on though, that's what the radio had been saying, clean sheet in the first half, and a late goal, they'd have less time to equalise ... I pass classroom after classroom, I eventually snap out of my thoughts, realising that all of their doors are closed. Silence ... I check my watch ...oh my God ...

'And you think you're getting out of here at 3.00 p.m. this afternoon?' said Foster, my teacher in P7. One of only three male teachers at the school at the time, he was by a good bit the eldest and the strictest. After years of young, liberal female teachers, all prepared to encourage flair and tolerate tantrums, Oakbank prepared you for the real word of secondary school with a year at the hands of a first-class disciplinarian. Any unscheduled chirping or showing off was anathema in Foster's tight and prescriptive world of order. And turning up late for anything, like now, was even worse. His big red, nodding face had an ironic 'I dinney think so, son' expression written all over it, answering his own question. This question drew to an end to a Foster rant, part one of what was guaranteed to be a severe and protracted bollocking that would span the entire school day. I've already got a lump in my throat as I sit down. What have I done?

'Ah'm no havin' it son, ah'm jist no havin' it!'

At the first opportunity, I attempt to explain what had happened, the fact that some high school kids had taken the ball and belted it down the road. This was the usual excuse for late appearances after morning breaks, but Foster had warned us all several times that he would not be held to ransom by this sort of nonsense. It was our job to get to class on time, after breaks, with or without our footballs. I knew I was on dodgy ground.

'Aye, well you better phone your dad at lunch time and tell him you'll be leaving the school with the rest.'

JESUS, please no. Not this. Send me outside the class for an hour; belt me, anything, not this though. It would ruin everything. According to Dad, we'd have minutes to spare even if we left bang on time. I sat for a minute without breathing, following Foster's white head as it bobbed around over his desk while he shuffled piles of papers around, waiting for some clue that he was bluffing, that this was an idle threat. What was I supposed to do if it wasn't? Just get up and go at 3.00 o'clock? What if he stood in my way, or pulled out a huge bollocking, did I have it in me to walk out through one of those? Could I enjoy the rest of the day if I did? Foster's silence goes on. He really must hate me. Half an hour comes and goes, and still no indication as to how serious Foster was being. It was starting to seem like the whole midweek football in Aberdeen plan was just too ambitious a thing to do, judging by the hassle this incident was causing. Deep down, Foster's reaction to it all only served to confirm a gut feeling I'd had for a while, that there was just something wrong, something cursed about this whole Wednesday night Pittodrie idea.

Perth had always been just far enough away from Aberdeen to isolate us from the rest of our family on school days. Even though it was physically possible to go to Aberdeen and back in the space of four hours, we'd never do it. We'd never needed to, and the emotional upheaval of the excitement in getting there and the downer of coming away again, just to spend a couple of hours there, would have been quite draining. And besides, part of living in Perth had been stoically accepting it was 80 miles from Aberdeen. Dealing with the reality of exile meant only going back at holidays, or at the very least at week-ends. But in Dad's overwhelming eagerness to get to the Bayern match, he was now taking on this immutable truth. He'd been going on for ages about the 'amazing technological and civil engineering advancements' that had in fact brought Aberdeen closer to Perth. This was right enough as the new dual carriage-ways went more or less all the way between Forfar and the city so that you could do the whole journey in around an hour and 35 minutes. But one thing my Dad was certainly not talking about with his 'technological advancements' was the P6. Even with the new roads, it was going to have to take a belting if we were to get from Perth to Aberdeen on time. I was always worried about breaking down anyway. The thought of spending a Wednesday night in a B&B in Forfar or Laurencekirk was pretty grim. Eighty miles was eighty miles, so there was only one thing for it, we were going to have to take a run at it. We'd both need to get some time off school.

No problem for Dad. His boss was from Peterhead, another exiled Aberdonian, and one with strong sympathies for our team and its European adventure. Dad had long bummed off about his good relationship with his boss, and according to his transcripts of their conversations they were familiar enough to call each other 'min', a sure sign of mutual approval, certainly in the North-East. For me though, it was going to be a different story. The news that I would be leaving the class at 3.00 p.m. on the 16 March, not 3.40 p.m. – normal bell time – to go to a football match, we knew was going to be met with some resistance from my teacher. But it was all arranged and agreed with McKinnie, Oakbank's headmaster. I'd meet Dad on Viewlands Road and we'd be off to the game. Just in case, I was warned to be on my best behaviour.

After the morning break incident, I knew I had no scope for any more slip-ups. Throughout the rest of day though, I couldn't concentrate on anything. Lunchtime had come and gone, and I had directly ignored Foster's instruction to contact my dad, setting up a guaranteed showdown when it was time to leave the class. That was if I had the bottle to get up and leave. As a quarter to three approached, I could feel my legs bouncing uncontrollably off the under- side of my desk. Then, I saw Dad park up on the road outside, it's 2.55 p.m., I knew I had to go for it. I stuck my hand up sheepishly, interrupting Foster – mid-lecture – and asked to leave.

'COME HERE!'

A massive sense of relief runs through me, I sense I'm to be released, although a final tonking is on the cards. I put on my jacket with as little controversy as possible, picked up my bag that I'd been surreptitiously packing for the last half an hour, and shuffled, head down, remorsefully, to the front of the class.

Foster wiped the floor with me in front of the whole class, with a ten-minute long dressing down. He criticised my irre- sponsible dad, and made it clear to everyone else that it was wholly inappropriate, for any reason, to depart early from school. At five past three, still attempting to look as contrite as possible, I noticed out of the corner of my eye, my dad marching purposefully across the empty playground, staring up at our classroom. I knew he was going to be anxious about the driving and getting there on time was going to be tight anyway. Besides, he'd already been waiting for ten minutes; he was not going to be in the mood for any nonsense. I could tell by his strides that he was coming for a show-down with Foster. A cold sweat came over me as a hundred of my dad's tirades towards the referee flashed through my mind. Christ, I can't have this in front of my classmates … Stern footsteps approach the door, then a knock, the door opens.

'I've come for Stuart,' instructs my dad assertively, staring at Foster with probably the most impressive Paddington Bear stare ever. Foster's tirade towards me stops, he deliberately blanks my dad, says nothing for a second, his normally crimson countenance now purple with rage, then …

'GO!' he shouts, upstaging my dad's measured thunder, causing his jowls to wobble uncontrollably in his anger. I walk out of the class, and close the door. I'm free.

'BASTARD!' blasts Dad shortly after I'd finished my summary of events. I'd fairly pumped up and embellished my verbatim account of what Foster had said to me and in particular the charges he'd levelled against my dad. When we got on our way, Dad wasn't saying much. I was already feeling bad about this. Other than roaring 'bastard!' I don't think he said anything at all. This was supposed to be the ultimate adventure but it had started disastrously.

This was no time for me to be twittering anyway. Even if we'd got away on time, it was going to be tight. I could sense Dad's tension as he raced up and down the gears, exploiting every half chance to burn off the farm vehicles and articulated lorries on the way. He rarely broke the speed limit, but even upping the pace by ten miles an hour or so seemed to transform the P6 into something much more complicated, judging by the increased concentration it demanded from him. There was something impressive about it though, his focus, his eyes darting rapidly from rear mirror to rev counter to wing mirror and back again, meticulously preparing each commitment to overtake like he was landing a 747.

Sitting in silence in a car bursting with Dad's intense concentration, I sort of realised that he was driving that night much like Aberdeen were going to have to play if they'd a chance. When I thought about it, the whole sense of anticipation about what I was going to see was different. For the first time in my life, I was going to a competitive game involving Aberdeen, in Aberdeen, and I was expecting to lose.

For a start, this was a German side. A side full of guys with first names like Wolfgang, Dieter and Klaus. And they had two players I knew all about. Karl-Heinz Rummenigge and Paul Breitner. They were among the top 50 footballers in the world, and they had the medals to show for it. Between them, they had done literally everything in football. Played in, scored in, won and lost World Cup and European Championships Finals for Germany, league championship and cup medals with German and Spanish club sides, European Cup winners and losers with Bayern Munich, European Players of the Year. A wee bit more than Ralphie Milne and Davie Provan then, and we'd sometimes struggle to contain even them in the domestic game. On the other hand, I wondered who the Bayern fans would be worried about in Aberdeen's side. Willie Miller? They'd maybe have known him from the World Cup in Spain 1982. But then again, he seemed best remembered for his part in the 'Benny Hill' sketch he played out with Alan Hansen in our last (as usual our third) group game against the USSR. They had collided, attempting to reach the ball on the touchline, and ended up in a pile like a pair of clowns, letting the Russians in to score their second goal. All that was missing was a circus style thud on the kettle-drum or a couple of toots on a kazoo. Of course, it wasn't Willie's fault, but anyway.*

When we finally arrived at the Bridge of Dee with half an hour to spare, it seemed to me we'd made it. But Dad still wasn't taking any chances, and took a bewilderingly circuitous route as we went tearing through Aberdeen, drawing on all the backstreet knowledge of the city that he'd acquired from his boyhood paper round. We park the car behind the university, lock up and march off. Dad's still saying nothing, as he storms along at a pace that requires me to do a few daft skips every ten yards or so to keep up. At least we're here ...

As soon as we got into the South Stand, I immediately understood the rush. With a full 35 minutes before kick-off, the whole ground was already packed. No wonder Dad was so annoyed with Foster, another ten minutes and we've have been standing for the whole match. Being 3 foot 6 tall I'd have seen nothing.

'Made it!' barks Dad defiantly, his Herculean efforts to rescue me from Foster, beat the traffic and get there on time now vindicated. And he's finally recovered the power of speech. We stand looking at each other, savouring his achievement for a moment, before we both burst out laughing. What an adventure this has been already, I knew it was all worth it for that moment, whatever the score.

That night, it was as if I'd turned up at someone else's home ground; I'd never seen it like this. Everyone was standing up and there was already something approaching hysteria all round the ground, which was constantly erupting into song. The whole place seemed like the Beach End when the Old Firm

* Judge Stuart Cosgrove of the BBC's *Off the Ball* concurred in a review in July 2004 that it was Hansen's fault, not Willie's.

visits. We join in immediately, chanting and singing, as we home in on what seem like the last seats, right in the very front row of the South Stand, behind the corner flag. This is fantastic, as Dad and I sing and shout through mouthfuls of our homemade ham and mustard sandwiches and clap palm of sandwich holding hand against free hand. This was our chance, our only chance of a generation, to watch the Dons challenge at this level of football. We were all going to make the most of it, it seemed.

And there they were ... Rummenigge and Breitner, limbering up on the pitch, the best, most decorated players I was ever likely to see live. They were really here, Aberdeen the city was really here, we were here. With the atmosphere around the ground now deafening, the game starts ...

We harry and hustle in midfield in the early stages, but everything we do seems lumbering, awkward, stilted. The class gulf is massive, right enough. Mark McGhee in particular seems well out of his depth. He's having a nightmare. Poor Mark. My fears of Munich's towering superiority are already confirmed and it's about to get worse. With 15 minutes on the clock, the Germans get a free-kick in the middle of our half, following the mid-pitch attempted murder of Dieter Hoeness by Rougvie and Cooper combined. The French ref seems more disgusted with the assault than any of the German players, judging by the exaggerated animation in the severe bollocking the Aberdeen players receive. I suppose this'll be the first time he'll have refereed in Scotland then. Play restarts; Breitner knocks the ball into the path of the enormous Augenthaler, 25 yards out. He advances tentatively ... then, knocking the ball deftly to the right he wrong-foots the entire Aberdeen defence on the edge of the box (literally about five players, including Miller and McLeish) ... he strikes, his blistering shot bends perfectly, high into the Aberdeen net. One-nil Munich. Silence for the first time.

Augenthaler, Miller's opposite number 6 … a defender? In Scotland the back players could only normally score with headers, appearing like lighthouses in the box, tall objects against which to rebound the ball at close range. Are Bayern going to need Rummenigge or Breitner tonight? The Germans are even better than we thought.

The ground soon starts bellowing in hopeless belief again though. There's a gritty determination in our mood, we seem to know that pure willpower is going to have to take over if we've a chance. The South Stand swings into the performance of a lifetime, singing ironically 'Here we go' again and again and again. But the team seems buoyed by the crowd, as they battle and bustle. We grind out a series of corners, but still no real goal threat … As half-time approaches, we gradually open up a few shots on target and, for the first time in the game the sheer determination of the team suggests they think a kill is possible … Not me, I still can't see it, even though the intensity in the ground is now going off the scale … A Munich defender loses the ball to McGhee who for once keeps his balance, sends in a deep cross, a powerful header towards goal from Black, parried by Müller … but the ball falls kindly for Neil Simpson, arriving like a train, who careers the ball, himself, and a Munich defender into the back of the net! That was it, we *can* score against them, we *can* do it! The ground goes ballistic, our roaring and shouting was more than worthwhile. One-one at half-time. Me and Dad catch our breath. This is something else …

Twenty minutes of the second half pass, Bayern are starting to control the game from midfield. Del Haye breaks up the right wing with Dremmler, past Stuart Kennedy on his way into the Aberdeen half. A cross is fired into the box, McLeish seems to have headed clear, towards the unmarked Pflugler

on the left, but he's miles from goal. Phew! That was close
... Peering through the red and white frames of players blocking
my view, I see Pflugler up in the air, as if poleaxed from below
by a scything Doug Rougvie leg. But there's no one near him
as far as I can see, what's happening? He disappears from my
view in a sea of flailing, but somehow coordinated limbs ...
I catch a glimpse of a taut left leg that thrusts at the ball and
in a flash, it bounces and smashes into the back of our net.
God almighty. What a goal! Two-one Bayern. Deafening
silence.

That was surely it. The Germans were playing with us.
Elaborate dramatics when goal opportunities presented themselves, unnecessary acrobatics when they'd loads of space, and
the ability to score unthinkable goals from anywhere on the
park. They could just up a gear and score at will. We're out
of our depth. Only, now we know that for a fact.

This is what you meet then when you reach the quarter-
finals, I conclude, it's men against boys. I knew about this
already. Every now and then our Primary 7 class would end
up playing some Primary 4s or 5s in playtime playground
matches. We'd do exactly the same as Munich. You just knew
when it was a 'no contest' game. The precociously gifted, such
as me, would attempt seemingly impossible solo 'keepy-uppy'
efforts all the way from our own half to be finished off with
a spectacular volley; goal efforts from bicycle-kicks, overhead
shots on goal from throw-ins at the halfway line, that sort of
stuff. I'd been there. That's what's happening here. Bayern must
have seen us coming, some lucky minnow that had somehow
got through the quarter-final net. Now in Aberdeen they were
just doing what they perhaps could not be arsed to do in
Germany. The worst thing of all is that they couldn't even be
arsed to kill us off early on in the match. They're that sure.
Maybe so, but there is something different about the Aberdeen
people tonight. We pick ourselves up immediately. Pittodrie

has become a cauldron, different from anything I'd ever seen, the fans are unwavering in their support, still screaming, still willing on the team, still creating the hostility that Pittodrie so lacked for domestic fixtures.

Still fighting, with 15 minutes to go, Strachan and McMaster are poised over a free-kick just outside the Germans' box. They both looked like they were going to take it. Maybe a chance … the rest of the team, bar Jim Leighton, are in the box. Desperation … They both run up towards the ball, both run beyond, then stop and look at each other. A squealing frustration rises from the ground, Dad tuts. That just sums it up. We're so outclassed, the gulf so massive, we're struggling even to organise ourselves for a routine set piece. It's all so obvious now.

But, just as I'm giving up in my mind, trying to find a meaning for my own disappointment, Strachan wheels round in a flash, stabs in a cross, the Germans are off their guard, and an enormous, red lighthouse rises in the box, it's Alex McLeish, he dives, and scores!

Pandemonium. Complete and utter pandemonium. Ten thousand Captain Cavemen, locked in a heaving caveman mass of wide open, shrieking mouths, bulging eyes. I can see my dad's face of shock, before the joy kicks in, shaking his head in disbelief. We've scored! Again! We just won't give up. The elation of the surprise quickly transforms into a determined belief, the doubts are exorcised, we *can* do it! We're going to do it! All of a sudden, a great gasp of anticipation from elsewhere in the ground draws our attention, mid-celebration, back to the pitch … WHAT!

Eric Black is back in the box, right in front of me at the front of the South Stand. He's not marked, he's hanging in mid-air, awaiting a perfectly flighted cross … ONE THAT'S ACTUALLY ON ITS WAY TO HIM … he meets it perfectly and thunders a header towards the top left-hand corner, Müller makes the save of his life though … but it falls to Hewitt, he's slipped! JESUS … he gets a half shot in, the ball bounces straight at Müller … THROUGH HIS LEGS! … WE'VE SCORED AGAIN!

If it was pandemonium before, then there are no words to describe what happened in the South Stand at that point. It was as if something atomic had been dropped into the ground, all the space had disappeared, there seemed to be three times as many of us in the South Stand as there had been before, fans pouring on to the pitch, policemen dancing behind the goals. I discovered later that I smashed my hand against the stone wall at the front of the South Stand, but I didn't notice at the time. We hadn't even had the chance to take in that at 2-2 Bayern would still win the tie. That 40-second period had teleported us from losing the tie on two counts, to leading with one jump. We could not believe our eyes. Neither could the cameramen, who, caught up in the excitement themselves, missed the whole build-up to the second goal. I've still to meet someone who actually knows how it happened.

We gradually calm down, rounding off our celebrations. 'Unbelievable, HERE WE GO! – nae real – HERE – WE – GO!' Some are laughing, some look like they're about to cry … That 40-second period had also carried us from praying for time to stop, to praying for the remaining 14 minutes to disappear in an instant. But we didn't need to, it transpired. To the extent we could concentrate at all, we were about to see again what Aberdeen's long lauded defensive qualities were all about, stifling and sweeping up any attacks the Germans tried to mount. We had done it. We had beaten one of Europe's biggest sides in the quarter-final of a European competition. We wait inside the ground, imploring the players to come out for a lap of honour … when they do the standing ovation goes on for what seemed like an age. We felt invincible, we wanted the next match to start immediately, no one wanted this amazing sensation to end.

We eventually got back to the car, both hoarse, and set off down the road, listening to Radio Scotland as it fell over itself with superlatives to describe just what the Dons had done. The unthinkable had happened, and Fergie's Dons were in the semi-finals of a European trophy. One of the last twelve teams from 130 that had started all European competitions that season. The only Scottish, the only British side left. Incredible.

Somewhere on the way down the road, my skinless knuckle eventually started to register some serious pain, I couldn't understand how I'd managed to smash my hand like that and not notice. But once it healed, it left a mark, a battle scar that is still faintly visible today. Every now and then, as I scan for inspiration across my splayed hands on my computer keyboard, its irregular crumple catches my eye, smiles up at me, reminding me I was actually there that night, the night of Pittodrie's finest hour.

Two days later, the draw for the semis was made. We'd drawn the Belgian Cup holders, a team called Waterschei, avoiding the favourites Real Madrid. The bad news was that the first leg was at home. The only plus about this was that it fell on the first Wednesday of the Easter holidays, which would mean I'd be spared another confrontation with Foster. Instead, I'd have my Aberdeenshire grandad to contend with and that was just about as bad.

Chapter 11

Easter Retreat

'Doing anything over the holidays Gordon?' asks George, as we finally wind up the pleasantries following my late morning piano lesson.

'Aye, wur gan up fur Vaterski tonight.'

For crying out loud. Dad insisted on saying 'Vaterski', the *correct* pronunciation of the Belgian side Waterschei that we'd be playing in the Cup-Winners' Cup semi that night. Correct according to John Stasson, his Belgian teacher friend at school. I'd a fairly good idea of what was coming next from George.

'Waterskiing? Oh, excellent, far div ye dee 'at, Loch Earn?'

'No, em ... Watershee? Or Watershy?' repeats Dad, now trying hard to say it more like he'd heard it pronounced on the TV. That was probably the best bet; he must have thought George had maybe heard the name in the news, perhaps pronounced less perfectly than the authentic Flemish of John Stasson. But even after this, George was clearly none the wiser. Dad goes on, '... The Belgian team the Dons hiv drawn in the semis o' the Cup-Winners' Cup.'

'Ah, of course!'

Finally all on the same wavelength, we dissolve into hilarious laughter. It wasn't that funny though. In fact, in normal circumstances, I wouldn't have pretended to find it funny at all and certainly would not have encouraged them any more by laughing out loud with them. But with every step through

George's front garden towards the car, with every chortle, the imminence of my release exaggerates how amusing it all seems to me. This was a liberation I'd been pining after for four and a half days.

The Easter holidays had started officially on Friday last week. I had been condemned, however, to music camp with my trumpet right up to the day before. The particularly unfair thing about this was I'd missed the St Mirren game at home (where we lost 1-0, missed a penalty and ultimately threw away the title). The only good thing about music camp was that it ran over my usual Monday afternoon piano lesson.

I'd taken up the piano at the age of nine when my mum was offered the loan of a piano from a fellow teacher at her school. Although lessons and practice were too much like school, getting to play the piano in class and on stage at Christmas shows was a perfect outlet for my show-off side. But when the chance came along to be taught by the legendary George Donald, the pianist in 'Scotland the What?', a comedy act from Aberdeen, it seemed too good to be true. He was full of infectious enthusiasm and he thought I was great, continually bumming me up about my talent. All this was fine until things like today happened where George would go out of his way to accommodate my music camp timetable by offering an extraordinary late morning session. In the holidays? Not just that ... on the day of our European semi? I needed the whole day to prepare mentally for football, especially European football. So my holidays are only starting now and I'm savouring every last second of the build-up before they kick in for real. And not only am I free from my days and hours of musical commitments, we are leaving directly from George's to go to Aberdeen for the European Cup-Winners' Cup semi. But first, we'd spend the rest of the day in Kemnay, home of my grandparents. This alone provided enough excitement for a lifetime.

Kemnay was the ultimate escape from the crapness of life

in Perth. It was our very own secret holiday village, tucked away about four miles inland from the main Aberdeen–Inverness drag. Even Aberdonians slagged it off for how out-of-the-way it was. The house itself sat back, elevated from the road, cloaked in its own protective canopy of enormous horse-chestnut trees, out of sight. Once up the steep drive through the trees, you'd see the top of the 'Queen', an obelisk in Queen Victoria's name that Granda had found in a ditch and restored. Nothing underlined how different it was from home than its almost perfect, countryside peace and quiet. This to the extent that when we stayed there I'd be wakened up almost every morning by a silence broken only by a single cooing dove, and would then lie wondering how it could be that I could sleep at all through the constant stream of rattling, squeaking articulated lorries, free-wheeling their way down the A9 outside my bedroom in Perth. But there was one thing that made the Kemnay experience more exciting than anything else, especially today. It sat in acres of grassy space that were crying out for someone with excellent ball control to do them justice.

Along the back of the house, there ran a rectangular swathe of plush lawn. A perfect mini football pitch, it was the most tantalisingly playable surface available to me anywhere in my world. The bit I would always forget was that it came with an almost impossible series of obstacles and obstructions. Firstly there were the moles, who would regularly carpet-bomb my pitch with dozens of enormous black mounds during the night. Secondly, unlike my facilities in Perth, there were no walls that could play the part of crosses from Peter Weir. On one side, three bent rusty wires partitioned me from a field and an ever-present herd of curious, masticating cows. The only thing that linked my bovine spectators to my fantasy football world was perhaps the stench that seemed to linger around them, which reminded me of the toilets at away grounds. On the other side, there was a window that ran the entire length of the lounge, with only a two-foot section of wall below it, guarded by flowering plants, all personal friends of my granny's. There was one potentially excellent goal area at the bottom of the garden, delineated by a curtain of tall conifers. But piled up on what would have been the six-yard area, was a mountain of car doors, distributor caps and leaking sumps, making a goalmouth impossible for even the most powerful imagination. But the sheer outdoorness, the sheer Aberdeen-shireness of it all, meant that on each visit to Kemnay, I'd make a go of it. Today though, I was discovering there was another problem. Granda himself.

According to what I was hearing in the car, Granda had been campaigning since our last visit that I was now far too old to be playing football in his garden. This was on account of the dirty ball imprints on the lounge windows, dents in scrap car doors and reports from the farmer next door who'd apparently complained about someone he'd spied through his binoculars from the other side of the field, drop-kicking a ball at the cows from point-blank range (wasn't me). So he was decreeing that any football was going to have to be played in the park, five minutes away. Absolutely no way. The park was crap, having even fewer facilities than Granny and Granda's house. Agoraphobic hell for a one-man game. And in any case, I was a far superior player than I'd been last time, quoting verbatim to Mum in the car the remark made by Grimmond (the Oakbank football coach) that I was 'one of the best dribblers we had' and that 'I should run with the ball more often'. These remarks were made following my match-winning performance in our Perth School Cup victory over the notorious Caledonian Road (the most mental primary school in Perth). In other words, my ball control was so good now that there was absolutely nothing to worry about. All the talk in the car on the way up the road led to my sister pleading to be allowed to play too. I could not believe this.

My sister had only once before expressed any interest in anything to do with football, and that was fairly short-lived. She'd been asking for weeks earlier in the season if she could come to a game with us. Against my advice, Dad eventually decided to take her to the relatively civilised venue of Dens Park; only half an hour away from Perth and a guaranteed Dons victory, so as safe a match environment as possible for Lynne's first game. But as I had anticipated, it did not work. All she did was plead from the very start to be taken for a pie and, of course, when Dad eventually gave in, he missed Aberdeen's second goal that sealed our 2-0 win. Typical. But her insistence in the car to be allowed to play with me once we got to Kemnay eventually resulted in a compromise: we'd ask Granda if we could both play and we were careful. Obviously, this was far from ideal, but I realised immediately that it did have some advantages. It meant that she could be blamed for almost anything that went wrong, even though she hardly ever got (or was given) the ball.

But I was hoping more generally that tonight's match would soften Granda's mood. Surely today, the sense of occasion, the significance of our historic achievement, would affect Granda too, and he'd relax his stance, loosen up and warm to all things football related, including my re-enactments in the back garden. Reaching the semi of a European trophy was not something we were likely to do again and, let's face it, getting to the Final was still very unlikely. Everyone would surely be bowled over by it. This was the pinnacle of football in the North-East of Scotland, probably for ever. I had my doubts though. I had known for some time that today would be a sort of day of reckoning for Granda and his relationship with the game. If anything was ever to expose the truth about whether he cared for it at all, it was going to be today.

I'd only ever known him to express an interest in football during the initial cursory minute or so of polite chat. By the time the bags were in from the car, Granda would normally have already worked through his standard string of platitudes about the Dons, the only time he was known to voluntarily bring the subject up. You could tell he couldn't really be arsed though. He always asked me if I thought the Dons would win 'the cup'. Now *the cup* traditionally was the Scottish Cup. But there were also the League Cup and the European Cup trophies we competed in. And then there was the league championship, much more important, that he never mentioned. On top of this, it almost seemed that he didn't know when 'the cup' (assuming he meant the Scottish Cup) was played, since he was capable of asking this question anytime through the year, even during the summer. And when I'd asked 'which one?', attempting to get Granda to clarify the exact trophy he had in mind, he'd wink at me and maybe laugh, before moving on to something else. And my dad did little to help, and seemed to sense how little Granda really cared about the Dons. He'd keep his football reflections to a surprising minimum when with Granda, but would happily return more than the favour by spending the remainder of our time there talking about Granda's passion ... cars.

He was, by all accounts, an extremely talented engineer and I knew from experience that this chat could go on for as much as five solid days. This was the backbone of his relationship with my dad – Granda was the master car mechanic and Dad his willing apprentice, and the pair of them would enthuse over everything from tie-rods, ball joints and big-ends, manifolds to air filters, petrol tank senders and coils. They'd come up in the lounge, in the enormous garage at the bottom of the drive, over dinner, in the shops. It had often occurred to me that it was a good job that Granda never came to Pittodrie with us, where no doubt they would have discussed

the same things. I could just imagine what might happen –
Granda holding court, presiding over impromptu Q&As in
the South Stand, like I'd seen him do in his Kemnay kitchen
when other 'apprentices' were present. But then again, there
was no danger of any of that. It was not lost on me that
Granda, who had resided for the majority of his life within
20 miles of Pittodrie, had not been to a game since 1934.
God only knows how on earth he'd managed this – he literally must have gone out of his way to avoid it.

But surely today would be different. Surely he'd be wanting
to talk about the game tonight? Finally in the grips of the scale
of our achievement, the sheer amazingness of it all, he would
catch up with Dad and me in our area of expertise? Surely?
We arrive in Kemnay and I immediately head for the bedroom
to change into my stuff. All kitted up I opened the bedroom
door and braced myself, hoping not to bump into him on my
way outside – we had an agreement with Mum, but Granda
was still capable of overruling this. Tentatively approaching the
back door, I could see Dad and Granda from the dining room
window, both down at the door of the garage, far enough away
for me to escape out to the back unnoticed. Superb. It seemed
to be going perfectly. The other half of the plan involved Lynne
disguised in plain clothes (unlike me, wearing my 1982/83
away kit). She had retrieved the ball from the car, and was
already in place in the back garden. But as I emerged from
the side of the house I found her standing in the middle of
the grass, staring at me apologetically, with her left hand
covering her mouth. I realised that disaster had already struck.
The ball was sitting in the field, and between it and us stood
12 large Friesians.

I could just imagine exactly what had happened. She would
have placed the ball in the middle of the grass and taken about
ten steps back. Then she'd start her run-up, with a few unnecessary hops and skips on the way, like she was taking a rugby

penalty from the halfway line, the only way she seemed to know how to kick a ball. And for possibly the first time ever, she had actually made perfect contact, toe-poking it high and long over the herd, ending up a good 20 yards into the field. I stood and mourned my disastrous situation for a moment, while my sister whimpered away seeking approval, and one cow mooed, before yodelling a little at the end, a noise that just summed it all up. Ten minutes we'd been here, ten minutes. Without even kicking the ball myself, we've either to wait till the cows disperse and move far enough away to get it back (these were the largest living things that I'd ever seen in the flesh – apart from the odd football fan – so 'far enough away' was quite a distance) or, if we want a result now, we'd have to get my Granda. I reluctantly turn and head for the kitchen, where from the window I could see him and Dad about to have their coffees. As I approached the door, I caught the tail end of their conversation, '... and as soon as I turned the key, the rocker heid gasket jist blew.'

I stood staring in disbelief at them both. It was true. We have been back here all of ten minutes or so, and even now, all they can find to talk about is cars. I knew at that moment that my Granda literally could not have cared less about our team, our historic night or generally about anything to do with football. And now I have to ask him to go into the field and get the ball.

'Weel, you'll jist hae tae wait til the coos move awa!' chuckled Granda at the unexpected and pleasant news I was bringing him, quite happy no doubt for the cows to stay where they were for the rest of the day. And, of course, they did. The afternoon came and went and the cows had not budged. By the time teatime came round, any lingering doubts about my Granda's interest in Aberdeen were dispelled for ever. When the table should have been bouncing with nervous energy, and our talk dominated by one thing, the onset of the biggest night in Scottish club football history for almost a decade, we were still talking about flywheels and alternators, peppered with anecdotes from Asmara and Baqubah, where Granda had learned much of his trade.

Once on our way, my complaints about his obsession with cars and his lack of interest in the real business of tonight's football were slapped down immediately. I was reminded that it was Granda's experience and tips that had contributed to our having years of operational P6 Rovers that took us to the games and that listening to him pontificating about them was a small price to pay. But soon I'd stopped listening as we entered Aberdeen and the real reason for our trip hit home. We were approaching Aberdeen for a match from a North-East base, the way it might always have been. I looked down the traffic stretching the full length of St Machar Drive. Streams of Dons fans on foot join the main route to the ground, accompanying the rolling traffic. It must have been what all other build-ups for European nights were like in Aberdeen. Other cars were thinking we'll have come in from Dyce or Kemnay, and, of course, tonight they'll be right. It was as concentrated an occurrence of Dons fans as you'd see anywhere, and here was I, not only among it all, but acknowledging and being acknowledged between the car windows, lads my age, older and younger, mouthing the words 'Aberdane, Aberdane' (this is how we pronounced Aberdeen when we sang at games).

Three hours later, however, we were all back, stuck in the same traffic jam on St Machar Drive, only this time going in the other direction. Dad turned up the radio when they replayed Davie Begg's commentary of a frantic goalmouth melee late in the game. Dad and I relived the magical moment when the ball, that seemed to bobble about in the box for an age, was finally poked home, causing our stationary P6 to list and dip and my mum to frown at us unnerved, like we were a pair of juvenile chimpanzees. We might as well have been. But no different to the boys and dads in the jammed up cars crawling along adjacent to us towards the lights, their faces like ours, bug-eyed, stunned, hysterical, riotous, as they like us received the commentary, the reconfirmation, of what we'd seen. It was one goal in the game, but it was a goal of unimaginable importance. It was our fifth goal. We had won a European semi-final 5-1.

Something special was happening at Aberdeen to fan, player and manager alike. Stuck out on the edge of the North Sea, a distant beacon of light, properly isolated from the rest of the civilised world, our team soared to the top of the European game with a bristling confidence that seemed to defy everything that I had come to expect from Scottish sport. A transformation that seemed only to happen in the darkness of a Wednesday night when there were just us Dons fans there, packed into our modest 24,000 capacity stadium, hiding out of the reach of our historic demons of self-doubt. Now, barring a disaster, we – Aberdeen FC from Scotland – hardly on the radar screen at home let alone anywhere else, had already reached a European final. Half an hour later, once free of Aberdeen's traffic, we arrive back at Kemnay. Mum and I whisper our good nights to Dad and head off to bed, Dad makes for the lounge where Granda is still up. On my way back from the bathroom I pause while passing the open lounge door and I pick up their conversation.

'… an' then, pit it back oan *aifter* the rocker heid gasket and 'at should be jist richt,' advises Granda.

'Aaaah, of course!' welcomes Dad zealously, his mind feasting on yet another gem from the oracle.

That was it. There was absolutely no doubt about it now. Not the first time, and certainly not the last, I was just going to have to accept it. Even today, even now, football and Kemnay was just never going to work.

But when school started ten days later, I would find myself

catapulted from one extreme to the other. Even before our place in the Final was assured, the promise we'd already shown had become the property of everyone at Oakbank Primary. For me this was great initially, but as the run-up to the Final got underway, it all started getting out of hand.

Chapter 12

Playground Stand-off

'I'm Mark McGhee the day ...' asserts the burly figure of Ricky Hamilton.

What? No way. Absolutely no way. Today is the day of the Cup-Winners' Cup Final itself so he can fuck right off if he thinks he can get away with this. 'No, I'm Mark McGhee, I'm always Mark McGhee!' I spit back at him, taking care though to step out of the reach of Hamie's imposing frame, in case I pick up a kick or a swipe for my cheek. Hamie was well harder than me and we both knew it.

'C'moan then!' threatens Hamie turning towards me, squaring up. I can't believe this. No one had ever tried to be Mark McGhee before, a title that had been mine, unchallenged, for at least two seasons. Certainly not the likes of Hamie, a notional Hearts supporter. His family were from Edinburgh, although he didn't go to the games. And even if he had, it would not have made any difference. Being Mark McGhee in the playground for me was more than simply taking a player's name.

'I'm no' playin' unless I get to be Mark McGhee ... '

Fortunately, I had the ball as a hostage, which meant that no one else was playing either until we got this sorted out. As far as I was concerned, the fact that I saw McGhee play every other week meant that I *was* Mark McGhee, or I might as well have been in the playground at Oakbank. I'd already

been to over 50 Aberdeen matches. This meant that I'd naturally benefit as a player, watching the best football in the
country, but also that I knew McGhee's game and peculiari-
ties better than anyone else. I'd even perfected the peculiar
stoop and protruding lower jaw that he often seemed to take
on, as he'd run back to his own half after scoring. And today
of all days, the very day of the Cup Final itself, Hamie expects
to be Mark McGhee?

'C'moan Stuart, gie us the baw man!'

He's not joking about this either. I turn and grimace disbelief towards my two fellow 'pre-Euro glory' Dons fan
comrades, Moir and Spunk. The fact that the three of us
were the original Dons fans would bring them to my aid
and I knew neither of them really approved of Ricky Hamilton
anyway. Surely they'll argue my case; they won't have any
of this. They had at least seen Mark McGhee largely (but
not exclusively) thanks to the fact that Dad and I had taken
them to quite a few games, so I was hoping they felt that
they owed it to me to take my side. But it becomes clear,
as they avert their eyes from me and gaze at the ground
that they're not going to. Brilliant. Some mates. Some Dons
fans. They'd rather side with Hamie, the walking side of
beef, who had the ball control of a blind man on a runaway
horse, Hamie who they ridiculed behind his back, over me?
This was the final straw. It was only a matter of time now
before a massive tantrum was unleashed. The stand-off
continues, as I start to contemplate how ridiculous it had
all become.

How things had changed since we'd come back to school
after Easter. The first couple of days had been truly amazing.
As much as anything else, all my classmates seemed blown
away by the fact that we had been able to score five times in
a single European semi-final match. Not even the big English
sides, that we all knew everything about, could boast anything

approaching this – certainly not in our memories.* And since I'd been at the game the others in my class couldn't get enough of it. This allowed me to spend hours reliving the semi-final drama, interrupting playtime games on the invitation of others (or not), organising re-enactments of the build-ups to the Dons goals and making sure that I played the lead parts on each occasion. I was in my element, and everyone else seemed quite happy too. And then when we lost only 1-0 in the second leg in Belgium, sealing our place in the Final against Real Madrid, everything changed again. Now, Aberdeen were about to capture the imagination of the country in a way that was beyond all expectation. Everyone, everywhere was talking about my team, countless Aberdeen strips appeared in sports shops all over the country and then on the sports fields around the High School and Primary. And it was around then that it all started to get out of hand.

I'd never believed I'd come across a situation like this. Not that half of them had opinions about my team; they'd always had them. But now they all spoke about the Dons like they'd become the national team, like they had a stake in the Cup-Winners' Cup Final, like Aberdeen had become their side. Now, they were even prepared to argue with me about it all,

* In fact, at the time of writing, this had only happened on a total of 15 occasions across all post-war European competitions, including semi-final play-off games in the old Fairs Cup. But only one other British side had managed to score at least five in a semi-final match, Manchester City beat Schalke 5-1 at home in their European Cup-Winners' Cup semi in 1970. Four other British clubs have been on the other side of five or six goal hammerings in semi-final matches though, three of them Scottish. Rangers remarkably conceded six in both legs of their European Cup semi against Eintracht Frankfurt in 1960, Hibs took a 6-0 walloping at the hands of Roma in the Fairs Cup semi-final play-off in 1961 and Dundee conceded five away to Milan in their European Cup semi-final tie in 1963.

ready to dismiss my first-hand accounts, my summaries of South Stand wisdom, my general superior knowledge of all things to do with the Dons. It was unbelievable.

The Doug Bell arguments were probably the most ridiculous example. Fergie's Doug Bell gamble in the semi had turned out to be the masterstroke of the decade. They just could not cope with him as he dominated the game, dribbling everywhere and setting up three of the five goals. That gamble had been all about whether the Belgians had ever seen Doug Bell in action before, and they hadn't so this was not something that could be repeated against Madrid. At school though, they were having none of it. How could Aberdeen choose not to play such a lethal player, someone who could do that in a European semi? It was so simple for them. So I made it my business to make sure that I challenged every instance of incorrect Doug Bell forecasting that I came across. I argued and argued and argued, they argued back just as vehemently, accusing me that just because it was my team, that didn't make me a know-it-all about the players. They'd seen the highlights too, and I was talking out of my arse.

And when all of this spilled into the classroom after breaks or at bell time, it eventually drew the attention of Mr Foster. 'You jist pipe doun, son. We've a' heard enough aboot you'n yer team,' interjected Foster, assuming I was the ringleader, that it was my fault we were always talking about Aberdeen. And quite predictably, none of my classmates came to my defence, to explain to Foster that they were just as keen to talk about this as me. But there was much more to Foster's slap-downs than this. I had learned a couple of weeks ago who Foster supported. It just had to be Dundee United.

I knew he had never really forgiven me for my controversial, Dad-sponsored skive to get to the Munich match back in March. But on the very same night, something else happened that was to make things even worse for me. Dundee United had been in action in the UEFA Cup quarter-finals, and got knocked out. He had to be particularly pissed off with this. I knew from Arabs I'd met that they really fancied themselves as Scotland's European specialists in recent years. They had reached the UEFA Cup-quarter-finals the year before, beating teams like Monaco 5-2 away and hammering Mönchengladbach 5-0 at home. So it would have been bad enough that this year they'd be knocked out by some crap sounding Czechoslovakian outfit. It was also true that Bohemians of Prague were hardly comparable with the decorated and star-studded giant that was Bayern Munich who we'd beaten on the same night. But the fact that Dundee United had never got beyond the quarter-finals, and now we, Aberdeen, were in a European Final, would have made things fairly unbearable for them. The Cup-Winners' Cup Final to boot, number two in the pecking order of European trophies, second only to the big one, the European Cup itself, not the crap UEFA Cup for serial 'also-rans' like Dundee United.* Everything was conspiring against me. And now I can't even be Mark McGhee?

---

* There is a conflicting argument that says that the UEFA Cup should have been recognised as the second trophy ahead of the Cup-Winners' Cup. It is argued that the teams that end up in the Cup-Winners' Cup are weaker than the UEFA Cup qualifiers on the basis that many continental countries did not take their domestic cup competitions as seriously as the Scots or the English. The UEFA Cup teams on the other hand were typically the second and third strongest league sides. However, I don't think anyone could doubt the quality of the teams in the Cup-Winners' Cup in 1982/83: Real Madrid – European Cup finalists in 1981; Bayern Munich – European Cup finalists in 1982 and Barcelona – European Cup-Winners' Cup winners 1982 (Michael Crick's book about Fergie, The Boss, lacks attention to detail on this front). In any case, the perception at the time certainly had the Cup-Winners' Cup as the second most prestigious European competition.

'Och, come oan Stuart! D'you really think it matters if
you're no Mark McGhee? Let's face it – yees are gonnay get
TANKED!' shouts Bally jolting me out of my self-pity, as my
classmates now all seem set to flock to Hamie's cause. And
what he's just said must be the worst thing of all. No one
really cared about the result, and no one had any faith. They
all wanted a piece of the excitement that Aberdeen's European
success had whipped up, but none of them would be picking
up the pieces tomorrow, next week, in August or September
or January next year if we *did* get tanked. I would though.

Even the highly respected Mr Grimmond said the same
thing. I'd overheard him reflecting on the Final with Mr
Gallespie (another Dundee United supporter) in the corridor
yesterday lunchtime, 'Naw, naw, they've got their work cut
oot the night. Ah mean, it'd be good for Scotland like, but ah
cannae see it,' he commented to his older colleague in the
corridor. This was particularly hard to bear, since out of
everyone I knew in the world, he was by miles the best placed
to judge our chances tonight, having been on Dundee FC's
first-team books for three or four years where he'd even got
to know Gordon Strachan. But before I was able to get a
chance to hear his expert analysis on this, Mr Gallespie had
to interrupt him prematurely, 'Oh yes. My auld freen Alfredo'll
have them sussed, I reckon.'

I sensed Grimmond pausing, like me, wondering who on
earth Gallespie's 'old friend Alfredo' could be, and then the
penny dropped. It was the legendary Madrid striker Alfredo
di Stéfano of their great 1950s side, now manager of Madrid.
This was confirmed when Gallespie starting recounting that
he had seen him play at Hampden in the European Cup Final
in 1960 when he'd been taken there by his Dad.

'Oh aye. Nae bother tae Alfie!' jokes Gallespie emphatically. That was it. That was why Gallespie and Alfredo were
'auld freens'. And that was all that was needed to cause both

of them to forget all about tonight's monumental game, as they went banging on and on and on about that 1960 European Cup Final. How it was the greatest European Cup Final ever, the majestic performances from di Stéfano and Puskas who scored all seven goals for the Spaniards, how Madrid won it for the fifth time and how flattered we all were in Scotland that it should happen at Hampden, on our turf. Fifteen minutes this went on. Fifteen minutes! On the eve of our finest hour, they've no more than a few derisory seconds for us, and that was just to dismiss our hopes.

'Stuart! Stoap bein' a dick!'

Staring into space in a daze, I started to wonder if it was all a daft dream I was having ... I'll be watching the TV tonight in the lounge, and Mr Foster will march across the screen on to the Gothenburg pitch, wagging his finger and shaking his head towards the Dons players. 'Naw, naw, naw, naw, you boys shouldnae be playin' here ... ' The players comply, heads down and leave the field, only to be replaced by an AC Milan or a Juventus, some realistic Euro Cup Final material and more in keeping with these apparently legendary Spaniards we were due to play. And then I'd waken up ...

'GIE ME THE FUCKIN' BAW!'

That was it ... I'm over the edge ... I take four long and calculated steps, and then welly the ball as hard as I can over the concrete playground, aimed at the High School roof. For a split second, the whole playground stands and follows its flight, to see if my kick can defy gravity, before they all turn and look angrily in my direction. I bolt for the school doors, slowing to a canter when I'm safe, checking over my shoulder a couple of times, just to make sure. Fuck them.

Somehow the next eight hours came and went, I escaped school unpunished, had tea, got changed and went downstairs into the lounge to watch the game. Dad and I squashed into the two-man sofa, replicating our South Stand circumstances (rather than him sitting in his armchair and me on my pouffe – our normal TV viewing seats – but taken up by Mum and Lynne right now). Here we were – a live European Final involving my team, my Scottish team. The four of us sit in silence as the seconds tick away. At 7.30 the game starts …

Bang, bang, bang … 'Ma – drid!'
Bang, bang, bang … 'Ma – drid!'
Bang, bang, bang … 'Ma – drid!'

The Madrid fans start their chant right from kick-off and continue for the rest of the match, more or less unbroken. They're that good. So good, their fans don't even need a range of songs. 'MA-DRID!' That says it all. I suppose at least the Dons fans find themselves in the rare position of having more songs than the other side's supporters. If nothing else, we'll win on the singing front.

Aberdeen mount their first attack, the ball goes out for a throw-in. The vibrating TV thunders nervous roars from the Dons fans into our lounge, you sense they're trying to force a manifestation of belief from somewhere, to convince themselves, the Madrid fans, everyone that it *can* be done. Every challenge by a Dons player is welcomed with gutsy roars that many Pittodrie goals would have been jealous of. Exaggerated boos when free-kicks and throw-ins go the wrong way. We're booing and shouting at the TV too. A hopeless 40-yard blooter by Neil Simpson is met with massive applause as we try to believe that this is happening, that we're actually there. The stress of the occasion is laid bare for us all to see as the camera pans to a gaunt-looking Fergie.

Then, a racing attack up the left led by Strachan, he crosses, Black smashes an acrobatic mid-air volley first time, we're up on our feet about to celebrate and my dad's jitters cause the coffee table to slide halfway across the lounge and almost knock over the TV. Black's shot hits the bar. We've never seen him do anything like that before. We *can* do it. We *can* do it. An enormous OOOOOOOOOOOOO rings in the air, prolonged to try to squeeze out all our doubts. Maybe that was our chance, though. Maybe that's the sort of chance we need to take against a side like Madrid …

… Five minutes gone, you'd think Black's effort had actually put us 3-0 up, judging by the noise the Dons fans are making. At the first chance to take a breath, I realise that Dad and I are both in the South Stand mode, but it's not the same. Especially for Dad, there's little chance of him getting away with his usual abuse towards the ref. Not with Mum and Lynne sitting here with us … tonight more than any other, we're really going to need an escape valve. Our first corner, Weir crosses, McLeish arrives late, a powerful header … the goalie parries, the ball falls to Black who wheels round and SCORES!

An ornament on the unit behind us falls to the ground, and the whole lounge shudders under the stress of the three-man pounding Dad and I deliver along with my sister, who seems somehow to know how to celebrate a goal. What a start! We calm down and take up our lounge terrace seats again, and focus back on the game. An anxious miaowing comes from the closed lounge door. The cat, who'd been asleep under the bay window, is not …

The whole momentum is with us. We're winning free-kicks, everything. 'Aberdeen, Aberdeen, Aberdeen,' boom our fans. I look at Dad. The goal hasn't helped the anxiety, there's even more at stake now and there are still 83 minutes to play, if only it could stop there. Di Stéfano's grim Latin countenance fills the screen, as he embarks on an enormous draw of his cigarette. It almost runs down to the cork in a oner. We lash out at him, 'You're finished!' But there's an unnerving calm about him, he is the legendary Alfredo di Stéfano, the one that

Grimmond and Gallespie were getting so excited about earlier. His sense of himself is written all over his face.

The Spaniards, now coming back into the game, are committing more and more fouls. Born-again Dons fan Ian St John complains about their Latin antics, reminding us how Liverpool dealt with this excellently two years previous in the European Cup Final. Right enough, they've been in a European final that recently. How can *we* win this? Thanks for that Saint, just when we were starting to believe ...

Fourteen minutes gone. McLeish – sturdy, flawless Alex McLeish – clears up a failed Madrid attack and passes back to Leighton in goal. Shit! The ball stops dead in the rain-drenched pitch, sitting up perfectly for the on-running Juanito ... he's only got Leighton to beat, he rounds him ... Penalty ... surely? Penalty it is! Juanito strikes, and it's there, 1-1. It's over. A 'real tragedy' acclaims St John, ironically. There's silence in the lounge. The cat might as well come back now, I think.

> *Bang, bang, bang ... 'Ma – drid!'*
> *Bang, bang, bang ... 'Ma – drid!'*
> *Bang, bang, bang ... 'Ma – drid!'*

Same rhythm, same song, only louder this time as their side is reinvented. They own the midfield, the slick pair of Gallego and Stielike slip the ball around, 'total-footballesque', showing off their incredible, effortless touch and control, on the chest, traps, passes. The Dons revert to agricultural-style sliding tackles from 40 yards, booting the ball into touch whenever they get a glimpse. The false confidence of the Dons fans is now unveiled. Four to one we outnumber them in the ground, but we've disappeared, and we're about to feel the might of a European giant as it gets into its stride. I look at my mum and my sister as I wring my hands and fidget relentlessly. They're totally caught up in it too.

Twenty minutes gone and the ZX 81 they use for match info has the score over the screen. Over to the bench, Fergie still looks like he's suffering the most drawn-out heart attack in history. 'Aberdeen, Aberdeen, Aberdeen' gradually makes a comeback, but it reeks of a defeated, half-hearted rally, the enormity of the occasion diminishes us. They know and we know it's going to be a pounding. Saint seems more exasperated than us, complaining about a lack of urgency, tutting in frustration, and giving Peter Weir a pasting.

The game loses its pace, as Madrid keep play in the middle of the park, slowly building for an attack. The Dons fans turn their attention to other things and now try to hijack the Spanish drummer's beat, with some success ...

> *Bang, bang, bang ... 'AB - ER - DEEN!'*
> *Bang, bang, bang ... 'AB - ER - DEEN!'*
> *Bang, bang, bang ... 'AB - ER - DEEN!'*

At least we're having laugh. We had our chance at the beginning, but now the truth is out. We've no belief, and they're the biggest thing in world football. Half-time comes.

Just to buck us all back up for the second half, Brian Moore keeps getting Rougvie and McLeish, then Weir and McGhee mixed up. No wonder. What does he know about Scottish football? Why on earth have they given him this job, tonight of all nights? And he's reminding us that Gallego and Stielike dominated Cooper and Simpson in the first half. And then he starts playing the British card, that Aberdeen would be the sixth British team in history to win the Cup-Winners' Cup! We want some partisan bias for our team, not some impartial neutrality; this is a Scottish night, nothing to do with Britain. Dad rants and complains, we all agree heartily.

We know the Dons fans are digging deep when they start to sing, 'Come on ye Reds, come on ye Reds' to the tune of

'Auld Lang Syne', where did they get this from? Or maybe
they're playing a Scottish card, great, that'll surely have the
Spaniards quaking in their boots ... Mum and Lynne titter
nervously when the camera pans round the ground to zoom
in on a flag with 'Rougvie never lets a dago by' written on it.
More ironic was that Rougvie was most likely the player who
would be struggling with any swift, fleet-footed 'dago'
attempting to get past him. In any case, I'd rather not be
reminded that we've anything as primitive as Doug on the
park at this time. I do not laugh, neither does Dad. We are
not expecting to laugh for some time ...

Ten minutes gone in the second half, and Aberdeen open
Madrid up for the first time since we scored, through a Strachan-
led attack. This is new. The fight comes back to the Dons fans
at the game. A corner swings across. Dad and I are now on
our feet. The seating accommodation can't deal with our nerves.
A goalmouth melee, the ball breaks to Strachan, who rockets
a volley towards goal, it's on target, the goalie blocks, it falls
to Doug ... another corner. COME ON! COME ON! We're
looking strong for the first time. This was much more
dangerous than anything we'd seen from Madrid. COME ON!

Three minutes later, Peter Weir is deep in our half, he wins
the ball from a first Madrid player, he beats a second, he's at
the halfway line, he nutmegs another, he's thundering up the
left wing in the Madrid half, he shimmies in front of a fourth,
beats him, he's now at the penalty box, he crosses, it takes a
deflection over the defenders in the six-yard box, it's dropping perfectly for unmarked Eric Black at the back post, COME
ON! ... a header with only the goalie to beat, and our best
headerer ... over the bar ... That was definitely our chance.
We've now missed two; it could have been 3-1. We'll pay for
this. Dad and I exchange pained glances, as we sense a build-
up for an almighty crash back to earth. No ... please, no ...

'And Juan José clears, no sloppy backpass from him,'

comments Moore. What? 'Get him off the air now!' I shout, 'Why is he reminding us of our only mistake in the game? Whose side is Moore on, is he really that indifferent? And where is this place "Pittoodrie" he keeps referring to? Fuck's sake.'

'STUART!'

'Sorry Mum ... '

The nerves are now unbearable. Unless Real Madrid are playing with us (surely not, not in a European final), we've seen that we have the measure of them. So if we don't capitalise now it'll be worse than if we'd taken a hammering from the start. Madrid will, no doubt, be back in many more finals. Will we? No way. We have to do it now.

Dad and I sit down again, as the second half gets bogged down in midfield. It's 1-1 at full time. Moore and Saint are talking about penalties. 'Nae penalties' pleads my dad, already writhing agonisingly at the thought ... still 1-1 at the end of the first half of extra time. The Dons still seem to have the edge, but everything is untidy now. Score in the next 15 minutes or penalties. This is hell ...

The players all look knackered. During the break, the Dons fans are still preparing for defeat with loyalty anthems, 'You'll Never Walk Alone', 'The Northern Lights of Old Aberdeen' and even 'Flower of Scotland'. We join in at home in the lounge, hands up, defiant. Come on! Brian Moore keeps reminding us that *Domino Principle*, the Wednesday night film, will be shown later on after the *News at Ten*. Who on earth would be caring about this? This guy is on another planet.

Seven minutes into the second half, Weir wins the ball deep inside our half, beats his man and, just before he runs into trouble, he lobs the ball 40 yards to McGhee. There's only one player between McGhee and the goal, Hewitt races unmarked through the middle, the best chance we've had ... McGhee takes on the last defender, gets past him at the edge of the box, he crosses, the goalie's coming out towards Hewitt, the ball hangs between them, it slips past the diving hands of Agustin, Hewitt makes contact with his head, on target is it? Or is it going past? It's past the post now, but is it in? Then when we see the ball lodge in the bottom corner of the net … we know IT'S THERE!

You'd have thought my mum and sister had been football supporters all of their lives, as the four of us lock into a volatile embrace, gripped by the elation of our goal, a family huddle in a front lounge that's never seen anything like it.

Eight minutes to play. We're praying. We are up on our feet twice within the next three minutes as McGhee then Hewitt agonisingly squander two excellent chances to kill the match. COME ON! We're so close, will we regret those misses? Please, no! The clock shows that time's almost up, then a free-kick is awarded to Madrid 20 yards from goal. It's their best chance in extra time, their last chance?

The Aberdeen wall assembles; Moore reminds us that if we can withstand this it's ours. Thanks Brian. The free-kick is taken; it hits the wall and is cleared. PHEW! What? It's got to be taken again? WHAT? The tension is now total as time stands still for an eternity … the wall reassembles, the Spaniards, panting, take their time discussing it; they know this is their last chance. Gallego runs up, thumps the ball … it speeds through the wall, Leighton launches himself hori-zontally across the goal, it's beyond him … it's going into the net … it misses, by an inch, that's it surely! Goal-kick taken … the ball hangs 30 feet in the air, a whistle starts … it's long, the camera pans to the ref, he has his arms in the air, he's pointing to the middle of the stand … WE'VE DONE IT!

The lounge is no longer big enough for us, we run through the house, scarves in the air, YES! YES! The phone starts ringing, and rings for the rest of the night as what seems like the whole of Grampian region is phoning to speak to me and Dad – even my Granda.

Aberdeen FC: European Cup-Winners' Cup winners 1983. Amen ...

Chapter 13

Defying the Divine Right

It's the beginning of the close season, late May of 1983. Rangers and Celtic are not happy. For the first time in a quarter of a century, Scotland's Old Firm have had to finish the season fighting over the scraps, the tawdry old League Cup. The New Firm have carried off the big prizes of the Scottish Premier League and Scottish FA Cup. And above all, the Glasgow giants, along with the rest of Scotland, and England for that matter and I suppose much of Europe, have been upstaged by Fergie's Dons, the sensational winners of the European Cup-Winners' Cup. It's as barren, as humbling, as it has ever been for Scotland's Old Guard.

They've tried everything, but it's not working. Other than orthodox football rules, they'd resorted in desperation to head-butting our players on the park, trying to intimidate them in the tunnel after leaving the field of play, even the tried-and-tested methods of their fans – lone assassins, or mass inva-sions and riots in and around football grounds … all hopeless. They had even failed to kill my dad, me and many thousands of other Dons fans. They had their chances, I know, I was there. But, of course, they're not finished. This is the Old Firm, after all. As the dust settles on 1982/83, news breaks that Celtic's premier Billy McNeill has been axed. Now, the directors of the provincial clubs around Scotland start to sleep uneasy. They know that a supernatural phenomenon is stirring, one that has the power to redress this imbalance in the Scottish game ...

Again and again, they are visited by a nightmare in which a great storm of apocalyptic potential sends tremors shuddering through their humble, rickety old main stands. They and their crap grounds must brace themselves and pray that they are spared. For they know that one of them will be singled out, when a humungous cloud-finger will form, massive and dark in the sky, and point towards their ground, and one of them shall hear the booming command:

'YOUR MANAGER SHALL COME ...'

Tonight the great divine digit appears in the dreams of a Paisley-based man, but not at Love Street, home of provincial St Mirren. This time, it's the owner and manager, not of a club, but of a provincial pub, a Celtic legend by the name of Davie Hay. The provincial clubs of the Scottish game, for once, are spared.

But what about Rangers, the other Old Firm colossus? New blood is urgently needed at Ibrox, too. Surely the provincials cannot escape again? In the end, Ibrox boss John Greig remains in his seat although it is known that more than a premonition has reached the Aberdeen board about who might be the next Rangers manager. But no celestial command is issued. By late autumn, when the new season gets underway, the storm has passed. Or so it seems ...

It's a windy, winter afternoon, Saturday 5 November 1983. There are about two minutes to play of another superlative Aberdeen victory away from home. Johnny Hewitt even scored a hat-trick in our 5-0 pounding, a record away win for me. And it all happened at Muirton Park, home of St Johnstone, a mere 20-minute walk from our house in Perth. Normally our home town was a place where the worst thing that could happen to me was a bollocking from my mum or a scraped knee playing football in a concrete playground. It was a sanctuary of pamperdom. Not now though. As the final whistle approaches, I am in the face of the unavoidable, mortal danger that we'll confront on leaving the ground. I am shitting it more than ever. And this time there is good reason.

As the final seconds of the match tick away, I bite my lip nervously, chastising myself for my big mouth. This time, definitely this time, it is going to happen: Dad and I *will* be battered. I had been warned about it for weeks at school. If the Saints fan nutters from school see me after the game, I'll be killed. My biting intensifies as I remember how I'd fanned the flames, telling them if they didn't shut up, I'd make sure an extra-large contingent of Aberdeen casuals came down. As if I could command extra casuals. As if I even knew any of them. But whether they believed me or not, what they said they'd do in return had been terrifying me all day: their Saints fan brothers, uncles and cousins would be there and they'd been given a description of me. The ref is now wandering around with the whistle in his mouth, constantly flicking his wrist. This is it! I glance enviously for one last time across the bank of our fellow Dons fans inside Muirton, as they joke and laugh, relaxed after a thumping victory. What I would give to be one of them right now. They all quite sensibly live in Aberdeen, have parked cars or buses in a Dons fan area, or will get the Dons fan train back to Aberdeen. In other words, all safe in Dons fan numbers. I look at Dad, taking in the final seconds … my mind toys with asking him to see if we could get on one of their buses and maybe get dropped in Scone where we could phone Mum and get her to pick us up? I knew he wouldn't though. I work out that all we can do is break away from them once outside, to merge and disappear seamlessly into the larger flow of our fellow Perth residents and somehow avoid my school casuals. Impossible. The final whistle goes. My heart rate moves up a hundred revs ... they all clap as we amble along towards the exit, I just walk, staring at the ground. And even before we get outside, everything is already going wrong.

As we approach the bottleneck at the exit of the terracing, my panic levels go off the scale when I realise I've been sucked into a bizarre sort of fast-track stream of bodies, being shoved to the very front of the exiting fans. 'Dad!' I shriek. No response. Now I realise that I am among the first handful of Dons fans to be out of the ground. Before I am free to control my movement again, I can already see what awaits us outside ... Jesus ... hundreds of Saints fans stream past our gate, the full width of the road, frozen, scrunched up angry faces, all staring at us. They've lost to Aberdeen, 5-0 at home, a humiliation I can barely imagine, and now they're surely at breaking point, and we're surely dead. They start to sing and chant to the pace of their march, 30 abreast, hundreds deep, the agitation is electrifying. I scurry around to the edge of the gate, and cower behind a couple of other loiterers who'd been exited prematurely like me, trying to avoid the Dons fan identity parade I've found myself in as I wait for Dad. Then, it gets as bad as it could. I spot the three people in the world that I know I have to avoid today if I am to escape at all. And they are definitely about to see me. Farkie, Logie and Tommo are at the head of a large group of Saints, glaring at us as menacingly as possible, although they still haven't spotted me. They are three serious nutters I had started secondary with at Perth High, all former pupils of the notorious Caledonian Road Primary School. We had all heard for years that at that time it was the hardest Perth primary by a mile, and we all understood why when we met them at the big school.

They had set out their anti-establishment stall right from the very first day of first year, without even saying or doing anything. Like everyone else from Oakbank, I turned up in a shapeless pair of standard issue Markies flannels and a plush navy blue blazer. 'Smart' in the old-fashioned sense of the word (even more smart than the other squares from Oakbank, on account of the fact that my mum was a teacher at the same school). Meanwhile, Archie McLinton, Farkie, Robbo and a handful of others, all from Caly Road, turned up in their burgundy Sta-Prest, flouting the school's well-publicised sartorial code. Sta-Prest were all the rage at the time and implied a rebellion in whoever wore them (this to the extent that I'd be banned from wearing even black versions to school until sometime in third year). The Sta-Prest incident told us that these guys meant business, but over the following weeks we'd come to realise that this was just the tip of the iceberg. We'd learn about the famous lunchtime ambush of St Ninian's Primary school in P7 last year, where, according to the most exaggerated accounts, they'd stoned all the school windows and battered all the P7 boys who'd stood their ground. The same sort of organised assault was carried out on Craigie, one of Perth's more suburban primary schools. But something else had supposedly happened there that I found more chilling than anything else. They had gone after the jannie. They were prepared to try and batter a man.* It wasn't just that they were capable of it physically; it was more that they would even consider a fight with a fully grown adult. One like my dad, who they had an excellent chance of identifying right now ... Jesus ... the thought of visiting him in hospital, broken, in tears, him, all of us ... Mum, Lynne ... how they'd taunt me for years to come, revelling in another adult scalp. How it would suit them that it was my dad ...

And then it happens ... 'Duck!'

I was Duck. A nickname I'd invented around two months

---

* Over time, we'd come to conclude, through an absence of Craigie or St Ninians witnesses, that most of these claims were not true.

ago in a panicked split-second when, during an early physics class, my new peers at Perth High, who all seemed to have nicknames, turned to me for mine. We didn't really do nick-names at Oakbank. Why 'Duck'? Well, my surname is Donald. Enough said.

'You're fuckin' claimed!'

All of a sudden, it seems like my luck has finally run out ... the three of them look left and right in preparation to bolt out of formation across the road towards me ... Panicking, I turn to move back in amongst the exiting Dons fans, but it's hopeless. Behind me now, I find an impenetrable rally of Dons fans, now exiting Muirton Park in full flow all singing and pointing, 'Are you Rangers in disguise?' at the tops of their voices towards the Saints fans at the other side of the road. And guess who is at the very front? His hands raised in the air, an enormous smile over his face as he sings, with his enor-mous scarf thrusting out of his jacket (as usual the only man-made thing that can be seen from outer-space, along with the Great Wall of China). It had to be the proverbial red flag to the bull. It is going to happen now ... I immediately look away from him. It is all I can do ... I know if Farkie and Co. realise that this scarfer at the head of the casuals is my dad, I'd die there and then and so would he ... But just when my bladder is about to give up the ghost, yet another change in events comes to my rescue ... Just in the nick of time, the sight of our nutters emerging along our side of the road causes the bulk of the older Saints fans to pick up the pace on their side, with a great surge sweeping Logie, Farkie and Tommo back into line, on their way into the town centre, for official business.

'Yoos're fuckin' gettin' it later!' Farkie fires back at me. 'Yoos' he had said, not just 'you'! He'd already worked out who Dad was! The serious nutters now on their way into town, we cross the road, and join the flow of Saints, heads down, funnelling through the shortcut onto the Crieff Road. No one says a word; we seem to have gone unnoticed. But Dad's scarf is still the biggest threat to us. Surely this time … surely here he'll not make a scene if I ask him.

'Hey min, Ah'm an Aiberdeen supporter!' trumpets Dad in response, for the benefit of the whole Tayside region. Christ! It's worse than ever, he's out of his mind! Almost immediately, three or four ugly stares from the Saints fans surrounding us turn and fix on him for a second or so, a bloke in his mid-20s launches an inter-continental grochle from the other side of the road over the gridlocked traffic that lands a foot away from me. This is it. This is it … my autopilot security system kicks in, and I start to move out of the immediate pocket of fans we are with, further along the pavement away from him, where we can't be linked. The risks of this were huge as well, I knew I might well come across another classmate, maybe not a Caly Road headbanger, but anyone that recognises me would still probably blow my cover. But still, being with Dad in his 'kamikaze' mood, now even away from home, still seems a much higher risk … Walking six abreast, now separated from him, I look round every now and then to try and locate him, but each time I look back immediately when all I see is his scarf, which is still not only visible, but fluttering in the wind … God almighty … I clench my teeth in dread as I imagine Dad's scarf latching onto lampposts, enveloping and mauling the heads of Saints fans around him – as if possessed by Rod Hull's Emu. With every heartbeat another second passes, no noise from behind, no violence, not yet, but it must come.

We reach the entrance to Feus Road, still two miles to go, still surrounded by thronging Saints masses in a cloud of absolute dejection. Still nothing … Halfway along Feus Road, someone shouts, 'Sheep-shaggin' bastard!' very loudly about five metres behind me, where Dad must have been. A lump hits my throat, I can't even look back to see if he's OK I'm so scared … It could well be Farkie and Logie. I start running. I reach the Glasgow Road ... Five minutes later, I turn right and leg it towards the house ... no one follows. I finally get up the drive where I wait on tiptoes at the elevated entrance to the vestibule, where I can follow his striding figure as he walks up our street, no one follows ... still no one ... he's at the bottom of the drive now, safe at last ...

'What are you playin' at Dad?' I shout, standing in the hallway, facing the open door as he arrives. He looks at me with a confused frown, closes the door then hangs up his jacket and scarf. 'Did you realise that we'd been spotted by the Caly Road boys?' Dad grins, I stare angrily back. 'Do you know what they did to the Craigie Primary jannie?' Dad now winks at me patronisingly, as if to say as a teacher he could cope with lads that age. But I doubted that, Crieff High was a country school, so there was no way in my mind they had a feeder primary that came close to the very mental and urban phenomenon that was the Caly Road. 'And did you hear what that guy shouted at you along Feus Road?' Dad has still to say a word and seems to be fairly amused by my strop, laughing, shaking his head. 'Look Dad, why can you not just hide your scarf after games, what's wrong with that?' Finally, I seem to have struck a nerve as he prepares to break his silence, his joviality dismissed as he clears his throat.

'Listen min. Ah've been waitin' a' mi life for 'is, and I'm nae hidin' ma scarf fae onyb'dy! OK?' he says, staring at me square on, his eyes tightened. I stand looking at him, hands on hips. He really means it. This was totally beyond a joke. I turn and run upstairs and begin a sulk that would see me not speak to him for the rest of the weekend. Mum sussed out something was up within hours and gave us a proper lecture over tea along the lines of it was one thing coming home on Saturdays and being in foul moods when we lost, but when we won 5-0, away from home, we really needed to stop and think about it all.

Mum was right. At face value, it was inconceivable that we could be falling out. That week, we had rebooked our place in the last eight of the Cup-Winners' Cup, and today's result against Saints put us two points clear of Dundee United at the top of the table. But what my mum didn't know and what I didn't understand was that Dad was just starting to come to terms with something else that had happened that week, something that could turn him into a headbanger at any moment for weeks to come. He was three days into what he saw as the most famous victory Aberdeen had ever got against the Old Firm, arguably the most unlikely story that happened during the golden era. In time, I would come to realise that this event was as important as Gothenburg in redefining who we were at Aberdeen. But back then, all I cared about was retaining the Cup-Winners' Cup, killing Dundee United and this year, surely this year, winning the league. That was all. And those final months of 1983 would see Aberdeen hit a purple patch in form, the richest, deepest, purplest spell of form we would ever see, making my unreasonable set of objectives seem perfectly attainable. For me, it all started at the beginning of the previous week ...

'STUART! WHAT ON EARTH ARE YOU DOING HERE?' gasped Mum.

'Shit!'

My mum was not pleased, to say the least. She was a teacher at Perth High, and right now she was mortified to find me standing outside a classroom door in an empty corridor. I'd been sent out as a punishment for inappropriate behaviour. This was bad enough, since my teacher would certainly have grassed me up to her, behind my back. But that day, I had being rumbled during my penance by my mum, in person. Hence the mid-corridor bollocking I was about to receive, and my disbelief at my uncanny bad luck. In spite of this, I was still confident my mum would find in my favour that Monday morning, once I'd explained to her the injustice I'd just suffered. That day, I just had to bring the programme from the Celtic match into school.

In the first couple of months at Perth High I had already discovered a huge diversity of football allegiances, much more than at Oakbank. A Hibs fan, a real one from Edinburgh, a Notts Forest supporter (justified on the basis that he'd lived there for a while, fair enough), a Man Utd supporter (no such justification, and they weren't half the team they are now, so no excuse at all), a few Dundee fans, even a Forfar Athletic supporter, and of course, dozens of Dundee United, Saints, Old Firm and Aberdeen fans. Apart from the supporters of the local teams (Saints and United), I was still the only long haul, professional fan. But my new school pals just wouldn't believe me. Aberdeen and back each Saturday, every Saturday. With your dad! In a 1975, P6 Rover, a car considered an old banger, even back then.

'Awa tae fuck! How come ye' dinnae bring in the programmes then?'

I would have, but bringing a programme into secondary school ran enormous risks. I'd already seen what had happened to one of Lavo's prized Notts Forest programmes: Nottingham Forest v F.C. Köln, the European Cup semi match, first leg, 1979, home (3-3). The sort of thing that I, as an Aberdeen fan, could relate to. I'd been there, European semis, I knew what this meant. But it had been stolen and taken hostage. Lavo had been forced to beg and plead for days around his Caly Road suspects. He'd eventually thrown caution to the wind when his desperation got the better of him and squared up to Logie, who he'd eventually worked out was the thief, in the PE changing rooms.

'Gie me it!' he forced through clenched teeth, fighting back the tears, foaming at the mouth. That was all he said. And that was all that was needed. Logie and Farkie gave him an excruciating, public scant-lift on the spot in the changing rooms, leaving him squealing like a piglet on the ground for his crimes, his programme tossed on the muddied wet floor next to him like some sort of trademark, mafia-style punishment. And he was lucky. Other stuff they stole from you, not only programmes, could just simply disappear. For ever. And there was absolutely nothing you could do about it, if you wanted to avoid a scant-lift or, worse, a kicking. You'd maybe pick up one of these for good measure anyway. I'd seen all this first hand, so there was no way I would risk it with our Dons programmes. Until today.

Aberdeen had been asleep since way back in May. In fact, if I was honest, we hadn't played well since the night of the Cup-Winners' Cup Final itself. I was certainly talking a good game at school, still pumped up by our European dream come true. But the truth was we'd been stumbling and stuttering, the way that big teams often do early on in the campaign, so I'd convinced myself. But we'd dropped points to the likes of Motherwell, and by the penultimate game of the first quarter of that season we'd even hit the sorry depths of losing to Hibs. Hibs? It was first time I could remember losing to them. Gothenburg seemed a distant dream that Saturday. And I got my comeuppance following that result for all the trumpeting and chirping about Aberdeen that I'd foisted on my new PHS classmates for two months now. The Hibs defeat seemed to have caused an inter-denominational group assault on me back at school. Rangers and Celtic fans, Hard-cunt and Square, Dundee and Dundee United supporters, all otherwise impossible alliances, all rallying to rubbish Aberdeen and its rep – me. In fact, I even found them rehearsing for my arrival in our registration class the following Monday morning, breaking into a rendition of 'Your so bad it's unbelievable' ('shite' used normally in place of 'bad', but the teacher was there) as I came in the door.

It was a different story today though. No taunts, no jeering, not even any eye contact, as I drift six foot tall into the register class. That Saturday, 22 October 1983, our league title challenge had been launched more boldly, more emphatically than ever. It had been the day of the great reawakening. As I took my seat in the classroom, I looked around at them, my mind full of what they'd have seen of the game on TV – Pittodrie, purring with an intense satisfaction, waves of enchanted applause flushing up and down the ground, as the champions elect stroked the ball around, turning the match into an exhibition, now leading 3-0 with another goal beckoning all the time. And my silent classmates would have seen the pass of the century on the highlights too. We'd all been conferring among ourselves in the South Stand about who had made the glorious first-time, 40-yard pass from the middle of the pitch that beat the offside trap and led to the definitive second goal. We were all fairly sure it was Tommy McIntyre, playing only his second full match at right back. He'd been put in at the deep end against Celtic and had already played a blinder. So how impressed they would all have been to see that we had this sort of unknown quality in the reserves, ready to drop in, even against Celtic, and make a pass like that? Final score: 3-1 to Aberdeen. This was more like it. They, like me, knew what this meant. It was the most emphatic win over Celtic at Pittodrie for almost three years (although we'd been doing it at Parkhead on a regular basis). Celtic left Pittodrie that day in tatters and we were back, stronger than ever. They would believe now as I did, that this year, surely, the league title would be ours. Now the programme would be going to school on Monday morning, whatever the risks. It was time.

As our English class got underway, my programme got passed furtively between the desks while the teacher's back was turned.

I tried to monitor and absorb the reactions to it as it made its way between desks around the class. I was proud. It was proof of my loyalty (there was little other explanation as to how I could get the programme so soon after the game if I had not been there). And I had quite rightly predicted they'd be impressed by its glossy finish. It was a statement of just what Aberdeen was. You could tell the serious teams by their programmes – only Rangers could rival us for slickness of programme in Scotland. After about ten minutes, it's heading back in my direction, at some pace, now being greeted with muffled titters. There was something they found particularly amusing, that made me suspicious immediately. As it was slipped back into my hand from behind me, I could already feel there was something inside, something warm, bulging in the middle pages. I opened it up between my legs hidden under my desk, and to my shock found an enormous greener corroding its way through the glossy paper, like a lump of molten cheese. My Dons programme. My Dons programme from the best Celtic game ever.

I blew a fuse. I immediately got up and marched towards the front of the class, mid-lecture. This was what Lavo should have done. Straight to the authorities, no messing. And as I did so I heard someone snarling and muttering in the background, protesting his innocence even before being accused. I knew it. It was Tommo, our class's resident Caly Road nutter.

Standing, trembling with rage, I stood with the centrefold open right in front of her, my programme 'exhibit A', as the grog starts to disintegrate, dripping on to the floor. She hesitates, before surely, interrupting proceedings to demand to know who had done this. I'd already turned towards the class, ready to offer advice to her, maybe pointing out those kids who were not to be accused …

'Get out.'

'Me?'

'YOU!'

So there I was in the empty corridor. By the time I'd delivered half of my account to my mum, I realised that her flaring eyes and dropped jaw were not expressions of sympathy for the outrage I was relaying to her. I knew what was coming and so drew my defence to a close.

'BLOODY FOOTBALL!' she roared. Not 'bloody Caly Road boys', or 'bloody football programmes' or even 'bloody stomach-less Mrs Fox'. 'Right boy, we'll see about this tonight,' she says chillingly, prodding me repeatedly in the chest, before storming off down the corridor.

I knew what was coming tonight. I'd been warned that if I got into trouble once more, I'd be sent to the Academy, the Perth secondary school for poofs, saps and toff kids that spoke with English accents (so we had already convinced ourselves before we even left primary). The thought of this was as appealing as losing a Scottish Cup Final to Dundee United. It was that bad. But the whole thing was so unjust. I realised I'd come off worse than even Lavo. At least he got his programme back, undamaged. Where he picked up a scant-lift (of which I'd already had many more than him), I'm now at best on parole, at worst, facing expulsion. And on top of this, I've to face Tommo. One thing was sure now: I'd be claimed, by him and most of his old Caly Road pals. There were few acts more treasonable to them than grassing someone up to a teacher, whatever the circumstances. And, of course, this was literally the first thing that happened when he passed me once the classroom door finally opened and my penance in the corridor was drawn to a close. But at that very moment another, much more significant door had just opened. It was the door to the manager's office at Ibrox. Rangers had just sacked John Greig. Little did I know at the time, but this act was to carry massive consequences for the rest of my life, the first of which I would discover later that night. At 4 o'clock, just after Dad arrived

back from work, I sneaked into the dining room and hid behind
the kitchen door to eavesdrop on my fate.

'This is the fourth time this year he's been in serious
trouble, and it's nae even Christmas!' ranted Mum. 'How I
am supposed to get on with my job, get other kids to behave
if he's actin' the goat a' the time?' I hear her assert, tapping
her nail repeatedly on the laminated breakfast bar table, with
the same chilling purpose I had sensed from that same finger
when it prodded me in the chest earlier that day. 'And what's
behind it all? What's at the bottom of every instance?
BLOODY FITBA!' she blasts, pointedly at Dad, stopping
short of laying the blame at his feet because she needed his
agreement for her newly hatched plan. 'So I'm gan tae spik
tae the Academy Rector the morn and find oot if the Academy
can take him from January.'

JANUARY! I immediately struggle to pant in silence as my
heart hits 200 beats per minute. So soon!

'Och, look …' says Dad, sounding like he was to argue for
some middle ground, '… it'll die doun afore lang.' I could
see my mum through the join in the door, looking at him,
confused. I'd no idea what he meant either.

'Listen, he's been warned again and again to leave football
at home and he jist disna seem tae care,' says Mum. 'Every
time he … '

'At's nae fit I mean,' interrupts Dad. Mum stares at him.
'D'ye nae ken fit happened the day?' says Dad. 'Rangers hiv
come in for Fergie.'

Mum could see in Dad's face that he genuinely believed
he'd dropped the bombshell of the century. She turned away
from him to look out of the window, biting her bottom lip,
fuming. I wished Dad hadn't said that, God knows what the
consequences would be for me now. Even I could see that she
was trying to canvass support just to allow her to do her job
properly at school and all Dad can do is turn things back to

football, the very subject matter that was at the bottom of all this. But Dad wasn't even finished.

'And we a' ken fit 'at means,' added Dad. 'Fergie's a gonner, and that'll be the end o' a'thin. You watch fit happens. Finished.'

'Right, well you bloody well spik te' him!'

I was off the hook for now. I knew Dad would speak to me about this in the car on Saturday, and he did, although he seemed more concerned about the damaged programme and if there was a way to get another one than anything else. But I just did not get this. Our form had turned the corner, our team was injury free and there was no indication that any of the players wanted to leave, so what if Fergie left? I mean, I didn't want him to go, but I couldn't see what the fuss was about. However, I discovered at Dens Park the following Saturday that most of the other Dons fans seemed to be as messed up about it all as Dad. They chanted and pointed, 'FERGIE MUST STAY! FERGIE MUST STAY!' on and on throughout the whole game. The urgency in their voices stepped up at the final whistle as he walked up the touchline, just in front of us. But he blanked us and made a clapping gesture instead towards the Dons players leaving the pitch who'd just impressively beaten Dundee 3-1 to put us top of the table for the first time that season. He didn't look at us once as we watched him turn and make off down the players' tunnel. We stayed on, all of us, and continued to chant desperately, in case a few extra bursts might help him decide. But you could tell that in the hearts of the people around me that he's already gone. Monday and Tuesday came and went, no decision, and then on the Wednesday, both Aberdeen and Rangers were to play their second-round ties in the Cup-Winners' Cup, Rangers away to Porto and Aberdeen at home to Beveren.

On the way up the A94 to watch the second leg against the Belgian side, Dad was trying now to be philosophical about it. The only reason it hadn't been announced yet was because of our European tie. That would be unfair on the players, especially since we'd such a fantastic chance to get through – we'd drawn the first leg 0-0. I agreed. Much more of a concern was our usual mad dash to get to the midweek game on time, especially tonight, since for some reason it was not all-ticket and there was still a good chance that we wouldn't get in. We picked up Uncle Geordie, parked the car and dashed down Merkland Road to find to our horror that the queue was halfway up the street, about 400 yards from the South Stand's back gate. I'd never seen it this far up.

Ten minutes later, we could hear the turnstile clicking tantalisingly, around 50 yards or so from the gate, but now the tannoy announcements had already warned us twice that the gates were about to close. First Geordie, then I get through and into the open area next to the pie stand, the atmosphere is overpowering, European nights seem to get better and better. We're still waiting for Dad who's taking ages. Oh my God … What's going on? I can see him mouthing, 'Fit?' disbelievingly, they're not letting him through. A split-second of 'lost-in-Marks-and-Spencer' panic from years past runs through my mind. He's still conversing with the guy in the turnstile booth … Come on, please let him through … he drags himself clear of the clicking barrier, and explodes in uninhibited goal-celebration mode as he runs towards me. What? He must be the last to get through …

'Fergie's stayin' min! He's stayin' wi' the Dons!'

Party Poopers

'Ah mean, how could he stay wi' us? It's jist nae real min …
I still canna believe it …' remonstrates Dad as we turn out
of Stonehaven on the last leg of our journey to Aberdeen for
the Rangers game, still beaming as if Fergie's decision to stay
at Aberdeen had just happened yesterday and not ten days ago.

'Ye ken that naeb'dy has ever rejected 'at job?'

If Dad had made this point once, he'd made it a thousand
times. He went on and on and on about it. Not once in the
history of Scottish football had anyone ever said no to the
offer of a job as manager of one of the Old Firm sides. I stare
at him, starting to wonder if he will ever come to terms with
it, still shaking his head, still refusing to believe, still in a sort
of euphoric denial that it could have happened.

'Jimmy McGrory teen fae Killie by Celtic jist aifter the war,
Jock Stein pinched fae Hibs in 1964, McNeill fae us in 1978
… and 'at's jist the managers they've pinched o'er the years,'
says Dad, casually sifting the abundant evidence that predicted
that Ferguson should have left Aberdeen. 'And Rangers, fit a
platform? Fit a platform to ging on, and dee even mair than
at Aiberdeen! If you're brutally honest aboot it, you couldna
hey blamed him really!'

Blame him? If Fergie had left Aberdeen, he'd have been
damning him every day for the rest of his life. Dad was simply
not in the 'brutally honest' game when it came to Aberdeen.

'But it jist shows you what the Dons hiv become if someone
like Fergie can say no tae the Old Firm. You'll understand
eventually min,' nods Dad, well aware I was yet to be convinced.
I was still none the wiser about exactly what a manager did,
and I'd given up trying to understand. But I had accepted that
there was something else I wasn't getting because of how all
Dad's generation, the TV, radio and newspapers had reacted.
All this motivation, management stuff was beyond me. For
me, playing football was self-motivation enough, and I couldn't
see what Fergie or indeed anyone else could add. Dad on the
other hand seems to have become a supporter of Alex Ferguson
FC, as opposed to Aberdeen FC. All the other amazing things
that were happening to our team were all secondary to Fergie's
decision to stay. According to him, the 4-1 liquidation of Beveren
– our most accomplished, most stylish, most clinical European
scalp to date – was all about Fergie's brilliantly timed disclosure, half an hour before kick-off, that he was staying with
us. And, the way Dad spoke about it, you'd have thought that
the ceremony that Fergie attended in Paris, where Aberdeen
were presented with a 'best team in Europe' award was for
Fergie himself, and not the Dons. All of it, everything, seemed
to pale into insignificance against this single act, or non-act,
by our manager. If Fergie stayed, we'd have years and years
of the same to come. If he'd gone, it would be over in a season
or so.

'Maybe we've made it, we've made the big time, ken?' says
Dad with a huge beam, flitting between the road and me.

And this, more than anything, was what was at the bottom
of Dad's euphoria – the idea that Aberdeen were now able to
compete with the Old Firm on a level playing field. It was
this, the big club feeling, that was ratcheting Dad's sense of
everything to do with Aberdeen to a new level of hysteria,
the same hysteria that fuelled his behaviour last week outside
Muirton.

Today, he'd been up to it again on the way to the game. He can't help himself, wagging his finger condescendingly at the convoys of Rangers fans on the old A92, with their cocks out at the back window of the bus, wearing his cheeky, patronising smile (the same one he'd use for road ragers he'd encounter, until a few years ago when he got chased by one, ending up in a two-hour stand-off at a bus stop outside Perth police station). The Gers fans, enraged by Dad's taunting, piled over to the nearside at the back of the bus, causing it to lurch and threaten momentarily to keel over on top of us. But Dad dropped into third, the old P6 screams up to 6,000 revs, before springing the clutch, causing the Rover to bob and list like a boat, before eventually steaming past them.

But there was something else about today's game. It was about more than simply rubbing Rangers noses in the fact they'd failed to pinch Fergie from us. Rangers had finally got a replacement manager, and that was as significant for historical reasons as everything else. It was Jock Wallace, the man who'd led Rangers to their last league title (and Treble) in 1978. I knew that, but what I didn't know was that it was also that season that the Rangers fans had rioted at Motherwell, a story he'd told that day up at June and Arthur's. The riot (according to my dad's version of the story) apparently started after a special nod from Big Jock, so terrified the Motherwell players that, although 2-0 up when it started, they eventually lost the match 5-3, earning Rangers two points – the margin by which they finished above Aberdeen at the end of that season. And the Dons had a better goal difference.

As we reached the Old Bridge of Dee, the purpose of today's game was becoming clear. Today was as much about celebrating the fact we had withstood a Rangers raid to take Fergie as revenge for 1978. Today, Rangers, the team, their fans, their manager, would be made to eat humble pie like never before. And timing was perfect for a revenge killing. How fitting that they should be the next victims of our purple patch of electric form, crushed by Aberdeen, the new order, as we'd make another massive stride towards our rightful title. We were both so pumped up we stopped speaking. We needed to get to the game. We just had to get to the game …

One Jock Wallace!
There's only one Jo-ock Wallace!

What? Not today! No way! I think, as we shuffle painfully slowly through the South Stand turnstile. They're supposed to be embarrassed! We get inside and the ground opens up in front of me to reveal the packed Beach End. But on the pitch in front of the Beach End goal, there stood what was exciting them so much. It was the man himself.

One Jock Wallace!
There's only one Jo-ock Wallace!

How on earth had he been allowed on to our pitch? My eyes lock on to the portly, grey-haired figure in a long black coat at the opposite corner of the ground. He claps side-on, towards the legions in the Beach End, as he walks nearer them beside the goal for a minute or two, lapping it all up. You'd think he'd been their first choice all along, judging by the reception he's getting. But why? They wanted Fergie did they not? None of this made any sense.

'Get 'at cunt aff the park!' blasts one of those rare specimens with 'fog-horn reach' in his vocal cords. It was what all of us were thinking … we need to all sing something like that now. Instead, to my disgust, a round of half-hearted booing picks up – not really what I had expected for our opening song on a day that is supposed to be a party for us. And I hated booing myself, my 'boos' were still too high-pitched to make a proper contribution and I'd often get paranoid if I caught the eye of any smirking adults around me. But right now all inhibitions are thrown off, my self-consciousness kicked into touch, we have to stop the noise in the Beach End, by any and all means, we all must conscript, we all must boo to neutralise the Rangers fans ...

> *One Jock Wallace!*
> *There's only one Jo-ock Wallace!*

They sing ever louder, so loud now that I can barely hear myself think, let alone boo. This is hopeless I realise, now standing arms folded in silence. How could they dare do this? Have they no shame? I mean, surely at some point the Rangers fans would realise that we were now out of their league, that they couldn't match us on the pitch? Why are they not subdued by the depressing reality of it all? Still clapping above his head, Jock finally starts walking slowly off the pitch, and they continue their tumultuous applause well after he'd disappeared down the tunnel. Now it was surely our turn, our turn to power up the volume, surely today we'd be able to reproduce the atmosphere of our European home games, dominate the whole place with our overwhelming majority, put Rangers in their place for the remainder of the afternoon. But within a minute of Jock's departure from the scene and before we'd even half a chance to get going, a farcical string of pre-match incidents start unfolding.

A few shrieks and whistles quickly explode into an urgent roar, spreading to all areas of the Aberdeen support inside the ground. Then I see what all the commotion is about. I cannot believe my eyes. A lone Rangers fan has vaulted the wall at the Beach End and is cantering up the middle of our pitch. Uninhibited, he continues to trot nonchalantly, scanning his stretched out Rangers scarf left and right so we are all left in no doubt that it is a Rangers scarf he is holding. I keep looking along to the end of the South Stand, expecting to see the thousand or so casuals at the far end of the South Stand breaking on to the pitch … but nothing … no action from anyone, only shouting. The lone Ranger walks into the centre circle. By this point the shrieking, screaming and squawking suggests that the place was about to erupt onto the pitch en masse … but still no one reacts, no pitch invasion from us … what's wrong with us?

The Rangers fan even has enough time to stop in the middle of the pitch, do a final revolution with his scarf to the whole ground, before bending down and laying it in some sort of ceremonial act around the centre spot. Finally, two policemen run onto the pitch as the bellowing peaks into a thunderous, demonic jeer. Suddenly I realise what this means. It is a carefully choreographed act representing the Motherwell pitch invasion, a symbolic reminder to us that they knew too that they had stolen the league from us in 1978. They knew it, and they were revelling in it. And there was absolutely nothing, nothing at all, we could do about it. Judging by Dad's body language, he knew it as well, standing wearing his special, pre-Vesuvius face, lips rounded, very slow left and right head movements, silent. It was a face that only came out when he had been pushed to the limit, one that was still so fearsome to me, I didn't want to be near him when he was wearing it, even though its appearance right now had absolutely nothing to do with me, and right now, I was as angry about it all as he was.

'Can ye imagin' if onyb'dy'd dee 'at it Ibrox?' shouts an old guy at the front, looking round for some response. But no one says anything back, although we are all thinking it. No one would ever dare do this at Ibrox. We all knew what would happen there, hundreds of them would massacre you on their pitch. But here, what was our response to the same act? Nothing.

Absolutely nothing. Defenceless. At home, huge majority
already in the ground, but totally and utterly impotent. Today
of all days. When surely we stood taller as a club over Rangers
than ever. When there was so much payback due and such a
perfectly timed opportunity to mete it out. Gradually, all around
me, I start picking up tutting, clicking of fingers, body language
of desperate frustration, bursting for an escape route. Some
stand snorting in silence, others mutter and rant with their
friends, most bellow and shout disparately, uncoordinated, at
the Rangers fan now being walked off the pitch, hands held
behind his back. Meanwhile the perfectly orchestrated Beach
End rounds off its prolonged clamorous, standing ovation for
their martyr, now bouncing with more vigour, more energy,
more glee than ever, delighted at his nerve, his sacrifice, his
true blue sacrifice, and even more pleased at how upsetting
they can surely see it is for us. It felt like they'd just scored
their third goal with two minutes to go. BASTARD! Burn
him! Lynch him! They shout round about me, now realising
that his removal by the police is far from satisfactory as a
punishment, as he is escorted to the large red gates between
the Paddock and the Stand, and out of the ground. And then
something even more unexpected happened.

'Hey min!' roars a fat Dons fan with a furrowed brow
pointing back up into the crowd about three rows in front of
me and Dad. At first, it looks like it may be some attempt at
a deadpan greeting towards some long-lost friend he's just
recognised, but then, 'Fit are you dein' here? Is section's fir
Dons fans!'

Sitting three rows directly behind the Ger, I could see
exactly what he would have seen at that moment. Hundreds
of heads, started turning, all at different speeds, some from
standing bodies, some seated, some surprised, some glow-
ering. It was fairly common to see small pockets of Old Firm
fans (all suspected of being local turncoats) in our end and

it would normally be tolerated without incident, albeit with a fair amount of abuse. Not today. I gulp as I am swept away by the unhealthy intrigue of the moment, as if I was the object of their interest.

'Hey min, did you nae hear? Fuck aff!' shouts a man about Dad's age, arriving with three burly companions and gesturing towards the Beach End. But the Rangers fan ignores it all, sitting, pretending to bite his nails, blanking us, his body language underlining a defiance that personifies his team, the immovable, non-surrendering Glasgow Rangers, too big for us, too big for anyone ... He's asking for it now and he deserves it too, after what we've been subjected to today. The barracking his presence is causing now attracts Dons fans as far away as the King Street End, all competing to deliver bursts of swearing, as volley after simultaneous volley of, 'Fuckin' Rangers Bastard! Awa back tae fffuckin' Glaisga, ffuckin tink!' rings out ... It all merges into a shrill, angry jeer that gets louder and louder as more and more of us stand up, conscripted by the infectious revenge it offers ... I feel myself drawn to join in too. I've never seen anger like it, certainly not in the South Stand ... everyone is up for it though ... it was about time too ...

'Fuckin' Rangers ANIMAL!' Vesuvius had blown ... out of the corner of my eye I sense my livid dad, his whole body shaking, shedding itself of a build-up of nervous tension ... there's just something not right about this, something alarming about men in this mood ... the very same one that had me shitting my pants before away games. So what though? I'm safe, Dad's safe ... and this was different ... this Rangers fan is asking for this. This is the very least of what they would do to one of us in the wrong end at Ibrox, wouldn't they? Fly with the crows and expect to get shot down, that's what Mum always said. But with every second that goes past, things seem to get more intense, darker. The Dons fans are losing their patience, every single one of them now shouting bile and hate at this figure with the Rangers scarf. All of a sudden, I grab my dad's arm pulling him back, I want them all to stop as I sense we've passed the point of no return and now I'm about to witness something gruesome. The mood turns yet again, descending into a mass hysteria, a spine-chilling bloodlust ... 'Fuckin' heid kicked, fffuckin' deid ...' 'KILL UM, KILL THE CUNT! FUCKIN' KILL UM!' There's no way he'll get away with a couple of skelps to the face, it has gone well beyond that ... something much nastier, much more brutal ... a mouthful of sick races up to my throat as a vision of the birth scene from *Alien* that had terrorised me since I'd seen it on Brookie's video in 1982 races through my mind. The Ger has to get out now. Biting on my bottom lip, I urge him in my head to get up and go ... Jesus ... I'm shitting it ...for a Rangers fan? I don't care ... he just has to go ...

Finally he gets up, slowly, cowering, shuffling apologetically, almost as if not to provoke us any more with any sharp or jerky movements. Please let him out ... he approaches the end of his row, where another very fat Dons fan stands up too and does everything he can to block his way out, swivelling his fully unrestrained belly round to make his escape route non-existent ... Jesus! The Rangers fan has no option but to force and squeeze past the enormous gut as gently as possible to get to the passageway. Now he bounds like he's running for his life down the steps through a gauntlet of searing, vituperating, pointing fingers, a shower of spit and at least one guarded attempt to trip him. His rubber legs cause him to collapse onto the wall, before hurriedly straddling it to get trackside, where he is greeted by an anxious looking policeman, who helps him over and escorts him round to the Beach End. Within 30 seconds, his courage is back, and he starts pulling a series of Paul Gascoigne style circus faces towards the waves of ranting, pointing shaking South Stand bodies, still caught up in the mood of the moment, that follow the escapee round the ground to the Beach End.

Even though it felt like he had won, Rangers had won, I knew deep down that I didn't care. I was just relieved that I'd been spared watching something I sensed might haunt me for the rest of my life. But as soon as the game had started, the familiar routine on the pitch had us all immediately reabsorbed into the real business of the afternoon. Rangers had maybe won – and maybe would always win – the pre-match bravado, but now we watched their side taken apart, as Aberdeen raised the bar yet again winning 3-0. It was a day that reconfirmed that the tables had been well and truly turned on the old guard, and seemed firmly bolted down on the flipside for the foreseeable future. And more importantly, it was confirmation that our title challenge was as strong, as real as ever. We were still only one point clear of Celtic and United at the top, but this year, with form like this, surely we'd win the league. And now would come the biggest test of the season. In two weeks, 26 November 1983, we were to meet the champions Dundee United at Tannadice. It was a fixture that had been tormenting me from the pocket-sized fixture list that I carried with me everywhere. I'd been here before. The Dons soaring, the fans bubbling with confidence, and then, enter Dundee United to spoil the party.

Chapter 15

A Bet ye a Punch in the Pus

Narey looks up, launches an inch-perfect pass to Ralphie Milne on the right wing, he beats Rougvie, he beats Willie Miller ... WHAT? Miller skinned? Oh God no ... Milne's now racing towards the box, he flicks over a dangerous cross, SHIT, Sturrock! He has his back to goal, 18 yards out, he launches himself in the air and smashes the ball in an overhead kick. Leighton dives, it slams into the top of net, the United fans are delirious, it's the best goal I've ever seen, and it's now Dundee United 4 Aberdeen 0. I turn to Dad in the Aberdeen end ... Lynne? Tommo with a Dons scarf on? Wait a minute, what are they doing here? And it's a bright sunny day – this is Dundee in November? Where's Dad?

I spring up in my bed, sweating and panting; it's 3 o'clock in the morning. It was the same dream almost every other night that week. Only the goal they scored seemed to get increasingly spectacular and the clues that it was a dream ever more ridiculous. At one point, my Dad appeared as a substitute, taking instructions from Fergie on the touchline, pumping his knees, about to enter the field of play. And each dream seemed to remember that the night before, I'd had a similar dream, but that this one was definitely real.

It just did not make any sense. I should have been over the

moon. As boyhood football experiences went, mine was surely second to none. Dundee United was the only blemish in a perfect football world, a perfection that seemed to break new barriers every other month, to become even more perfect. Our purple patch had more than matched my wild hopes for the season so far: back in the quarter-finals of our Cup-Winners' Cup, top of the league, and, in a couple of weeks we'd play Hamburg, the European Champions, at home. If we win, we will officially be the best side in Europe. Literally, the best side in Europe, so they said. What more could you have asked for? And then there was the other world, one of guaranteed failure and disappointment, in which, in spite of everything else, we'd end up playing second fiddle to Dundee United. Or that's certainly how it felt. In 36 hours 22 minutes, the game will already have started. The tedium of the arithmetic sends me back to sleep immediately ...

Friday 25 November 1983 – Main doors of Perth High, 8.30 a.m.

'Yes, he's here!' I gasp under my breath, making a beeline for the festival of cagoules and anoraks congregating at the school's main door. Standing around a mountain of enormous schoolbags bulging with football trainers and outsized Tupperware boxes, were my square mates. They were everything that the Caly Road boys were not. Discreet and attentive in class, never got claimed, never claimed anyone, and always handed their homework in on time. The smart kids. With evolutionary efficiency, they'd chosen as a breaktime haunt the foot of the draughty main doors of the school. Efficient in that this was out-of-the-road and inhospitable enough to provide safety from the marauding packs of Caly Road predators. Ones that might otherwise see their gathering in a more visible, temperate location as a challenge to a fight. They'd leave their safe house at lunchtime to migrate

en masse, across the exposed grass up to the blaze, to re-camp
their considerable baggage, eat their lunches, and reveal just
how enormous their Tupperware boxes really were before
playing football. I'd regularly join in, and take great pleasure
in unleashing my Oakbank-honed dribbling skills, in particular against a stoic, sturdy defensive little terrier from Errol.
Ewan Proudfoot, or Prunie, Perth High's number one first-
year Dundee United supporter. We seemed to have grown out
of announcing to each other which players we were, but in
our minds it was Hegarty against McGhee, every time we
played. We were never in the same side, and we rarely spoke
otherwise. Needless to say, this guy was far from a mate. And
he is the reason I'm so excited this morning. He's been hiding
from me and now he's been rumbled.

He'd been an enormous problem for me since I'd met him
that autumn at the big school. A season ticket holder at Tannadice
for a start, he went to every single home game with his dad.
That in itself made him a competitor. I had taken badly to
discovering that I was no longer the only professional fan of
a Premier League club at school. But like the rest of the
squares, destined to become the successful fund managers,
accountants and lawyers, Prunie had a brain and he could
intimidate the thick kids and late developers (me belonging
to the latter, of course) without having to batter or even threaten
to batter them.

Most of the verbal abuse I had to put up with as an Aberdeen
fan was fairly hopeless. For some reason, it often seemed as
much about saying this new word 'fanny' we all seemed to
have discovered at the big school. 'Duck, Aberdeen couldnae
score in a bucket o' fannies.' Just not true, we were always
top scorers, or thereabouts. 'Aye, Duck, we'll wrap yur fannies
aroon yur necks at Muirton oan Saiturday!' Again, rubbish,
whether that had to do with football or fighting, Saints had
no chance. I suppose I was more intrigued about what I had

yet to learn about a fanny if you could do this with it. Prunie, on the other hand, was above this. He just knew his stuff.

'So Duck, when have Aberdeen ever beaten United in games that *really* mattered, eh? I'm talkin' League Cup quarter or semis or finals themselves, crunch league games, when Duck?' Right enough. As far as I could remember that's how it worked out, all those League Cup defeats, the important league games, including another one this season at Pittodrie which we'd both been to see. They beat us 2-1 in early October; a result that left us trailing them by three points. Mind you, that was before we hit form. 'I mean, have you ever stood and watched Willie Miller lift the Premier League in Aberdeen, in your own back-yard?' No I hadn't. He was right. Whatever we did, however much we improved, there was no way round it. They always got the better of us. But today, I've got a fantastic card to play; Dundee United had suffered a shock defeat on Wednesday night, 4-0, away to St Mirren. This material was just too good; he'd have no answer to this.

Struggling to temper my excitement on my approach, all the pastings I've taken from him fire me up as I hastily prepare my attack. 'Awright Prune?' (ironic smirk), 'No bad team St Mirren, mind you we did kinna hammer them 5-0 at home a couple of weeks ago . . .' or, how about, 'Good defensive record you've got, pity about Wednesday night?', or maybe, say nothing, maybe simply a smug smile?

'Och, jist fuck off Duck!' snaps Prunie, as he turns his back seeing me approach with gloat written all over my face, and waddles through the cagoules and Tupperware to the other side of the group. I didn't even get a chance to speak, after all the shit I've taken from him. I slouch off. 'Aye, come ahead anytime! Yoos are gonnae get it tomorrow!' I bark in my false hard-boy accent. Twat!

Break-time, 10.20 a.m.

'Duck! You got a len o' 6p?' asks Tommo.

'Aye, sure,' I respond eagerly, hurriedly tidying my kit away. The soiled programme incident and the post Saints match debacle were in the past. They had long disappeared into the unwritten annals of a thousand other threats and violations meted out to me and my property by Tommo and his Caly Road fellows. And now Tommo and me were mates.

He was already a smoker. I'd been going round to the music department with him now for a couple of weeks, I'd hang around as he'd scored tabs for both of us off big guys, normally for 6p a pop. That was the deal, I pay for the tabs, Tommo handles the dealers. Concerned about being caught in the act of buying a cigarette – surely guaranteed to send me to the Academy in one fell swoop – I'd get Tommo to score for me too. I get a relatively risk-free moment of coolness; Tommo gets a free tab on me. We turn up at the music base.

The area around the music base is full of experienced hard boys, as many pairs of burgundy Sta-Prest as standard black and grey ones, each of them with school tie interpretations that would never get out of my front door. Some are pumping exquisite smoke rings from pouting baboon faces, others gob with a marksman's precision. The most highly skilled could alternate between baboon face pout to pinpointing droplets of gob, through the bullseye of their smoke rings. And then there was me, blazer, pristine satchel, spluttering over fake drags, often with my hand over my tie, hiding dribbles of spit, or averting my gaze in horror from my often misdirected spray that would land on the trouser-leg or shoe of some unwitting hard boy. But my shortcomings didn't seem to matter. My street cred was soaring, I'd never felt so fast. When girls I secretly fancied came wandering past, I'd hurriedly make sure I was visible, taking a drag on my tab so they'd see just how cool I was too. On top of all this, there was constant football talk. Mostly Saints fans, they'd go to the home and some away games, and they spoke about their football experiences like they cared. Cared like me.

The squares spoke about football endlessly too, but not like this. The smokers' corner crew would head and swipe their way through the last 20 minutes of their historic Scottish Cup game against Rangers in 1981. Their eyes would light up as they relived the moment when they genuinely believed they'd slain Rangers, up 3-2, about to knock them out of the cup, only to concede a late goal tragically in the dying minutes to draw. They'd talk with even more pride about their heroic 2-1 victory over Hearts in last season's First Division title decider at Muirton Park. Better still, they'd always as much to say about the fighting they'd seen and allegedly caused. Post-match battles in Perth, Dundee, Edinburgh, when the Rangers, Hearts and Dundee fans totally shat it, faced with the gameness of the outnumbered Saints fans, my new mates leading from the front on each occasion. Although my presence there seemed to be tolerated, I'd be wary about saying too much. I knew I could get away with being a sort of warbling talker of shite in the safety of the classroom. But out here, I was a known Dons fan, I was aware of my blazer and satchel attributes and my mum was a teacher, clearly not strong hard boy credentials. But today the conversation has turned to Dundee United, who they hated with a violent passion. Brilliant.

The last match they all seemed to have been at, including Tommo, was their lowest point of the season, two weeks ago. They had seen Dundee United mince them 7-0. According to them, if Johnny Brogan had just scored that header in the first five minutes, they might have won. Aye, right, I thought. But still, I'm on their side here, Dundee United was the enemy. After the game, one of their friends had been hospitalised in the post-match skirmishes and Telly and Tommo had gone on the rampage for revenge 'doun' the Hilltown', a notorious part of Dundee, on their way to the station. Enter me to help with their small time woes …

'Aye, I ken what yees mean. Fuckin' Dundee United bastards. They beat us in all the important games as well, like the League Cup final in 1980, the semis and the quarters in 1981/82 and 1982/83, the league game aifter the Bayern match, and then this season at Pittodrie, and that was after we won the Cup-Winners' Cup man! Dinnae worry though, we'll put one over the bastards for yees tomorrow!'

This was the business. Four hard cunts, three Saints fans and one Dons fan, all tabbing, all gobbing, all united, against Dundee United. I was proud of how effectively and recurrently I'd sworn and was fairly confident I'd shown them I was all right. I had generously dedicated a predicted victory over Dundee United to their team, poor little Saints, already relegation bound, surely endearing myself to them, bringing some 'big-team' clout to our wee gathering. And I could have gone on. That day, the day of their 7-0 drubbing, we had already been helping them, since we had beaten Rangers, who were still only three points ahead of Saints at the bottom of the table as a result. Until …

'What are you sayin', ya wee parrrick?' laughs Telly with ironic disbelief, as he launches at me, grabbing me round the neck with one arm, and rubbing his knuckle furiously against my skull with the other. I was laughing initially too, surely just some harmless hard boy toy-fighting, maybe a hard cunt initiation thing. But while I was staggering around in Telly's arm-lock and the friction from the knuckle treatment seems like it's going to penetrate my skull, I could hear Tommo and Co. laughing too, and caught a glimpse of my satchel as they booted it about the concrete. Eventually it ripped, spewing out its contents of jotters, pencils, rulers and pens that were then in turn blootered about the same area.

'Aye Duck, you're a prick,' derides Tommo, sidling off in

Telly's wake with the others, sliding right up Telly's arse, more like. The bell rings, leaving me on my own to collect my scattered affairs.

Religious Education, period 6, 1.40 p.m.

Tommo and Roddie are playing 'compass roulette'. They splay their hands, one after the other on a desk, close their eyes, and then stab a compass recklessly between their fingers, one after the other. The winner was supposed to be the one who lasted the longest without stabbing one of their own fingers. Or so I had originally thought. It was really another hard cunt bravery test, and if you never ended up impaling your hand (only recognisable by the drawing of blood), then you were eventually accused of 'sapping out'. The real winners were those that were hard enough, game enough to lose, and lose properly. Needless to say, it had been weeks since I'd been invited to play.

Watching them thumping their compass into the desk with even more abandon and vigour than usual, demob happy on a Friday afternoon, my mind drifts over the view from Perth High's fourth-floor windows. I'm imagining with one eye closed, that I can see through Kinnoull Hill and the Sidlaws all the way to Dundee, 20 miles the other side. I'd be able to see right into Tannadice where McLean, Luggie, Ralphie, Bannon would be training, discussing their tactics, how they plan to outwit Aberdeen on Saturday. Ralphie will be practising his special right-wing run that I'd been dreaming about and had actually seen many more times. He'll do it tomorrow … He normally does … Three thuds, then a yelp, someone's lost at compass roulette … or won, depending on how you look at it. Miss McNaughton turns up, class starts.

Here we go, pointless RE. I pretend to take down notes anyway and make out I'm concentrating, but I'm really thinking about Prunie's theory that United always beat us when it matters. It has really been bugging me. I scribble down the scores and dates of games I can remember on the inside back cover of my jotter and 20 minutes later, it was clear. However I cut it, however I'd try to corrupt my stats, only counting games I'd seen, only those I hadn't, changing the review period dates, Dundee United had the upper hand. Prunie was therefore right. We had maybe done the unthinkable in Europe, but we didn't have to play them to do that. In fact, as far as I could see, it was just as well. We have to win tomorrow. We just have to ... The bell goes, off to art for the last two periods of the day. Good, art ('fanny-fart' as the Caly Road boys called it, another amazing thing fannies were reputed to do), particularly on a Friday afternoon, was a right old ramy.

Art, periods 7&8, 3.00 p.m.

'Naw, naw, mind Farkie batter't Archie ootside the chippie?' argues Tommo.

'Aye, right enough, must be aboot third then, eh?' recommends Roddie. Roddie, the master compiler, is leading the weekly revision of the league table. I was maybe in a strop with them, but this was fascinating stuff. The Caly Road lads had established a classification of hardness that ran to a list of around 20 first-year boys at Perth High. No official records were kept, but among them a general consensus seemed to be achieved by the collective memory of fights that had taken place over the previous year or so. What was even more amazing was that they seemed also to have command over data relating to kids from other schools. Data that could be factored into the new, global, Perth High league table. For example, second on the new revised Perth High list was Figs, a laddie from Dunbarnie, a local county school. How on earth could they know that Figs was that hard? I mean, outside of the Caly Road boot camp – surely the most effective training arena of all of Perth's primary schools – how could they be confident enough to allocate second place to a teuchter?

'What? D'ye think you're harder than um, Duck?' Oh here we go. Why did I ever speak to them? And what's worse, they sense that they've got to me. 'What ye daein' at the weekend Duck, getting a new schoolbag?' I might have expected that. 'Goin' tae Tannadice?'

'Yes', I blurt.

'Aye, yous'll get beat. Sorry Duck, ah think United'll skelp yees,' Tommo concludes, his face offering a ridiculous hint of apology, as if he was just telling the harsh truth, telling it as it was. Roddie's face does likewise, as they telepathically collude to round on me. Now that really pisses me off, he knew fuck all about football, he's simply agreeing with Tommo anyway out of 'hard cunt' respect, I'm not having any of this, time for a warble.

'No chance. Maybe a defeat, but not a *skelping*,' I respond, now reverting to a strict 'posh-kid' accent (still Scottish, mind), with particular posh emphasis over the particularly unposh word 'skelping', playing up to their perception of me as a toff, something I knew they despised. I go on to trot out my proud defensive record theory (that I'd be trotting out for years to come), that almost two years (about half of my professional Dons fan life to date) had passed since Aberdeen had conceded more than two goals in a league game. And if we lost, the score was almost always 0-1 or 1-2.

'Aye, right,' drawled Tommo, assuming I was making it all up. I'd no way of proving it, other than my own stats on the back covers of my jotters. I knew they wouldn't buy that, so there was only one thing for it.

'Right, I bet you, if we lose against United on Saturday, it'll be either 1-0, or 2-1,' I retort.

'Right, a punch in the pus, then?' snaps Tommo. What? A punch in the pus? As a bet? Why did it always come to this? They could have extorted hundreds of quid from the bets they got involved in. In fact, they could have done this anyway without the ruse of betting. I mean I'd been about to wager 10p or maybe even 20p. That would buy Tommo almost a week's worth of morning break tabs. But now, instead, if I agree and we won or lost 2-1 or 1-0, then I'd have won the bet. That would mean I'd have to smack Tommo in the face, which in turn would guarantee me getting claimed. On the other hand, if I relinquish my right, I'd get claimed anyway for 'sapping out'. And if I didn't turn up for a claim, I get claimed again. Alternatively, if we lost 2-0 ... no, that's not going to happen. Fuck it, I thought. I've had enough ...

'Right then, a punch in the pus!'

'Right then ...' confirms Tommo. The bell goes, home time at last.

Home in the lounge, 6.00 p.m.

'You must be a Dundee United supporter by noo, bidin' doun here?' jokes Uncle George to me as we all sat down in the lounge before dinner. They'd come down especially for the weekend, so that Geordie could come to Tannadice with us tomorrow. I did my best to smile politely, but if this was the sort of joke he was going to make, they could all go right back home as far as I was concerned. But this was our Uncle George, one of those family members who could get away with saying almost anything.

Geordie, as he is affectionately known, is my great uncle on my mum's side. The eldest of his generation among our close family, he was alone in that he could swear repeatedly in front of my mum and make extremely un-PC comments about anyone, particularly Glaswegians and the French. Apart from his extraordinary purchase of a camel in Cairo in 1940 during the Second World War, the most amazing thing about him was just how long he'd been a Dons fan. He could remember going to Aberdeen games in the 1930s. He had a fond and vivid memory of a 3-1 victory over Celtic in front of an enormous 40,000 attendance at Pittodrie. Forty thousand at home, almost all Aberdonians too, what must that have been like I'd often wonder. And talking of this would remind him, every time, of how many of his 'turn-coat' pals ended up supporting Rangers who back then were attracting fans everywhere with the first of their many all-conquering sides. It was the oldest one of the many reasons I'd come across that explained why Aberdeen fans had such an intense dislike of Rangers. No wonder he was such good mates with my dad. But this weekend was supposed to be all about the United showdown, and the very fact that Uncle George, who'd suffered a serious heart attack earlier that year, was here for it said it all. But not content with accusing me of being a United supporter, Geordie started banging on about the talent of Milne and Sturrock, their remarkable achievement, blah, blah, blah. Dad nodded towards me, tilting his head as if to say 'see min?' as Geordie unwittingly corrob-orated more or less to a word Dad's own catalogue of pro-Dundee United reflections, about how marvellous it was that such an unlikely side could challenge the big teams. There will be none of this shite if we get beat – I'll be reminding them. Jesus!

Saturday 26 November 1983 – In the car, 1.30 p.m.

We're on our way. It's happening. From the back seat of the P6, I'm checking out all the other cars for football colours on the way to Tannadice. It wasn't hard, they were every-where, and they were all Arabs. Hundreds of cars packed with United supporters join the old A85 dual carriageway between Perth and Dundee, pouring out of the Carse of Gowrie villages: St Maddows, Errol, Inchure, Longforgan, home to many Arab supporters I now knew at Perth High. I sense their pre-match excitement, just like me and Dad leaving Auntie Helen's for a Rangers match, laughing and joking, they're off for another thriller against us, and their experience tells them to expect a win. They always do …

At Tannadice, 2.10 p.m.

'Fairly pishin' doun,' observes Geordie, looking across the rain drenched arena of Tannadice. It's ten past two but it feels like I've been here all week. We've deliberately arrived here an hour early to make sure we got under the covered part of this dump of a ground for Geordie. Just as well, as Geordie had already observed. Still, I'd rather be here than anywhere else.

2.20 p.m

Here he comes, I might have guessed it, ambling up the steps, pretending that it's just another one of those random encounters, pointing at us with the same surprised smile he'd pull every time he'd 'stumble' over us at Tannadice. It was Forfar. Originally an Aberdonian, bottle-top glasses and by his accent, exiled outside of the North-East for several decades. He was a pain in the arse. His chat reminded me of the old codgers in the Main Stand at Pittodrie, so boring it wasn't true. And he prevented Dad from singing, or talking sense to me, but Dad being Dad was too polite to do anything about it. Just now though, it doesn't matter, I wouldn't be talking to Dad anyway.

2.30 p.m.

The Dons end is still half-full, but then a hundred lads or so, all in their late teens, are marching, single file from the back gate of the terrace towards the barrier separating the two sets of fans. They're casuals. And today, because we've arrived so early, we're going to be in among them, one crumb of comfort on a day that otherwise had disaster written all over it. I was looking forward to this. At most away matches, there was normally enough space for fans to spread out, and Dad would normally steer well clear of them. At home games they'd normally occupy a full section of the South Stand, nearest the away end, miles from where we'd sit. But I'd usually make a detour to or from the toilet at half-time and stand behind their section for a couple of minutes, observing them, joining in with any songs or chants I knew that they'd be directing at the Beach End. It seemed to be unacceptable to say anything good about them, but I was secretly proud of them, especially since they were recognised by everyone as Scotland's biggest and hardest crew.

> *Scotland's number one!*
> *Scotland's, Scotland's number one!*

They burst into song, breaking their silence. The first sign of animation in our end takes a hold of me unexpectedly. The build-up of nerves and fear now burst out of me, shuddering and trembling, shouting and pointing towards Jim Leighton on the pitch, with more force than I thought possible. Until I realise that this song is not about Jim Leighton, Scotland's number one goalie (which he was) but about the casuals themselves (which they were too). They are all pointing across the barrier towards the 'Utility', their Dundee counterparts, not at the pitch. Still, the release it gave me made me feel a good bit better …

2.40 p.m.

Dad has now unbelievably met an old school pal he hasn't seen since 1962, they eventually conclude after what seemed like a lifetime of iterative elimination. Even Geordie was yawning as the two old school pals vied enthusiastically to upstage one another with snippets and memories from their last few years at Aberdeen Academy. It was 'Rose the Nose'. He was full of cheer, and seemed to make Dad laugh more heartily than ever. I discovered afterwards that much of the hilarity was caused by discovering an exact miniature version of his dad's beak in Rose junior, his son, about my age. I don't know if I can stand any more of this ...

2.50 p.m.

There must be at least 500 casuals now, hundreds of bright colourful jumpers, mullets, white trainers and light-coloured jeans, packing themselves against the barrier, pointing and chanting menacingly over the separation towards the United fans. The intensity of the casuals and their atmosphere and the ever building pre-match nerves fuels my imagination, I see them marching in sinister silence as I'd seen them do (particularly in Edinburgh) on their way up to the blaze behind Perth High. 'Fit eens, Stuartie, is 'at them? Is 'at him?' they might say, as I point out Farkie, Logie, Telly and my other Perth High enemies. I reckoned they alone could batter the entire city of Perth, let alone the hard boys and scarfers of Perth Saints. Let alone the first-year Caly Road boys of Perth High. But even they couldn't help me today ...

2.59 p.m.

There we stood, six eccentric scarfers in a hooligan sea. Forfar and Geordie, one trying to look more like Eric Morecambe than the other, the Roses – two contenders for the most prominent keels in Scotland – my dad and his Willie Miller moustache and me. Standing pounding, shrieking, the nerves bursting out of me, the electrifying, pre-match buzz at Tannadice gradually reaches fever pitch as both sets of fans brace themselves for kick-off.

Ten minutes after kick-off

McGhee picks the ball up on the 18-yard line with his back to goal and sends in a low cross, it falls to Doug Bell, who shoots, the ball takes a deflection, and into the net! The casuals bounce and cavort for several minutes, firing punch after punch at the Utility, I do likewise, alternating my swinging fist between the Utility on my right and the main stand in front of me, where I knew Prune and his old man were sitting, probably sharing a tartan rug. He must be thinking about me, I hope he can see or at least imagine me ...

Ten minutes into the second half

The restart brings back some of the pre-match nerves as we roar away some of our tension. No sign of Ralphie, even though he's on the pitch, they seem not to have any punch today. I'm still scared shitless though ... Aberdeen's midfield display is solid, imposing. Two more goals in the second half, that'll be about right. It's been a poor game, a bit of a letdown, but it's about a result and it doesn't matter to me a jot how it comes ...

Ten minutes to go

McGhee picks up the ball on the halfway line and lays on a perfectly timed pass for Strachan to run on to, he beats Dave Narey, he's rounded Hamish McAlpine, he must almost be at the by-line ... he manages to cut a shot back from the tightest of angles, and ... and it's in! We've done it!

One minute into injury time

Championees!
Championees!
Oh we are we are we!

It's their song, they are still champions, but all of us, every single one of us in the ground at that moment believes it, knows it, Aberdeen will be champions this season. Aberdeen feel like champions now. That's why we, Aberdeen, are singing this song. The game finishes. Never have Dundee United, players and fans alike, looked so beaten, so resigned to their fate as they flock from their pitch and their ground, heads down. We eventually leave the ground too, out into the mobbed Sandemans Road, arms outstretched above our heads, singing, 'Aberdeen, Aberdeen, Aberdeen'. What a day. What a moment! What a victory!

Ten days later, we went on to win the Super Cup, beating Hamburg 2-0 at home – the first time any Scottish team had managed this – earning us the official title of Europe's number one side. But to be honest, I just couldn't get too excited about it, in a world of established European trophies to win, of Dundee Uniteds to kill and league titles to finally clinch. And when 1983 drew to a close, both of these last desires seemed well underway. We were three points clear of Celtic at the top, and Dundee United were a massive seven points behind us now. It seemed like we'd won the battle against them. The struggle of the New Firm was over, for ever. And now, we would definitely win the league ... A punch-in-the-pus bet, anybody?

Chapter 16

Too Good

On the morning of Wednesday 4 April 1984, I was duly dispatched to music camp for the second Easter on the trot. This time, a year older now, the idea of four days away from my mum and dad seemed like a lot more fun than the year before. Now 13 years of age, and well into my first year at secondary school, everything seemed perfect. It seemed like it was only a matter of time before we won the league, only Dundee stood between us and the Scottish Cup Final and we were into the semis of the Cup-Winners' Cup too. But over the course of the next two weeks, I was about to discover a new force, one that looked for a while as though it might derail me from football, regardless of my team's incredible form. It was all down to a new mate I was to meet at music camp, who would change my life in more ways than one. He was Derek McKay. Our fate as mates at music camp was sealed when we were both detained at reception for three hours, at the mercy of music camp's Italian-style bureaucracy, before finally getting processed and allocated a dormitory. During that time, Derek basically rewrote the history of the world (or Perth), as I understood it.

To start off with, I remember being wholly unimpressed with him. He went out of his way to seem disappointed when I pointed out how lucky he was to have the same name as Derek 'Cup-tie' McKay – scorer of two of our three goals in

the Scottish Cup Final in 1970 against Celtic (also the winners
in the quarters and semis that year). It was also clear to me
that he hadn't noticed what I was either. I had secretly been
looking forward to music camp since, for the first time in my
life, I was going to be among the top ten hardest lads, certainly
out of the first years. And even if I wasn't, there were no
nutters there since being mental and playing a musical instru-
ment seemed an impossible combination. This meant I could
wear my Aberdeen soccer casual clothes, without worrying
about a shoeing. I couldn't wait. I could see myself walking
about, staring the squares out, white tennis trainers, bleached
jeans and a paisley patterned tank top. All cool ... all however
from my mum's Great Universal catalogue. There was no way
I'd dared wear this anywhere else outside the house, especially
not to football matches. I'd seen some of our own casuals
taking proper skelps to the mouth from our own Aberdeen
scarfers who seemed to hate them as much as anyone else.
And Derek was exactly the sort of Academy poof that I'd
expected would be fairly wary of someone that looked as tasty
as me. Not Derek though. I don't think he looked at my gear
even once. And there was, I was about to discover, a good
reason for this. Gradually, as we started chatting about other
things, I started to realise there was something different about
him. In fact, nothing about him was stacking up.

The first thing that made him stand out was that he was a
product of Northern District Primary School. It was one of
only a few Perth primary schools that had a reputation remotely
approaching that of the Caly Road. I knew this for a fact since
I'd only recently discovered that around five or six of the
hardest lads at school, who'd I'd taken for granted were Caly
Road boys, were actually from Northern District. But more
than anything else, the proof of its true standing came from
the fact that it commanded respect from the Caly Road former
pupils I'd met at Perth High. They had talked regularly about

what might have happened if the planned lunchtime battle with Northern District, who had been next on the Caly Road's fixture list before the end of Primary 7 last year, had actually taken place. I'd often heard them claim that it would have been so bad that they'd have had to close the Dunkeld Road, on which Northern District sat, to handle the carnage, with ambulances shuttling back and forth to Perth Royal Infirmary's A&E, that in turn might even have been closed to normal accidents and emergencies for a couple of hours. Yet this school had produced the extremely capable Derek McKay, a head boy in waiting if I'd ever met one, having already won the first-year dux prize at the Academy.

And that was another thing. I was finding out that my beliefs about life at the Academy, a place I'd long believed favoured and nurtured poofs and English accents, could not have been further from the truth. According to Derek, you could get belted for anything, even guys like him. But if Derek was worthy of respect for his martyrdom at school, what happened on the following morning had a much more profound effect on me. We had just met on our way out of the canteen following breakfast, and he seemed eager to get me on my own. He had something to tell me.

'D'you know Rania?' he whispered. Did I know Rania? Everyone knew who Rania was – half Jordanian, half Fifer and gorgeous, already a model having appeared in *Suzie* a couple of months before. 'Did you know that she fancies you?' This was the first time I'd ever been confronted with this sort of news. But even then I was still mortified at the idea of letting anyone know that I fancied her back, although I could feel an uncontrollable, undeniable glow spread over my face. But then, when two or three different people told me the same thing within a couple of hours, I knew it must be true. I was fairly flattered, but at the time I was getting off more on the fact it made my street cred soar among my peers. In any case, I didn't have a clue about what you did with that sort of information. So, I walked about with my new mate for the whole music camp, and did absolutely nothing about it. Just when it seemed like I'd missed the opportunity of a lifetime at the disco on the last night, we were pushed together by Derek and others, for the slow dance – Lionel Ritchie's 'Hello' [is it me you're looking for?]. We left the disco, and went to our separate dorms, me missing the chance to arrange to meet again. So what though? I thought – if I thought anything at all. Aberdeen v Motherwell the next day, Dad was picking me up on the way. Perfect. I was in a tremendously good mood as I met Dad and got into the car. But the nearer we got to the city, the more I started to realise that my state of mind had nothing to do with our usual Saturday routine. By the time I got into the ground, I realised something had happened to the Pittodrie file in my brain. It wasn't there. And I didn't want it to be there. By the time the match started, I wasn't really there either. I realised that I wanted to be where she was.

I wanted to be back in Perth, looking for her in the town centre or near her house, hoping to catch her coming in or out of her front door ... McGhee scores in 12 minutes, I stand up and clap ... make out it was random, bumping into her, but take advantage of the chance to ask her ... ask her what? What would I say? What if she was with some friends? Jesus. I realised that if I found her in a group, I'd be overwhelmed with embarrassment. I was well capable of just saying 'Hi' awkwardly, doing an extremely uncool Hitler style wave-cum-salute and walking on. How then would I deal with the spurned opportunity afterwards? No. ...'YES' shouts the South Stand, 2-0, Strachan, 37 minutes, clap, clap ... what was worse was that I'd managed to leave the camp without saying goodbye, and since she went to the Academy, I'd no way of contacting her ... Great ... Full time: 2-1. We drive home. Five or six days come and go, spent mostly listening to Lionel Ritchie's 'Hello' and cycling around Perth with Derek, being mildly amused by his impressions of Neil MacCorkindale, the rector of the Academy, and making him rehearse again and again how he would handle popping the question to Rania at school. Then, on the last Friday of the holidays, Derek appeared at my house with unbelievable news. He'd bumped into Rania earlier that day and she had asked if I was up for seeing her again! I arranged with Derek to call her midweek to meet up and ... who knows what.

'What was that Dad?' I shout anxiously, daring to poke my head out of the lounge door. It's Wednesday night, 18 April 1984. Dundee United are at Pittodrie for what was the Premier League's last chance of stopping us from winning the title. I was, as you might expect, crapping it. But I couldn't even do this properly since Mum had confined me to the lounge to swot for my history exam the next day. Dad, on the other hand, was in the dining room marking homework. The only radio he was allowed on was the one in the kitchen, deemed to be sufficiently far from the lounge that I could study unhindered. That meant that I'd been trying to interpret Dad's yelps and gasps to follow events. But now that Mum was out in the garden, I'd been sneaking every now and then to the door for hushed verbal updates.

'A shot fae Bannon, jist o'or the bar,' he whispers back. I breathe a heavy sigh of relief and allow myself to fall back onto the wall, closing the door. I was so sure they'd scored. I start pacing about in the lounge, fidgeting frantically with my pencil as the faint trace of Davie Begg's voice gnaws at me, teasing and torturing me that it was United on the attack and not us, mounting their comeback. We led by the seemingly comfortable margin of 3-1 at half-time but that just

made the nerves in the second half even worse. I knew we
hadn't beaten them at home for 18 months (the only home
victory I'd ever seen against them), and they are surely full
of vengeance after November. I immediately freeze, close
my eyes as the whine of Begg's voice suddenly becomes
discernibly more intense, signalling another attack ... It dies
down, nothing happened. When I open my eyes, I see my
mum, stopped with the wheelbarrow staring indignantly
through the lounge window at me from the front garden. I
point at my history jotter on the table and then to my head,
to imply I was memorising. She shakes her head slowly. She
was having none of it. Suddenly, just as I was about to sit
down again, a roar, a great thud as a seat is bucked against
the dining room radiator, and then the sound of a herd of
buffalo thundering through to the hallway ... I know what
this means, I dart a hysterical look at Mum, before leaping
in one bound to the door of the lounge, and rush to meet
Dad in the hallway.

'We've done it, min! We've done it!' Dad shouts. We stand
staring at each other, arms outstretched, motionless, silent.
Still locked in our gaze, we telepathically take stock of it all.
Now we could think it. Now we could believe it. Finally we'd
gone the distance. This time, there was no way the season
could peter out now like it did in 1980/81. This time, there
was no way we'd go through the exhilaration and then disappointment of our late run in 1981/82 or our even more
agonising collapse last year. This year, this time, we would be
champions. And before we even had time to move or say
another word, everything just got better.

And a wonderful ball, Rougvie must score . . . and he does!

Now we erupt, now we explode in a volcano, spewing out
flailing arms with rolled up shirts and pencils, springing in

and out of brief embraces, no words, just roars, shrieks, screams ... Eventually we calmed down, and stood panting for a split second, the commentary trapping us from returning to our swotting. 'Kitchen?' said Dad. 'Kitchen,' I responded. And so that was the end of the swotting, as we made our way from the hall, tossing our pencils onto the breakfast bar, both still gripped, both still silenced by the continued promise of yet more drama from the radio. There was no way we could do any more work now.

It was unbelievable. The promise of our form earlier in the year had more than come true on all fronts. Now we only need to pick up a couple of points from games against dross like Saints, Dundee and Hearts to become Champions of Scotland. We were back into the semis of the Cup-Winners' Cup, and were only down 1-0 from the first leg, second leg at home next week, and we were already in the Scottish Cup Final for the third year on the trot. And, if Dundee United didn't know they were dead before, they surely knew it now.

> ... that's it, 5-1 it finishes here at Pittodrie, what a remark-able result for Aberdeen against Dundee United, so often in the past, Aberdeen's bogey team ...

'United, oor "bogey team"?' said Dad. 'At's jist nae right, is it?' says Dad, smiling with not entirely sincere embarrassment at what we were doing to them.

'Why not?' I chuckled callously. For me, this was music to my ears. This was the fruit of all the hammerings they'd taken from us this season, as we'd battered them back down to where they belonged: destroying their retention of the title at Tannadice in November, knocking them out of the Scottish Cup in March (the first time I could remember us beating them in any cup competition), and now tonight, as raw a kicking as they'd ever taken. Their station was now definitely set in stone. Beating Aberdeen would now seem impossible to them. 'What is it you always say Dad? "Perception is nine tenths reality."' I added smugly. Dad shook his head with a disapproving smile.

'Aye, well, oor bogey team's got one foot in the Final of the European Cup, fit dis 'at say aboot us?' says Dad, thumbing in the direction of the radio. That was what made tonight's result even more amazing. In a week's time, not only would Aberdeen contest the Cup-Winners' Cup semi, but United were in the European Cup semi too. And now the commentators were drooling over the possibility that the New Firm could win both trophies by beating Man United and Liverpool in the Finals.

'At would jist be marvellous for Scotland, min, can ye imagine? Both a them beatin' the English sides in the Finals!'

Fuck that. It was one thing recognising that giving the label of 'bogey' to United was harsh, but the thought of them winning, or even getting to the Final of the European Cup, the ultimate prize in the whole of club football anywhere in the world, was a nightmare beyond comprehension. We could go on and win everything in front of us this season, but United even getting into the European Cup Final would diminish all of it. We'd then have to get there ourselves, just to even the score. I looked at my dad, still gobsmacked, still shaking his head, still being far too generous as usual to Dundee United. But tonight, it's OK. Besides I knew better than to reveal the true extent of my disloyalty when it came to other Scottish teams in Europe, Dad would have none of it. I headed off though to make my way to the lounge. Well, that's where I meant to imply I was going. I was going to tiptoe upstairs, to their bedroom, to make a phone call. And right now as I climb the stairs as silently as possible, all I have to do is phone Derek to confirm time and location. Two days later, I would go on my first ever date, 7.30 up Buckie Braes, Friday 13 April 1984.

In spite of a constant barrage of threats, my sister did not say anything to Mum and Dad, even keeping quiet when I eventually plucked up the courage to tell them my brilliant cover story (playing football with some mates). Soon I was off, walking the mile or so from our house to meet Rania to then amble aimlessly for hours around the wooded walk at the western edge of Perth. It was too warm for my soccer casual tank top (and too dangerous), so I wore my next coolest top, my prized Dons 'Hydrasun' hoodie – a bright yellow thing sporting the name of Aberdeen's then spon- sors. This top, or any football chat that I undoubtedly must have subjected her to, didn't seem to deter her interest in me that night and every other night for the next five or six days.

So by mid-April 1984, I had the lot – my team were offi- cially the best side in Europe, champions elect at home and back in the Scottish Cup Final for the third year on the trot. I was seeing Perth's hottest first-year girl, and next Wednesday Dad and I were off to watch our side secure a place in our second consecutive Cup-Winners' Cup Final. And there was no doubt about securing this in my mind. I'd never been so confident of a victory in such a high-profile match. Porto, our opponents, had maybe made the semis of a European trophy, but something had happened to them on the way that beggared belief. They had all but been knocked out by Rangers back in the second round, scraping through on away goals. Although they'd beaten us 1-0 in Porto in the first leg of our semi, and all the papers and Fergie had been very polite and cautious about our chances, being run so close by Rangers meant that I couldn't see how they could be taken seriously. We were surely through. And before we even left for the match, we already knew that Roma had knocked Dundee United out of the European Cup. It was so good, maybe too good! I couldn't have known it at the time, but as we drove north that April night, I was about to take the first of many painful steps on my way back to reality.

Chapter 17

Back to Earth

'What do you think you're playing at? How can you be so horrible to Rania?' rasps Derek at me down the phone.

'Look Derek, I was … '

'I mean, do you realise she was standing up at the gate to Buckie Braes for two hours last night? Two hours? On her own? How would you like it if … '

I removed the receiver from my ear and stared at it for a second while Derek's voice continued squeaking at me, before calmly putting the phone down as he spoke. At that moment, I solemnly committed to myself to never, ever speak to him again. OK, I had stood Rania up and maybe I should have tried to contact her. But I just couldn't, not after what I'd come through on Wednesday night. I lay back on Mum and Dad's bed with my hands over my face. I still couldn't believe it.

With the score still 0-0 (0-1 on aggregate) with seven minutes to go, we still only needed one goal to take the tie to extra time. If we were honest, we'd known right from kick-off that Porto were more than a match for us. And then the game disappeared into the fog at the other end of the ground, as it had been doing for most of the second half. This time, we heard gasps and screams from girls and women in the King Street End and South Stand, sounds you only ever heard at Pittodrie when a supporterless away side scored, or nearly scored. Immediately, we knew there was nothing 'nearly' about it at all. The Porto players visible to us jumped into the air, the goalie just in front of us provocatively turned and thrust a defiant punch towards us in the Beach End. The normal European night euphoria of the Beach End turned dark, as we jumped up en masse cursing and rounding on the goalie for daring to react with such a lack of respect. And when we'd calmed down, our inevitable defeat now stared us in the face despite the haar obscuring everything else. We now needed three goals to win, and we'd barely had three shots at goal, let alone three on target. That was it. Out of Europe ... with a whimper. No more Final for us. No more here we go. More like there we went. Or there we were going to go. Or thought we were going to go.

As soon as we got on the long road back to Perth, the real torture began. My mind insisted on casting itself back over the post-match glow we'd enjoyed for hours it seemed after the Ujpest game five weeks before. What a laugh Dad and I had. We'd spent most of the journey home talking about Willie Falconer. He was one of Fergie's new protégés, but we reckoned he wouldn't make the grade. That night though, he had turned the game for us, setting up the second goal that kept the tie alive. Willie had a dark Mediterranean complexion, but had one characteristic that made him stand out from any other living thing. He had a perfectly normal upper torso but his thunder thighs made his bottom half look like he was wearing the hind leg costume of a pantomime horse. We joked that Willie's destiny was to be onstage, playing the part of both Zorro and his horse at the same time. How on earth we ever found that funny I couldn't understand. But that night we laughed about everything and anything. Dad had got so carried away with the elation of it all, he kicked off on one of his favourite themes, the stunning Magyars of the 1950s, who'd captured the imagination (particularly when they beat the English at Wembley 6-3, their first ever home defeat), their legendary players like Puskas, and the mysterious tragedy of their defeat against West Germany in the World Cup Final of 1954. And all this simply to illustrate just how good we were now, if we could beat the legacy of Hungary's great footballing history and tradition, if we could beat their sons.

Tonight though, there was no history, no jokes, no nothing, until around Coupar Angus, ten miles from Perth. 'How on earth had this side lost at Ibrox, Dad?' I blurted out, breaking the hour-long silence we'd observed up to this point.

'Jesus min!' gasped Dad, with a dramatic lurch to the right, my outburst causing him almost to career off the road. That was all we said to each other all the way home, as we sat in silence, privately searching for an explanation for how this could have happened. Were Porto just so complacent against Rangers because they knew they were pish? If not, then what on earth were Rangers up to that night? It just underlined how hopeless they were. It didn't really matter though, we were out like Rangers. Out.

So there was no way I could go and see Rania that Friday. I knew neither Rania nor Derek could ever understand, and I knew I could never explain it. But this was just the beginning. Our exit from Europe was about to unleash a gloom on me that would smother everything else that happened for the rest of the season. Little did I know at the time as I lay feeling sorry for myself on my mum and dad's bed, but it was the beginning of a new football reality. This was to be the first step, of many that I would take over the next three years, as my life and my team gradually traded back down to its real station, the real world of Scottish football. I eventually got up and went downstairs. In half an hour, we'd be on our way to Dens Park where the rehab would start, the withdrawal from my years of Euro gluttony would smack me in the face.

We all stood still and silent, like a sad sprinkling of ancient, dilapidated tombstones in the away end of Dens Park, enshrouded in a cloud of mist that had followed us from the Porto game. And what a place Dens Park was for a crash back to earth. I looked around at its decrepit stands and roofs, hating them for how cruelly they underlined to me the grim reality of Scottish football. A world to which we were now condemned, now that we'd been struck out of, relegated from, our European one. As the game played out in front of me, I realised that our European journey had been going on for so long, it started well before the first time I'd come here, over three years ago. As we stood, I leafed fondly back over the highs in my mind, knocking out Ipswich, the UEFA Cup holders, in 1981, our Cup-Winners' Cup matches last year, our Super Cup games, our amazing quarter-final comeback against the Hungarians. As the game drudged its way through the second half, all I could think about was Porto, who'd be in Basle on 16 May 1984, to play Juventus – Platini, Boniek and Co. It was a date we'd been marking on our calendars, a date that the Aberdeen programme had confidently been publishing in its fixture list for weeks now. But now it was meaningless. Now it was over. Black scores with 20 minutes to go. Aberdeen win 1-0 undeservedly. I couldn't care less though.

'Cheer up min!' says Dad as we set off on our way back to Perth. 'Look at it 'is wey min, fa's the number one team in Europe?' Dad pauses, smiling as he looked over to me, trying to buck me up. 'We're the Super Cup holders, 'at's an amazin' achievement.'

'Look, no one cares about the Super Cup Dad,' I spat petulantly. 'Remember what happened in 1981?' I said looking out of the passenger window.

'What happened?'

'Liverpool and Dynamo Tibilisi couldn't even be arsed to

find two Wednesday nights to play their Super Cup ties and so the Cup was simply "*withheld*",' I said, pausing for a second. 'What sort of trophy that mattered could simply be "withheld"?'

'Ach, that only happened once. Aiberdeen and Hamburg certainly cared aboot it in December.'

'Did they?' I queried. Dad looks at me puzzled. 'Why were there only 15,000 Hamburg fans at their home leg against Aberdeen? Compared with 45,000 in the UEFA Cup tie against us back in 1981?'

'Listen min,' asserts Dad. 'Nae ither Scottish side has ever won 'at trophy,' said Dad pointing purposefully out of the window. 'Nae Rangers, nae Celtic. Naeb'dy! And they probably never will. Mark my words, min.' I looked at him, trying desperately to be swayed by his authoritative, morale boosting talk. 'And onywey, we're jist a couple a' points awa' fae winning the league now, eh?'

'I know,' I answered, still staring out the window. That was what made the depression at being knocked out of Europe even more galling. How could I be feeling like this given that we were just about to win the league? What a ridiculous state of affairs. Dad tutted and shook his head, fairly unimpressed with my gloom. And five days later the title was clinched at a rearranged game at Tynecastle. We couldn't go since my exam embargo was still in force, so I found myself standing in the kitchen on my own with the radio. In any case, I was still doing my best to get into the mood, full match kit on (Aberdeen away, what we'd be wearing against Hearts that night) under my Hydrasun hoodie, and my special matchday scarf, normally only used for games.

'That's it, this comfortable 1-0 win against Hearts sees Aberdeen crowned champions again,' announces the radio commentator with a backdrop dominated by boos and jeers from grumpy Hearts fans, almost smothering out entirely a faint chant of 'Championees' at the final whistle. I did a few jumps, punched the air a couple of times, going through the motions, trying to lock on to that vein of euphoria that seemed to appear naturally at every other trophy winning moment. It must be there somewhere. Dad appears holding his coffee mug, ambling through from the study where he's taken in the game too.

'At's it min!' says Dad. That's it? Is that all he can say? I've seen him more excited about a substitution. 'Is is jist rare min, winning the league wi' so many games still tae play. There's nae many teams dee 'at,' Dad said with a knowing look, switching on the kettle for another coffee. 'In fact, I wonder if it *his* happened afore.' He mulled to himself as he stood stroking his chin, waiting for the kettle to boil. 'Let's see ... ' he pondered, before disappearing with another mug of coffee.

I don't believe it. We've just won the league and all he can do is go and research some stats? What on earth was happening to us? Later that night, the footage on TV showed exactly the same thing at Tynecastle. An extremely sober Fergie, half-heartedly patting the players on the back as the league trophy was calmly passed around the team. This was not at all what I had in mind. I'd been dreaming of Fergie being carried shoulder high by Miller, Rougvie, Strachan, just like the United players had done with Jim McLean, parading him to the jubilant fans in front of the Dens Park main stand, packed with United fans all bursting with joy, when they clinched the title 11 months ago. The championship winning way, surely miles better than a great goal, better even than a cup final victory. It was the title, after all. The one we all want to win. Or so I had believed all my life. Finally Dad reappears from his study, having got so carried away with whatever he was looking into, he missed the highlights of the Hearts game.

'Got it!' he snapped, slamming shut with one hand the ancient Scottish football annual that presumably had given him the answer. 'Ye hiv tae ging back a' the wey to 1960 to find anither provincial that won the title with ony breathing space,' said Dad hovering over me, beckoning me to query.

'Right. Who was that then?'

'Hearts. A' the ithers, Dundee in 1962, Killie in 1965, us in 1980 and United in 1983, could have thrown it awa' on the very last day of the season. I tell you, 'is team's nae peaked yet. This is the stuff of the Old Firm, min.'

It was the stuff of the Old Firm right enough. And there was more on its way before the season was out. Within three weeks, we were back at Hampden, where we beat Celtic in the Scottish Cup Final setting another host of domestic records. It was our third Scottish Cup in a row – matching the record set by Rangers and Queen's Park and it also meant that we became the first team outside the Old Firm to win the domestic League and Cup Double. Once again, Willie Miller rose over Hampden, arms outstretched and solemn faced, like he thought that he was the statue of Jesus and Glasgow was Rio de Janeiro. Once again, my dad and his bleary eyed generation responded, belting out our emotional 'One Willie Miller' anthem to the sound of 'Guantanamera'. But this time, as I stood in among it all, smiling, singing, it wasn't enough. Not now. Even here, even at Hampden, the day we clinched the Double. Aberdeen standing tall over the rest of Scottish football, this time, this year, taller than ever. It wasn't enough. I'd thought at the beginning of the season that it was winning the league that mattered. Now we'd done that and won the cup too, but it still wasn't enough. What really mattered was Europe, and in 1984/85 we *had* to succeed in Europe again. That was it. As I stood clapping, that was what was keeping me from enjoying any of this, our Euro exit still eating away at me, still punishing me. The bar had been raised by Aberdeen themselves. Now I understood what we were and now we have to keep on proving it. Now, European success was a must.

Chapter 18

A Continental Perspective

'Awright son?' remarks an uncharacteristically upbeat Hilda from behind the counter in Drummonds. It's 6.30 a.m on Thursday 23 August 1984 and I've just arrived to collect my morning paper round. What's up with her? No. It can't be … Can it? No, impossible … I hurriedly shuffle around to open the first paper available to me. By the time I've even bent down, Hilda, sensing I didn't know the score from last night's game, had already sped round the counter with a copy of the *Daily Record*, holding the back page up towards me, peeking round from behind it, masticating her chewing gum enthusiastically in her eagerness to capture my reaction: Airdrie 3 Aberdeen 1.

My eyes leap with disbelief on to the page, attempting to find that they had rearranged the score and computed the wrong information to my brain. I'd been so complacent about the result last night that I'd forgotten to check the Radio Scotland news and had allowed myself to become preoccupied with my new ZX Spectrum. But now, even once I'd reconciled myself with the paper, I was still trying to believe that there had been a misprint. One paragraph into the match report, all hope was dashed. It was true. We were out of the League Cup. To Airdrie!

'No lookin' so smairt the day then son, eh?'

Three goals against Aberdeen? No one did this to us. NO

ONE. Almost three years had passed since we'd let three in against anyone (apart from a non-event, end-of-season affair against St Mirren in May when we were already champions, so that didn't count). And when I say no one, that includes Europe too. Airdrie were a First Division side, this was literally the worst result in living memory. The Treble, the most natural, most accessible progression for us following our historic Double last season, was already, less than two weeks into the season, out of our reach. I got through my normally tedious paper round in a daze, immersing myself masochistically in the shock of it all, reading the match report in each paper, including a notably gloating *Dundee Courier*.

I had expected some abuse from my classmates; I'd been prepared for that. I'd just have to smile, and take it on the chin. It was an absolutely shite result, there was no denying or defending it. It was so bad, I realised that I'd never had to deal with anything like this. But it also occurred to me that neither had my mates at school, and I was curious to see how they would all react. And right enough, by the end of the day, I'd miraculously bumped into – through no instigation of my own – literally everyone at Perth High I knew that understood the significance of the result. Even the teachers (mostly Old Firm), some that I didn't even know, had made a point of nodding or winking condescendingly at me in passing, or making some sly comment during classes. But before the day was though, it started to dawn on me what the result really meant to them.

They think they're saying that Scotland is pishing itself with laughter. But they aren't. They're actually saying something else. Something of how unpleasant it has been to share Scottish football with us, the unfaltering Aberdeen, to whom this sort of hilarious disaster had never seemed to occur. This reaction, to the fact that it *had* happened, was a backhanded compliment. Washing the dishes later that night, I discovered that

Dad had noticed exactly the same thing at Crieff High. As we analysed and deconstructed our day of abuse from his colleagues, my mates, his pupils and my teachers, we eventually pumped ourselves up to conclude that this rare blip had given us an unexpected insight into exactly how towering Aberdeen FC really was in their minds. Just as we were finishing up and everything seemed OK again, some irate swearing reverberated through the house from the hall.

'Fuck zem!'

Simply hearing this voice brought me crashing right back down to earth. It was Fabrice, one of two Perth High School French language assistants who were lodging with us for the year. God knows how I was going to explain all this to him. I'd been so excited about him coming to stay for weeks before he arrived. I thought I knew what to expect, having met so many foreigners of his sort of age over the summer. This was all thanks to Mum and Dad's summertime B&B business.

It was Mum's brainchild, something they'd started back in the summer of 1982 to help with the increasing mortgage costs of the house. Mum did all the cooking and front-of-house, Dad did the waiting and kitchen-hand work along with the shopping. They decided they liked it so much, they'd agreed with Perth High to take the two French language assistants as lodgers (and another guy called Hamish from Glasgow, a friend of a friend). My sister and I helped in the kitchen too, but spent most of our time befriending the guests. And so I had a captive audience of German, Irish, Italian, English and loads of other football-conversant guests. It was when I first learned what a truly international phenomenon football was. They appreciated that me and Dad were interested in and often knew a bit about their teams, and they all seemed to know who Aberdeen were because of our Cup-Winners' Cup victory in 1983. Many of them clearly remembered watching the game itself, and conveyed how much it meant to them and their

clubs that we'd outplayed, out-thought and beaten the ultimate football superpower, Real Madrid, that night. So the idea
of a new mate, like these sorts of guys, who would actually
be staying with us for a whole year, was almost too exciting
to take in.

Things looked very promising on the very first day when
he, Dad and I had a long chat about Platini and France's
European Championships success that summer. But fairly soon
it started to go rapidly downhill. Unbelievably, Fabrice quite
genuinely did not know about our European Cup-Winners'
Cup and Super Cup successes. 'Real Madrid? You dream!' he
uttered. Fair enough I thought initially, we all knew how unbelievable it was. But it would soon become clear that his atti-
tude was not about surprise. One way or another, this 'fact'
seemed to sit so askance, so at odds with Fabrice's world of
European football that, in spite of all the evidence he'd been
given, including the chance to watch the entire match on
video, he simply refused to accept that we were any sort of
European football power. And he'd tut patronisingly, dismissively at the suggestion we were expected at least to reach
the quarter-finals of the European Cup this season – very real
expectations, held by much of the rest of Europe too.
According to the French expert, this trophy was only for the
elite sides, Liverpool, Real Madrid, Ajax, St Etienne. When
he was asked to explain why on earth this French side should
be ranked with the other three, it brought out the only thing
that Fabrice was prepared to take seriously about Scottish football, the bizarre tale of the European Cup Final of 1976, played
at Hampden.

St Etienne, to him the greatest side in European football
history, reached their first (and only, it would transpire)
European Cup Final in 1976 when they played Bayern
Munich. The real score was 1-0 to the Germans but,
according to Fabrice, St Etienne had been denied at least

six goals, because of one thing, and one thing only –
Hampden's square posts and bars. He illustrated all this with
a trigonometric diagram that they'd clearly been poring over
for years in France, showing the different trajectories that
the countless headers and shots that hit the bars and posts
would have taken (i.e. into the net) had the goalposts been
round and not square. Because of this, France believed that
Scottish teams should have been banned from playing in
Europe until we could prove our goal-frames were up to
scratch. Bollocks.

By the start of the season I had already had enough. And
then last night my team contrives to produce the worst result
in living memory, completely undermining everything I'd been
trying to get Fabrice to take in. And if Fabrice had learned of
this at school, it was going to be more or less impossible to
square it away with him. But swallowing hard in preparation
to make eye contact with him as he came thundering into the
kitchen followed anxiously by Mum, it was obvious there was
something much more dramatic going on. I was going to get
a reprieve.

'I wear zis!' he bellowed at Mum, pointing defiantly inwards
towards his chest, referring to his worn out jeans, his cowboy
boots, faded leather jacket, and tattered shirt. This dishevelled
look was all part of Fabrice's campaign against imperialism
generally, but in this specific case it was about a stance against
the oppressive Victorian dress code he found at Perth High.
And it was my mum who was picking up the pieces behind
him. The school seemed to have decided conveniently it could
address its complaints about Fabrice's dress (and anything else)
to her, rather than to the combustible young revolutionary,
taking advantage of the fact that he lived with us. She was
already well aware that she had her work cut out and wasn't
happy about it.

'Look, you'll have to wear a tie, all other men and boys

do. That's just the way it is here, there's no point in trying to fight it.'

This particular episode would rage on for weeks, Fabrice ever more defiant, and Mum ever more infuriated in her impossible role as mediator. Eventually, some weeks and many hours of persuasion afterwards, he bought a tie, albeit the most ridiculous one he could find (a felt one), which he'd crumple religiously each morning before putting on, ensuring it was folded across the way in the middle, so it ended up looking like a sock hanging from his collar. That way, his contempt for the Perth High regime could be displayed vividly to anyone within a hundred yards. But with hindsight, what the school would really have been concerned about was something so in breach of its Victorian code of discipline, that no one could bring themselves to speak about it (fortunately for my mum). Not content with mere symbols of rebellion, Fabrice had opened up a new front of attack. He embarked on a rampage among the sixth-year girls of Perth High, overtly flirting with a good number of them all over the school, classrooms, common rooms, outside the rector's office, everywhere. This was bad enough, but each one of the sixth-year girls would respond, so electrified by the raw, carnal Fabrice, in a way that implied that if he had not already shagged them, it was soon going to happen. That night though, Fabrice was having none of it.

'Zees Engleesh education systeme, eet's so out of date, I 'ate eet.'

'*Scottish* education system,' intervenes Dad, assertively but politely, pausing for a second, then returning to his sink-full of dishes. He was applying all the diplomatic experience that he'd cultivated in these situations with non-Scottish guests over the previous three summers of B&B. As Dad had reflected melodramatically many times, 'English is a label we've been fighting off for a thousand years,' and so we had to continue the work – especially when it came to our sacrosanct 'education' or 'legal' systems. There was no question about whether these were Scottish. But then we got the shock of our lives. 'Ah non …' asserts the 19-year-old Frenchman followed immediately with three or four rapid-fire tuts and accompanied by an insolent, wagging finger, in Dad's face, 'in France, zere eez no différence. Scotlonde, Scotteesh, Englonde, Engleesh, Anglais, eez the same for us.'

And that was it. That was Fabrice's view. The customs of the French language and its nomenclature were what defined Scotland and its place in the world. It was just as bad as the football. He clearly believed he already knew everything about Scotland, and he'd nothing to learn from anyone else, not even us, Scottish people. It was now so infuriating it was beyond belief. Right now, Dad had to destroy him. I stared at my dad, my mouth gaping, trying to implore him with my frown to sit Fabrice down and put him straight. Surely he can't get away with this? But Dad, quite remarkably, just stood looking bemused for a second or so, smiled and turned back to get on with his dishes.

Mum, confident now the Frenchman had calmed down, escaped to the lounge, and Dad's silence seemed to have put an end to our conversation. I tried to mask my rage by staring at the floor and drying the last of the dishes, doing my best to blank Fabrice's arrogant French pus as it bobs about the kitchen, believing no doubt that he'd enlightened us with his views. And then, my reprieve came to an end.

'So you still win zee Cup of zee Champions, you believe?'

FUCK. OFF.

'Give me my trainer,' I pleaded, standing at the top of the stairs, towards Fabrice's closed bedroom door, Saturday 29 September 1984. I say plead, but that was really only to invite the sympathies of Mum and Dad downstairs, who would soon respond in my defence, especially since the missing trainer was now stopping us from leaving for the Hearts match in Aberdeen.

'Dad, are we ready to go?' I call downstairs. I hear my dad exhaling with an exaggerated sigh as he storms back into the kitchen, having stood in silence at the bottom of the stairs for ten minutes. By now it was clear that my trainer episode had turned into something of a siege that was threatening to make us late. I sensed though that Dad was deliberately avoiding the possibility of direct conflict. He was already furious with the Frenchman for borrowing the P6 repeatedly through the week to visit and shag the extensive network of birds he now had across Tayside and Fife, but had yet to put any petrol in. Dad knew if he tried to deal with Fabrice over my trainer, it could well erupt over into one of his once-in-a-decade Vesuvius performances. For me though, the idea of seeing the Frenchman cowering, diminished, in the face of the old man's formidable wrath and bluster was an attractive one. Fifteen minutes had now passed, and still we wait to get out of the house and on our way to Aberdeen.

'What on earth is going on?' intervenes Mum, no doubt on Dad's instigation, appearing from the kitchen, and fixes a glare on me from the bottom of the stairs. She sensed immediately that I was getting a fair amount of pleasure out of this. Too right I was. I had just exacted some revenge on the Frenchman. With much, much more satisfaction than I had expected. Shortly after Fabrice had come back from rugby practice that Saturday morning, I had approached his bedroom door. My grand plan, which I had agreed with myself some time after the Airdrie match, was starting to pay dividends.

I gradually came to realise that there was no point in trying to educate Fabrice about Aberdeen. What I'd been telling him about my team was true, our European success, our reputation, the fact we were seeded sixth in the European Cup that year, and so on – publicly available facts that he should already have known. So, I decided to ignore him, especially about football, and wait for Aberdeen to turn the corner and let the results speak for themselves. In the meantime, I'd keep quiet about it all. If our form started to pick up, then he'd realise through the results, coupled with my blasé reaction to it all, just how run-of-the-mill, how normal it all really was. How we'd coast through the early rounds in Europe as a sort of 'fait accompli'. If I was brutally honest though, my strategy offered another attraction.

The truth was that long before Fabrice's arrival or the Airdrie bombshell, I had had some serious doubts about how we were going to cope with season 1984/85 and achieve all that I wanted: league and Scottish Cup but especially Europe. How would we manage without Gordon Strachan, who'd signed for Man U before the end of the previous season? We'd shown that we'd get away with the odd game without him, and even pulled off some high-profile results (including a 3-1 at Parkhead in February 1983 and the famous 0-0 in Munich in March 1983) when he wasn't playing. But longer term? Look at how we withered after his injury back in 1981 when we had to play half a season without him, to finish the season with a whimper – the only trophy-less season in my career to date. And it wasn't just Gordon Strachan that had left, Mark McGhee and Doug Rougvie had moved on too. So, if the unthinkable happened, and we turned into a crap team, my attempt to appear blasé in the presence of the Frenchman could equally seem like indifference – indifference that would protect me from the Frenchman's shite. But then, suddenly, it seemed like Plan B would not be needed. The recovery gradually started to happen.

Four days after the Airdrie catastrophe, we won 2-0 against United with more ease and calm than I had ever seen. We battered Hibs at home 4-1, followed by an accomplished 3-0 win at Cappielow, our best result away to bogey team Morton that I could remember. But there was one thing that was obviously more telling and more important than anything else – progress in the European Cup, the one trophy that Fabrice seemed to be able to relate to. Four days ago, the previous Wednesday night, we'd beaten Dynamo Berlin 2-1 at home in the first leg of our European Cup tie. We obviously weren't officially through, but I'd been at the game, and I hadn't seen anything to be too concerned about. So today, I'd gone up to Fabrice's room to practise my new approach. But before I even opened my mouth, he'd already launched into another rant about how shit life was here.

'I 'ate zees place! Even zee rubgy eez sheet!' he snapped, standing, arms crossed, staring out of the window at the back of his room. This had been the main attraction for him in choosing Scotland for his year abroad. He was, as he said of himself, a 'rugbyman', a curiously English sounding word that I'd never heard before but that he used all the time. I knew how impressed he was with the enormous crowds that he'd seen amass for Scotland games at Murrayfield on TV, and the considerable and vocal travelling support that he encountered and got pissed with in Paris for the Five Nations games two years before. And the English friends he'd met at Montpellier had also told him that we played it everywhere, how passionate we all were about it and the high standards of rugby you could find in Scotland. But his experience was telling him otherwise, especially what had happened this morning,

'Eet's like training with a 'erd of cows,' he raved. Here we go again. I knew exactly what this was about. He'd often told me things like, 'Eet's necessary the big brain for the rugby. Rugby, eet's for the men who think,' unlike other sports, in particular football, he maintained. But his herd of cows remark was more broadly a metaphor for Fabrice's whole Scottish experience to date. Fabrice – the little genius prince, a sort of David Ginola character, surrounded by grunting bovine frames, bereft of skill, speed, flair, whether in the classroom, the bedroom or on the rugby field. And I had just about had enough of it all. So I launched into one.

'What did you expect? Scotland is a football country,' I asserted. It was true. Other than half-heartedly watching the Five Nations matches on TV, as boys we only ever came across rugby in PE at High School. But the fact that it was so close to football as a game: a ball, two goalposts, an oblong pitch, it seemed only to remind you of a missed opportunity to play football. And the hard cunts, who would invariably apply themselves more honestly than you'd see them do anything when it came to football, reverted to type on the rugby field, taking advantage of scrums to smack pusses, spit in ears, and generally turn the whole thing into a ramy. But no wonder, it was crap and we all hated it. Fabrice needed to understand this right now. I went on.

'You are lucky you are able to play rugby at all. You should see what my mate MacKenzie has had to put up with for most of his life,' I said now pacing backwards and forwards. Charles MacKenzie was a guy whose family were from the Borders, who I'd met at secondary school. He was the only other 'rugbyman' I'd known to date. 'He was still complaining well into second year that they never once got to play rugby in PE at his primary school. And you know what the teachers' excuse was? The school didn't even have any rugby balls apparently. And did they bother getting any? No, because they knew that no one else gave a fuck!' I said emphatically pointing at him. This caused Fabrice, who was still facing the window, to turn and frown angrily at me, encouraging me to go on. 'It was worse than that though. One time last year, he went into a week-long sulk, refusing to play lunchtime football with us when Ropes and McCrae – two of our Perth High pals –

knocked back the offer to go and watch Hawick v Gala with him and his Dad.' I pause again, Fabrice now looked at me expressionless. 'And d'you know why?' Fabrice raised his head impatiently as if to say get on with it. 'Because they knew there was a chance of coming with us to watch the Aberdeen game the same day.' I shrugged my shoulders in a 'that's life' sort of way I'd picked up from the Frenchman himself. 'But if he thought that was bad, he had another think coming when he met the Caly Road boys early on in first year at Perth High,' I went on. 'One day they started rounding on MacKenzie in the PE changing rooms, asking him if he was a poof when he claimed he didn't have a football team because he liked rugby.' I could see the temple on the side of Fabrice's head now pumping even faster; I sensed I was starting to get at him. 'MacKenzie couldn't help himself faced with that and came out with some guff about rugby being for "gentlemen" and football being for "thugs". The Caly Road boys let him finish, before battering fuck out of him.' This was a bit of an exaggeration. They gave him a trademark scant-lift. But it was a glorious moment, and I looked on with satisfaction, for once united with the Caly Road over the very game that divided us the rest of the time, as MacKenzie's pro-rugby stance that had irritated me since I'd met him was put in its rightful place. I could tell Fabrice had gleaned all of this from the satisfied grin my face was wearing, since his head was now shaking very slowly and his nostrils flaring. It was working … I was getting somewhere, getting under his skin! So I rounded it off just like the Caly Road had when they'd finished with MacKenzie that day in the changing rooms, 'Served the poofy wee cunt right!'

And with that Fabrice suddenly leaps in one enormous bound across his bed, arms outstretched as if for a mid-air rugby tackle. I shimmy away from his grasp and bolt for the door, he manages to grab my right foot but I leave him with only my shoe as I wriggle free and scramble out onto the landing. I stop halfway down the stairs when I realise Fabrice isn't following. He slams his door shut.

Half an hour has now passed and I haven't moved from my spot halfway down the stairs. But now Mum was getting somewhere, having opened up a dialogue with the Frenchman. After having to deliver a fairly stern lecture, including setting out to Fabrice that she was coping quite satisfactorily with the moral guidance side of educating her children, the door opened. Out struts Fabrice, to my hold my trainer over the banister for a second or so, before dropping it to me. With a look of disgust, and a sort of snorting noise, he feigned a spit towards me, before turning back into his room. I'd done it. I'd really got to Fabrice.

For the fourth morning on the trot I'm sitting in my pyjamas and dressing gown in front of the TV in the lounge, having wakened up in the middle of the night. It's 7.00 a.m. on Sunday 7 October 1984 and there's not a sound, no noise at all, apart from the faint whirring coming from the video machine. It is paused perfectly one frame before the instant in which the mid-air ball that is speeding towards goal, Willie Miller's penalty kick during our European Cup second leg against Dynamo Berlin, will hit the target. If it goes in, we progress to the fourth round of the 1984/85 European Cup. If it does not, sudden death penalties, then maybe we go out. Out of Europe for the second time in four months. Out of Europe at an earlier stage than ever before. Out of Europe, not at the hands of a Liverpool or a Hamburg, but to a two-bob, Eastern European side. Just as Fabrice would have expected. In fact, exactly as he had predicted. The frame I'd managed to freeze was the last frame, the last second in the normal, real world, of winning, of European football all season long, that I'd been trying so hard to convince Fabrice we belonged to for months. But if I press Play, the Berlin goalie will save Miller's penalty and we go out.* Now it is gone, as if it had never existed, only to be replaced with his world of partial or wrong information and unfounded beliefs. But now, he's somehow right. Suddenly, I hear footsteps coming up the drive, must be Fabrice after a night shagging one of his birds ... I hastily switch off the video that reverts to the TV and *Sesame Street* – I don't want him knowing how I'm feeling. This is the last thing I need. Fabrice comes in and sits down. Without even having to look at him, I sense he's wearing a mischievous smile.

'What eez zat?' Fabrice asks, pointing towards the two characters on the TV, Big Bird and Mr Snuffy, as absurd a sight on TV as you could expect to see.

I explain, 'Mr Snuffy is Big Bird's big invisible friend that no one else can see. Big Bird goes around trying to convince everyone that he has this great elephant friend called Snuffy and gets really annoyed when no one believes him.'

'Did zey base zees on you and zee Dons?'

Fair enough. I had to accept it. His version of reality had won. But it didn't change how it affected me. I stood up calmly, smiled, went upstairs to my room, closed the door and got back into bed. It was horrendous. Just like May, only five months ago, all over again, I found myself again staring at the ceiling in the early morning, the end of a European adventure that had been part of following Aberdeen for most of my life it seemed. This time, after only two matches. Now we had to face the rest of the season without European football. Now the willing, the yearning for the end of the season

---

* Strictly speaking, it was not Willie's miss that put us out (it was Eric Black's in the sudden death phase) but it felt like it.

starts, but this time we've a full eight months of it left, not a couple of weeks like last season. Eight months of a season that at best could only offer only what we'd won last year, the league and the cup. Because of that, the season could already have died a death there and then, had it not been for the fact that there was now doubt that we could even retain the two trophies we had. Yesterday we'd lost again, for the second time in four days, this time, at Parkhead in the league. As I slowly pulled the duvet over my head, a new torture, new questions and doubts were starting to set in. Maybe we'd lost our edge. Maybe the team without Strachan and McGhee couldn't win the big matches, the crunch matches when it mattered, even at home against Scottish opposition. And that was the beginning of it … the questions and doubts that would plague me every day for the rest of the season.

But soon we got back into the routine of winning again, albeit against the Dundees, Hibs and Mortons, some comfortably, some not so comfortably, keeping us at the top of the league. What I was really waiting for was 8 December, the next time we'd play Celtic, at home, to get the truth about the team, a proper feel for what they were made of now. Before that, we'd play Rangers at Ibrox. They were still in the title race (much to everyone's surprise), and had yet to concede a goal at home in any domestic competition. They'd also already won the League Cup. But what would really be a test for Dad and me was that we had finally decided to bite the bullet and break our duck. We were going to Ibrox with Hamish, our other lodger, who had organised it all for us. And it was to be another Glasgow experience that would change my life, opening the door on a whole new side of Scotland – one that I had never experienced before.

Chapter 19

Ibrox Incognito

We're in the main stand, there's a capacity crowd and I've never seen an atmosphere like it. It dwarfs everything, it makes the Bayern Munich match of a few years ago look like a primary school birthday party. And right now, I'm surrounded by a thunder, an outpouring that I've never seen at a home match because there's just been a goal … it's 1-0 after eight minutes. Breathing booze fumes down our necks, behind us sit around six or seven of what sound and smell like the largest mammals on the planet. I haven't dared to look at them yet; all I've picked up from the corner of my eye are their burly silhouettes and mulletted heads. They're half cut, and they're angry. Well, they had been, but now they're falling over each other, one of them gives me an almighty clap on the shoulder, as the delight of the goal spills over. It's 17 November 1984, Rangers 1-0 Aberdeen. We're in a Rangers section of the main stand at Ibrox … Ibrox incognito. And it is now all too clear why we've never dared come here before.

We're so terrified that Dad and I stood up ourselves, along with the rest of the stand, and are still clapping following the deflected free-kick that resulted in their goal. 'Stay standing,' I whisper through clenched teeth to Dad. He does a sort of nervous nod. The terrifying idea that they might sense what we thought of them, what we said about them at home made me realise that we had to stay standing as long as they did. Memories of the terror I'd experienced when we in the South Stand had exorcised an alien Rangers fan among us flood my mind. If we got rumbled here, it would be our turn, and here, there would be no mercy, we would not get away with a display of bravado. Their noise, their ravenous exaltation at their goal tell me that they *would* kill us. Gradually, my mind starts to flit circuitously from terror, to hate, to an envious exhilaration and back, as we stand expressionless, clapping and clapping. Who could come here as a neutral and fail to get carried away by this, the massive, impressive Ibrox Park, packed to the gunnels? This vocal power from 40,000 Rangers supporters, eight times as many of them that I'd seen at Pittodrie, was many, many times more awesome and intimidating at home. Now, the game beds down in and around midfield, but the mood of the crowd is far from settling, we're all still on our feet, as the cheering gradually merges with the first song following the goal, 'Hullo, Hullo', gathering momentum all around the ground, building up to the beginning of the second verse, as happens every other time I see them, hitting its climax, every one of them now bellowing, hanging on two enormous and drawn out Hullos.

HUUULLLO!
HUUULLLO!

Now they stamp and clap, as the main stand shudders to the swaggering beat of this, their favourite post-goal, battle-cry, pumping out the strange words of the other lines, about Fenian blood and the Brigton Derry boys. It goes on and on before gradually dying down after another four or five verses. But still now, five minutes after the goal, we all remain standing. I look at Dad, his face gaunt and expressionless. I'd never have believed I'd see him so reduced by his greatest of all enemies, but for once he's playing it exactly as I would wish. It seems like the only thing we can do given the circumstances. Amazingly, Dad's scarf is nowhere to be seen. I'd made him promise before we left Perth, or I wouldn't be going. It was clear now that there was no chance of any of his bravado today.

We all eventually sit down, a full ten minutes after the goal, just as the first glimpses of Aberdeen's threat start to peek through midfield. I work hard to remember to reverse all my natural reactions, clap when THEY get a throw in, tut when THEY put the ball out. And the more Aberdeen take over the midfield, the more the tension starts to mount, the more the Rangers fans sense it's far from over, a sense of angry urgency creeps back into their collective mood. Within a couple of minutes of sitting down, Aberdeen are looking lethal, especially down the right wing. Then the unthinkable happens. A cross comes in from the right and Starkie launches his frame, collapsing like a detonated chimney, to crash the ball spectacularly into the Broomloan goal. Silence behind us. Silence opposite us in the Govan stand. Silence all around us. Just a distant cheer from a tiny pocket of cheeky Aberdeen fans behind the goal and a couple of raised arms from some suicidal Aberdeen fans dotted around the main stand below us. I look straight ahead, biting my lip, forcing any trace of delight from my face. Within seconds of our goal, I suddenly realise how lucky we'd already been. When Hamish had randomly handed out the tickets, he'd inadvertently saved our lives. The seating arrangement was as follows:

Main Stand, Ibrox, 17 November 1984

Very Large
Angry Bears

Angry Bears	Row S seat 48 **Dad**	Row S seat 49 **Me**	Row S seat 50 **Georg**	Row S seat 51 **Hamish**	**Angry Bears**

Angry Bears

The Game

Hamish, furthest to the left, a neutral, would doubtless have engaged Dad in chat about the goal, with his strong, confident up-market West Coast voice, immediately blowing our cover. He had interesting and animated opinions about everything, and he was the reason we were here, having got tickets through ex-colleagues at the SFA where he used to work. Sure enough, he's standing up clapping, his whole body bobbing enthusiastically. Fortunately, he was too far away from Dad to converse, it seemed. Next to him sat Georg (the German boyfriend of Isabelle, our other French lodger). There was no way they were going to be speaking to each other. Georg and Hamish hadn't really seen eye to eye since they'd had a massive barny when Hamish claimed that Toni Schumacher – the German goalie – should have been banned for life after he put French player Battiston into orbit in the World Cup semis in Spain (a spat which happened after Hamish had got us all tickets).

Georg, sitting next to me, who didn't say much anyway, had said absolutely nothing since we'd left the car. I reckoned with hindsight it maybe had something to do with what Dad had said on the journey from Perth. Dad and Hamish were discussing the bad blood between Aberdeen and Rangers, the Doug Rougvie and Derek Johnstone incident in 1979, and more recently the high number of players sent off in the clashes between the two sides. Dad eventually got on to his 1961 Ibrox experience when a Ger had threatened to ram my Dad's bugle, one that he'd been tootering throughout the match, down his throat (this was the sanitised version, the bugle was going to go up my Dad's fucking arse, I discovered many years later), and how back in the 1960s, Dad and his mates would often end up in Aberdeen boozers post-match with Hearts, Hibs and even Celtic fans, but never Rangers people, for some reason. And then came the international incident of the day. Carried away with laughing about Rangers, Dad told his Rudolf Hess story. This was basically that the real reason Hess had flown to Scotland in 1941 was that he'd actually been a season ticket holder at Ibrox (as opposed to fleeing the Nazi regime). As soon as Dad finished his sentence, I saw his face turn green in the mirror. No one laughed; no one said anything for at least five minutes, apart from Georg, who made a loud single tut, and then stared out of the window for the rest of the journey. He'd been sulking ever since.

Right now, that was the perfect result. All that matters is that no one speaks. I'm just praying that Dad's violently bouncing leg and vibrating seat is the extent of his reaction to our goal, but could he contain himself? How has he been coping with all this? Surely he knows better than to speak, his Aberdeen accent would blow his cover instantly.

Then, from behind us, the silence is finally killed. 'Come on'n get in tae this shower a shite!'

It was loud and angry, but at least it meant the focus was on the pitch, and not us. The moment passes. We're safe for now. Fifteen minutes later, it's half-time, still 1-1 ...

I ...
WAS BO-RNE,
UNDER-A-U-NION-JACK ...

I had to look round. I just had to. I had to confirm the impossible, that the guy whose name was Tam, Tam with a Scottish accent, was the same voice singing this. My instinct was telling me not to dare, but my curiosity was getting the better of me. I just had to witness it. Eventually, I very carefully turned my head, looking just beyond Dad's miner's cap, along Tam's row. Even from the corner of my eye, I could make out Tam's large lips, rounding to make a trumpet shape, as he lusted and laboured the 'U' sound in the word Union, his eyes heavy, emotional, deeply engaged in the sentiment of the song.

A U-NION, U-NION JACK!

And it wasn't just Tam and his mates. All around us in the main stand, all the way from the Copeland Road to the Govan to the Broomloan, the entire ground is singing this? Forty thousand voices, Scottish voices, hanging, yearning over 'Union Jack', again and again. One of the worst things a Scottish person could think privately, let alone sing. When I'd heard this melody at Pittodrie, my mind had told me it was hearing, 'I was born under a wandering star,' words that didn't seem out of kilter with the other nonsensical stuff the Old Firm fans seemed capable of singing. It also made me realise that the 'God Save the Queen' and 'Rule Britannia' melodies I'd heard in the past were not simply melodies. Surely not 'God Save the Queen'? We hated that song, we had all booed it more vehemently than anything at Scotland v England games, we even booed it in the house when watching any England game on TV. But this also meant that there was more to the Union Jacks Rangers fans carried everywhere than a simple coincidence of colours, the only explanation I'd been given to date. How would Rangers fans live with themselves on the terraces of Hampden at Scotland international matches against England? Imagine how bad they'd feel if they somehow picked up the wrong flag on the way out the door to go to a Scotland game?

I immediately turn back, now terrified my disbelieving face would blow our cover. I now knew that I could not look at my dad again until we were back in the car. God only knows how his face is coping with this. One thing was certain though. If they got wind of any of our feelings, our shock, we would die more horribly than I could imagine ... there and then ... kicked to death in a gruesome frenzy, with the same zeal I'd seen from the Iranians on TV, desecrating effigies of Ronald Reagan and burning US flags. And then, everything changes again ... we break, looking more dangerous than ever, Cooper plays a through ball to

McDougall … a delicious one-two with Willie Miller on the edge of the box … Frankie's clean through on goal! He strikes, Walker dives, it's in! The exact same reaction that met the first goal spreads around the ground, but within a split second, disaster strikes …

'Oh, what a tremendous goal Gordon!' exclaims Hamish, compelled to his feet as his inspired eyes and clapping hands follow the goalscorer Frank McDougall, now doing a fly-by in front of the silenced Rangers legions in the enclosure below. It's going to happen. The large bearded head of Tam (I still didn't know what he looked like, but my mental picture had him with a beard) will appear from behind us, between Dad and me, asking, 'Right, which wan a you is Gordon then?' Finally Hamish sits down. I'd no idea that he'd get so carried away with Aberdeen, and behave like this … five minutes seem to come and go and not a cheap from behind us, I feel the sweat running down my back in the unbearable silence … it must come, a thud, a poke, a Chinese burn, something … then there's uproar in the stadium as Ally Dawson scythes down Peter Weir for the tenth time that day, giving the Dons a free-kick just outside the Rangers box. 'Dawson, you coudnay lace his fuckin' boots!' 'Dawson, you're a fuckin' donkey!' ranted and blasted the four big Gers fans behind us, bolting to their feet, to deliver in unison a tirade of grief to their struggling right back.

And just when things seemed to appear very slightly amusing, a new voice bellowed out, 'Dawson, yer fuckin' useless min!' Oh my God … Dad, what have you done … he might have tried to disguise his roots with an attempt at a Glasgow accent, but no, not Dad, who else would finish any sentence with 'min' here? Silent prayers, now mostly with my eyes shut to get me through to the end of the game … the minutes tick away, still we lead 2-1, still no contact with Tam and his mates whose attentions and frustrations are ever more desperately directed at their team's now inevitable defeat. The full-time whistle blows ... now we must get up and risk facing them. I keep my eyes focused on the pitch, avoiding all contact with those around me, in particular I try to stay as far from Hamish as possible. We eventually shuffle out of the ground, and Tam and Co. are nowhere to be seen. Now surely we're safe, although still surrounded by thousands of frustrated and subdued Gers as we plod on, all in silence ... finally the car comes within sight.

We get in and close the doors. Before I can even sigh in relief, Dad immediately erupts at the first real opportunity to release the pent up emotions from the previous two hours. He bounces between his seat and the roof like a man possessed, his head seeming to fill the entire inside of the car, like he'd become a self-inflating version of himself that had gone out of control. Hamish looks at my dad askance, pausing before driving off, taken aback it seemed, maybe shocked at Dad's swearing and emotional celebration. His silence after he'd regained composure seemed to suggest that he was left a bit embarrassed too. Eventually after much throat clearing, Dad's moment was erased from the collective memory and they all started talking about Aberdeen's superb performance. But as our journey back to Perth got underway, I was already preparing for school on Monday morning. It was to be the beginning of my new crusade against Rangers fans and their songs. A battle that would rage on for the rest of my days at school and beyond.

But when the dust settled on that weekend, the real business of the league campaign took over our thoughts. Beating Rangers was all very well, but the real proof in the pudding, the real test of mettle would come in three weeks. Then, Celtic would come to Pittodrie for the top of the table clash, the fixture I'd really been waiting for since our defeat at Parkhead in October. This would confirm whether we still had the bottle to go on and retain our League and Cup Double.

Chapter 20

Jammas

Standing at the bay window in my mum and dad's room, Saturday 8 December 1984, I watched over the constant flow of Saturday morning traffic sweeping down the Glasgow Road on its way into central Perth. Today is the day that Celtic were coming to Aberdeen for the first time this season. Today is the all-time day of reckoning and I'd never been as nervous about a high-profile match in my life. But something else had just happened that had my heart pounding so hard, it seemed like it was bursting out of my ribcage. Five minutes ago, I almost caused what might well have been the ultimate day of reckoning not just for me, but my whole family and everyone else in my house. It was a sign of the day I was about to have, it was a sign of the times our team now faced.

With half an hour to kill before we left for the game, I'd gone up to my mum and dad's room to check out a new jumper in the full length mirror before reverting to one of my private hobbies, sizing myself up for mentalness. This involved swaggering towards the mirror, beckoning and pointing at myself with a variety of aggressive, square go gestures. But then, carried away with how mental I looked, I turned to give the vics to the traffic on the Glasgow Road, when my eyes fell on a Celtic bus on its way to Aberdeen. Just the provocation needed to show how game I could be. I'd leapt into the bay window area, pumping massive double vics gestures with my left then right arm, up and down, until to my horror, the bus started slowing down and then stopped in the traffic queue backing its way up the Glasgow Road. I could see half of the bus peering and pointing out of the window at me, and some looked like they were moving to the door. Some were even arguing with the driver, surely to let them out … he was now my only defence against them storming up our drive, and then God knows what. But to my eternal relief, the bus pulled off. That was now ten minutes ago, but I'm still smarting, still getting over the fact that even here, in the bosom of my own home, and the very private, inner quarters of my parents' bedroom at that, I could still be scared shitless by them.

You had to admire it, I thought. It was yet more confir-mation of how different, how out of reach, how much more powerful the Old Firm were than us in so many ways. Just like the sheer number of fans they had, endlessly streaming past the bedroom window as I stood. Buses from Kilmarnock, Falkirk, Rutherglen, Bellshill, Alloa, Lanark and now Morecambe passing by on their way to the game. Morecambe? Fans in England? Not just that, but enough to form a supporters club? And their stadiums, both of which I'd now visited, that were so much bigger, so much more modern than anyone else's, they looked like they were built for a different sport. Just like the fact that they'd both won 30-odd League Championships each, and we'd won three – I'd be well into my 40s by the time we caught them and even then we'd have to win 30-odd ourselves back-to-back. I'd never thought of it all like that, I realised, folding my arms defensively. We'd no chance in the long run. They'd eventually come back and take over again … and maybe 'eventually' was now, since Celtic had just done something else that revealed what all this scale, all this power could do: they'd signed Mo Johnston. They could pluck one of Britain's top strikers from a high-flying career at Watford, a top six, English First Division side. They could even outmuscle an English giant like Spurs to get his signature to boot. And he was magic. I'd seen him running the Spanish defence ragged and then scoring twice in Scotland's 3-1 win in a crunch World Cup qualifier just days ago. And now he was behind the new Celtic, on fire in the league and in Europe too. Aberdeen were maybe still top of the table, but it felt like we were a shadow of what we'd been last year.

With the passing of the 28th Celtic bus (Ayr) in front of me, my dwam goes into overdrive ... these were the first green shoots of Celtic's, of the Old Firm's, inevitable return to dominate the game on the pitch as well as everywhere else ... maybe today, maybe this time, the end would begin. Maybe today they'll play us off the park like they had done for most of history, our dream over, our confidence smashed, back into line, hopeless, shite. Like the other Scottish sides. Maybe we will ...

'Stuart?' calls Mum from downstairs. I glide as weightlessly and silently as possible from their room before responding, so that my voice doesn't seem to be coming from there – I didn't fancy trying to explain to them what I'd been doing. 'Yes?'

'Uncle George has just been on the phone. Apparently it's freezing in Aberdeen ...'

'And?'

'Well ...' an intense pause, '... you better wear your jammas under your jeans.'

What! It's always cold in Aberdeen? I've never had to do this before. Absolutely no way. It was maybe going to be cold at Pittodrie, but this was beyond a joke. This was an unbelievably poxy idea.

'Aw, Mum!' I rage, as I make my way downstairs to argue my case.

'Look, yer father's got his on.' Dad's got his on? Dad, the

guiding light on football fashion-wear? The man who wears a battered old cap that makes him look like he'd arrived there from a coalmine? Dad tries to come at it from the technical side, going on about the value of 'thermal' protection in the face of sub-zero temperatures, and I'd realise once I was there that today was much colder than it's ever been. So what? I had serious street cred problems at school. Wearing pyjamas to a football match was beyond a joke. I could well imagine what would they say if they knew this. Why is she calling them 'jammas' anyway? I'm going to a bloody football match not a slumber party.

Worse still, my mum resorts to disarming baby talk. 'Mommy's little seal pup get jammas on?'

'NO. WAY.'

From behind my mum and dad's back at the back of the kitchen, my mum's reference to me being a tub reminds Fabrice to indulge his now daily attack on me, pretending to grope and lick a rack of fat boobs on his own chest. He knew this got to me intensely. I reckon now I would never have noticed my junior man-boobs had it not been for him. In fact, this was the reason I'd been in my mum and dad's room earlier on, evaluating a new school jumper I'd just got for its contour minimising qualities over these alarming mounds that had started to appear on my chest. All I can do is ignore the fact that he's there. But Fabrice is well up for sticking the knife in.

'If you don't wear zem, I tell Vicki ze whole story on Monday?'

I immediately freeze, and look at him from the side of my face, was I hearing things? Bloody hell … I didn't realise … how did Fabrice know that I fancied her, I'd told no one. What if he told her, or anyone else, that I fancy her? Christ almighty, I'd wear my pyjamas to school, over my trousers, if it would guarantee Fabrice's silence.

Vicki MacInnes had appeared like a bombshell in my registration class that year. I couldn't believe I'd never noticed her
but now she controlled my life at school, and I knew Fabrice
had a thing for her too. I'd wince with jealousy in French
classes when I'd be subjected to the doe-eyed Fabrice devoting
often as much as half of his lesson to helping her pronounce
French words. Getting her to watch his own lips, and then
lingering shamelessly over hers, as he'd help her pout. I finish
my toast, pretend that this had not been said and scuttle off
obediently to get my pyjamas on. Having struggled to get into
the tight fitting multiple layers of clothes, I realised that they
would serve to remind me permanently of my seal-pup status,
and probably made me look like one too. And just as we head
out the door, my mum, sensing the truth behind my sudden
speechlessness, captures the moment, with one of her affectionate sounding, but not entirely well meaning, jingles.

Stuartie's-got-a-girl-friend,
Stuartie's-got-a-girl-friend.

I literally could not have imagined a worse way to leave the
house for football. A victim of a spontaneously crafted, multi-
lateral pincer movement, Mum and Dad with their surprise
thermal underwear attack, Fabrice's boob miming and sensational outing of my crush, rounded off by my mum with
the killer blow, making sure I knew she'd picked up on the
Vicki MacInnes disclosure. It was the sort of series of knocks
that would have brought any man or boy to a fit of tantrums
or maybe simply to tears. Not me today though. As I calmly
put my seat belt on, blanking my mum and Fabrice waving
us off in the drive, the enormity of today's game was shut-
ting everything else out. It was as serious a day as I could
remember, and my intestines were already pulping my insides
to death. The only way to handle the anxiety was to try to

stay calm, silent, and focused. Unless, of course, you were my dad.

'Time to take 'is Celtic lot to the cleaners!' asserts Dad, as we reach the edge of Scone and the open road to Aberdeen. 'Like 'at 4-1 against them back in 1980, ken?' Here we go again, I sighed to myself as I looked across at his face, all lit up. He was ready for another morale-boosting two hours of positive reflection on our way up to Aberdeen, just the way we always did, particularly for showdowns against the Old Firm. But today? We hadn't played like that for well over a year now, he surely knew that as well as I did. Today I need a sober Dad, I need some truth, some level headed honesty about what was really going on. 'A proper barraload, ken!' summarises Dad.

But level-headed honesty was never my Dad's strong point.

'A barrowload Dad? Against this Celtic team?' I look across at him frowning. 'Dad, have you been paying attention to anything on the TV or radio?' Dad says nothing, as he concentrates on overtaking a tractor. 'Seventeen goals in their last three games, three different players scoring hat-tricks … They've even been comparing them to Jock Stein's Lisbon Lions.'

'Hiv they?' he queries. 'Fit a lot a rubbish.'

'Well, they are through to the quarter-finals of the Cup-Winners' Cup.* That's not rubbish in my book,' I said, looking out of the passenger's window. That had been the latest bitter pill swallowed in European football that year. Getting knocked out so early on in the season was hardly the end of it. Celtic,

---

* Or so we all believed. UEFA later made them replay the second round, second leg match against Rapid Vienna at Old Trafford, thanks to an empty quarter bottle of Bells that made its way onto the pitch via the Jungle. They inexplicably lost 1-0 and went out.

Dundee United and even Rangers all got beyond the first round in their campaigns. They each were involved and performed fantastically in barnstorming, end-to-end thrillers that came blasting through the radio at me. Each kick of the ball drip-feeding my festering, green-eyed gloom; Rangers beat Inter Milan 3-1, Dundee United stole the show versus Manchester United at Old Trafford in a thrilling 2-2 draw. That very night, I heard the Man United fans chanting Gordon Strachan's name, even after he missed a penalty, rubbing salt into the still open wound that was his departure. And that just reminded me of another massive problem we faced.

'No wonder though. We have to sell Strachan and McGhee, but they can go and buy a player like Mo Johnston?' I look back at Dad for some sort of response. 'How can we compete with that Dad?'

'But we dinna need Johnston, we've got Frunkie McDougall!'

I give him a 'get real' look; he surely couldn't mean that? McDougall, who we'd signed from St Mirren to replace Mark McGhee in the close season, had started scoring every other week, but none of us were yet convinced, given whose shoes he was filling. And we had other issues with him.

'You would choose "Sumo" Frank McDougall, over Johnston, Super Mo Johnston?'

'Hey min, fa's side are you on?' barked Dad. He was in no mood for any disloyal talk, even if it was only on Frankie's well-documented weight problem. I sensed that there was an unusual element of charge about his tone, and looking back, I might have heeded this given what was in store for me later that day. But I didn't. We were both going for it now.

'Fa's top of the league and wi' the best goal difference? And fa's scored all our goals?' asks Dad, rolling up his sleeves as he drives.

'All right,' I respond, 'who have we beaten then?' I'd been over this ground about our form at school and my classmates were having none of it. Deep down I knew that for once they were right. Archie McLinton summed it all up during a proper drubbing I took from them all in the changing rooms that week. 'Look Duck, d'you think if Robbo only battered the sappiest first-years, he'd stey toap o' the league? Would he fuck!' He was right. Robbo, the hardest boy in our year, managed to batter a near challenger or someone in a year above at least once every couple of months. That was what told us, reconfirmed to us, just how hard he was, punching at least at, or above his weight. Football was no different.

'Come on then Dad?' I prompt, now arms folded with my back to the side door so I could face him. 'Let's run through the list of the big games we've won so far this year.'

'Rangers three wiks ago?'

'Rangers? Since when have Rangers been a threat?'

'Hey min! Fit a bloody cheek!' spat Dad stroppily.

'Och Dad, you know what I mean,' I tutted, trying to appeal to Dad's sensible side. 'Look, the only big game we've won was the 2-0 win over United at Tannadice and that was way back in August, just after the League Cup disaster in Airdrie,' I stated. 'And d'you know what they say at school about that?'

'What?' asked Dad.

'That the United players were pishing themselves with laughter so much about the Airdrie result that they weren't able to put a performance together.'

'Ach, listen min, if you canna say onythin' sensible, there's nae point in sayin' onythin, ava.'

And that was the end of that conversation. Again I should have heeded Dad's unusually brittle response to what was meant to be a joke. But it was the same argument we'd been having for weeks. Only today we'd barely reached Laurencekirk by the time we'd stopped speaking, just about halfway. The longer the silence went on, the more entrenched our sulk became. It continued all the way to Auntie Helen's, and all the way to the ground. As I sat, denying myself the escape valve of talking gibberish to Dad, one thing was for sure. It was Baltic. Never before had I seen such a constant stream of hospital trolleys, carrying hypothermia ridden Celtic fans from the Beach End. As usual, each one of these attracted a few half-hearted verses of the Glasgow Slums song, 'raking yer bucket for something to eat, you find a dead rat and you think it's a treat …' a sort of 'Mexican taunt' a couple of years before its time. As usual, Dad chuckles away disapprovingly as the jokers round about us indulge their habitual socio-economic bigotry. 'It wisna a deid rat they needed the day, it wis clothes!' says one of them not far from us. But all I could see was another side of Old Firm power: martyr fans. Celtic had dozens, maybe hundreds of martyr fans, all so committed that they would risk wearing only their 'hoops' even to a game in Aberdeen in December. It was yet another indication of just who they were, and that sooner or later, we'd be crushed. As the game starts, it was all falling into place …

Just as I expected, with ten minutes on the clock we'd being drowned in wave after wave of confident Celtic attacks led by their new goalscoring machine. 'Mo, Mo, Super Mo' they all sing now in the Beach End, like we had done at the Scotland game on Wednesday night. He is everywhere, rosy cheeks, blond hair, crouched over the ball, causing the Beach End to buzz and boom infectiously in anticipation as he exploded menacingly in and out of the game. And then, with 20 minutes gone, still somehow 0-0, the touchpaper is lit for what would explode into the most mortifying thing that had ever happened to me. The one Aberdeen player who divided Dad and me more than anyone else comes into the frame … Billy Stark.

I could feel the hackles on the back of my neck rising as his very own mid-1980s afro (which was probably meant to be a mullet), his eight-foot-tall gangling frame and his daft gaping mouth over its retracted chin, comes drifting into my line of vision, picking up the ball for the first time in the game, on the right wing. Nothing epitomised our decline from excellence, our fall from grace more than this man … and true to form, he falls over, losing the ball, the way he always lost the ball, pushed over by an invisible feather duster when there was more or less no danger.

'For fuck's sake, Stark!' I rage, along with at least half of the South Stand, at the gigantic fallen daddy-long-legs, lying in an impossible pile of knees, elbows and chin.

'At's enough min, he's in oor team!' counters Dad from the side of his face, as Celtic tear impressively back up our half, stretching us yet again …

'Starkie! You belong in a fuckin' circus min!' bellows one of the many Billy Stark haters behind us, I turn and nod smugly towards Dad in agreement, Dad shakes his head ever more emphatically in disgust. When was Dad going to get it? When would he realise that Stark was not Aberdeen quality, Aberdeen material? I raged away to myself in my mind … No sooner has play resumed, a mishit goal kick by Bonner falls to Stark on the right … if he can only control it first time he could run-in on goal … Jesus Christ! He misses it completely. That was it. The anti-Starkie brigade in the South Stand has had enough, as thousands of us spring to our feet in the biggest anti-Starkie demonstration I'd seen to date. So big, it causes a few to start a new song to spread in patches down to our area. I'm so pissed off I'm among the first to join in.

> Stark-ie, get tae fuck!
> Stark-ie, Starkie, get tae fuck!

'Hey min!' bellows Dad.

I glance a dismissive tut at him. I'm not having any of his shit today. He should be agreeing, joining in. I mean it's hopeless, I go on …

Stark-ie, get tae fuck!
Stark-ie, Starkie, get tae fuck!

Stark-ie, get tae fuck!
Stark-ie, Starkie, get tae fuck!

I look round and to my horror all the other anti-Starkies have sat down, with only Dad left standing ... alone ... staring at me. He's even blocking the view of people behind us ...

'SIT DOUN NOW!' someone shouts.

But Dad takes no notice ... oh no ... I can see it in his face ... oh ... my ... God, I didn't realise ... it's Vesuvius time ...

'THIS IS AIBERDEEN ... OOR TEAM, RIGHT?

'Yes.'

'STARKIE'S OOR PLAYER, AND HE'S DEIN' HIS BEST FOR US, RIGHT?'

'Yes,' I whimper, praying for the ground to somehow swallow me up ...

'... YER MOTHER AND I ARE SPENDING HUNNERS A POUND A MONTH TAE TAK YOU TAE GAMES A' O'ER SCOTLAND, AND 'IS IS A' YE CAN DEE?'

I stare straight ahead, now that he's brought Mum into it, I can't even bring myself to speak ... it's the bollocking of the century, the public bollocking of the century ...

'I'M JIST NAE PREPARED TAE SIT HERE WI' YOU BEHAVING LIKE 'IS! WI' HINNA COME A' THIS WEY FOR YOU TO SIT AND COMPLAIN!

'**HIV WI?**'

'No.' Silence. Silence now for ten seconds. Twenty seconds. Dad eventually sits down. Just as it seemed it had come to an end, just as it seemed it couldn't get any worse, the whistle was blown on the pitch for a free-kick or something, causing a pause in the action and a lull in the atmosphere, framing

Dad's crescendo for the whole ground to hang on, allowing the dozens of voyeurs in the rows in front (and no doubt behind too) to compete for a glimpse, peering and stretching round each other to see if they could work out who the spoilt brat was and how he was coping, to shake an adult head in shame or sneer in disgust … with sweat now pouring down my back, all I can do is freeze, lock my gaze on to the mould on the back of the yellow South Stand seat in front of me … still the lull, still a punishing silence, now I pray that my mould teleports me away, but instead, it throws my imagination into overdrive: Billy Stark approaches the wall at the front of the South Stand to shout up at me, 'Your dad's right son. And d'you know how hurtful all that stuff you were saying about me is?' One of the hospital-bound Celts sits up in his trolley as he is wheeled past, grimacing and shaking his head, and then croaks, 'Here's me, dying o' hypothermia for my team and all you can do is complain about Billy Stark, you're a little cunt son'; the TV cameras above me under the roof of the South Stand focus directly on me, and a smirking Archie Macpherson comments, '… *there seems to be a bit of a distur-bance below me in the South Stand, where a chubby young lad is taking the ticking off of the century from his dad, well he'll be cringing when he sees this on the highlights tonight!*' My God, that *could* happen! The cameras often pan over the South Stand … everyone at school would see it, Vicki MacInnes would see it …

Finally the whistle blows to restart the match, still locked on to the yellow mould, all I know is that the free-kick is deep inside the Celtic half to my right in front of the South Stand. The kick is taken, a roar of anticipation – WE'VE SCORED! My public humiliation causes a delayed reaction in me as I get up slowly to clap, still minded to be as invisible as possible. Still smarting, but at least now not the focus of the whole ground. I still do everything gingerly, clapping quietly, calling decisions for Aberdeen without pointing, but our relent-less assault on Celtic's goal draws me out of my shell. One minute to half-time ... Celtic clear the ball from their box back upfield, only to our right back McKimmie ... he runs up, no way, he's teeing up for a thunder-blaster 40 yards out ... he strikes, the ball flies like a bullet, takes a deflection ... into Celtic's net! Now I escape from my doldrums, now I'm liberated from my penance as I and the whole South Stand go berserk. Two-nil? Against this Celtic side?

And so it went on throughout the second half, as we continued to tear Celtic limb from limb. Dad was right, he had been so right. It was happening, just like he had said it would. This was the Aberdeen of old, this was the feeling, that sense of on-pitch control and firepower that we hadn't seen since Strachan and McGhee had gone. This was the classic 'barraload', the Aberdeen trademark against the Old Firm, guaranteed to happen at least once a season. We still had it. It was still there, just like it's been all my life, only it's just taken till now to reappear. Final score: Aberdeen 4 Celtic 2.

Midway through our standing ovation, what seemed to be the 40th hospital trolley appeared in front of us on the track. 'Hey min ...' says Dad to me with a gentle nudge, 'I bet he's nae wearin' his jammas under his troosers!' I looked at him witheringly, but take the olive branch gladly. Fantastic. We were pals again.

And now we're back again. Five points clear at the top of the table; the league was ours for the taking. All the doubts could be laid to rest. Surely!

Chapter 21

Birthday Blues

For the last time, I stood and stared at it. It was the best bike on record to have appeared in the window of Perth Halfords, certainly that I had seen. It was Thursday 21 February 1985 and in two days' time it was going to be mine, for my 14th birthday. My grandad was coming down to pick it up for me and I'd been raving about it to him for months. And no wonder: fourteen speed – not twelve like my mates' bikes, it had the potential to change my life in all sorts of ways. It would effort-lessly slash my current paper round record of 22 minutes. And it could go some way to helping my street cred, compen-sating, offsetting my weight problem, maybe even helping me with Vicki. But today something was taking the edge off its unique chrome and gold metallic finish with its brown foam trim, as it stared seductively back at me. The closer we'd got to the weekend, the more our game at Parkhead started to loom over everything. It was an exact replay of the run up to the Celtic game in December. The doubts were back big time but this time, our form *had* fallen off a cliff. We'd lost twice to Dundee United over the winter, and had started drawing with rubbish like Dundee and St Mirren. If we lost to Celtic tomorrow, they'd be one point behind us at the top of the table. Then the league would be wide open. Could we hold our nerve throughout the final quarter of the season if that happened? I had more than a few doubts. But there was another

birthday surprise on its way that I would find out all about
tomorrow at school. A surprise so unexpected that it all seemed
too good to be true ... before my birthday weekend came
crashing down about my ears on all fronts.

Since Christmas, Fabrice and I had been getting on much
better. We'd spend hours playing pool, snooker, one-on-one
football in the back garden, cards ... everything. It was what
I'd imagined it was like having a bigger brother. No more so
than when he'd remind me not to get too carried away in
our regular play fights, when I'd draw glimpses of his short
fuse with the odd punch or kick. It was very impressive. You
couldn't have really called Fabrice hard (there was still something very French and so a bit girly about him), but as the
Caly Road boys would often underline, it's 'no so much aboot
being hard, but aboot being game'. He was game all right. I
had long fantasised about unleashing this side of Fabrice on
my enemies at school, but never really expected this to happen.
I was much more interested in trying to get Fabrice simply
to understand my side of things at school. And since my Ibrox
experience in November, this had been all about Rangers
fans.

   As the season had progressed, there seemed to be Rangers
fans falling out of the trees. It didn't really make any sense.
OK, they won the League Cup (beating Dundee United in
the Final, surprise, surprise), but they were going nowhere.
Aberdeen, Celtic and Dundee United were still the top league
sides, and we'd been at the top of the table all season, even
if a shadow of our recent past. In any case, there were at least
ten new Rangers fans in my year, having previously supported
Saints or United and even Aberdeen, and their explanations
took some believing. One guy, Steven McWhirter, a former
Dons fan in name, told me that he became a Rangers fan when
he realised that he was really a 'Glaswegian protestant', but

his Glaswegian-ness seemed all about an uncle that lived in East Kilbride (not even Glasgow, judging by the map). What sort of reason was that to ditch a winning team for a crap one? I suspected that this sort of stuff resulted from getting hooked just by going to the games. Since many were now regulars on the Perth Rangers supporters' bus (or more accurately, the 'Prince William Loyal' Perth Rangers supporters' bus), they'd surely have been sucked in by the amazing atmosphere at Ibrox. This was also why Peg Bain started to speak full time with a Glasgow accent that he'd simply 'picked up' by being at the ground for a couple of hours on a Saturday, so he claimed. But I also put a lot of the blame down to a guy called Peter McEwan who they all raved about, someone they'd met on the Prince William Loyal. He was a proper True Blue, a guy in his early 30s, and they worshipped him.

According to them, Peter knew all about Irish history, something they all seemed very impressed with. And he was proper hard, one of the only guys in Perth that even the fully assembled Saints casuals wouldn't go near. His most impressive exploit had happened last year during his summer holiday in Belfast, when he met the IRA in a pub (no doubt identifiable by their balaclavas). He'd been discussing Irish history with them which led to an argument, culminating in one of them smacking Peter in the mouth. But what my Rangers pals were really impressed with was how Peter had handled the situation. Apparently, his head banked to the left, absorbing the punch, and then redressed, slowly, with the same expression. I'd seen two or three actors' impressions of this incident, each one using a slow-motion special effect to underline his hardness, the slower the motion of his head as it came back after the punch, the harder he seemed. Even when the IRA (or the 'RA' as they were now sometimes called) pulled a gun on him, in what was surely a last ditch attempt to get Peter to back down and realise just who he was dealing with, he stood his ground. You had to admit, if any of it was true, it *was* fairly impressive.

But what had been causing us to fall out and fight among ourselves at school was something else about Peter. They all raved about what they had found in his lounge: one of the walls was painted edge-to-edge, floor-to-roof, with a Union Jack. The biggest Union Jack I'd ever imagined. And it was Peter's Irish history lessons that seemed to have persuaded them that there was nothing wrong with singing 'Rule Britannia', 'God Save the Queen and 'I Was Born Under a Union Jack'. Needless to say, we fell out constantly when they'd argue that these were just 'Rangers songs' and I'd argue that it was little wonder we'd so many problems with the confused foreigners like Fabrice and the English commenta- tors if Rangers fans would sing songs like these. And more often than not, our arguments would finish with me storming off in a rage and them starting up a rendition of one of the disputed songs, that they'd continue to sing until I'd disap- peared from sight. All this was bad enough and more than confirmed everything I'd seen at Ibrox in November. But in early February, Barry MacGregor, a long-standing Rangers fan, took things a step further.

I don't remember how we got on to the subject, but I recall his words perfectly, 'Scotland v England games? The result doesnae matter tae me. They're baith British teams like.' I stood looking at him, smiling, waiting for the punchline. But the punchline never came. Instead he walked off, unaware that I continued staring at him, still expecting to find that he was pulling my leg, until he made his way out of the school's main door. I had to speak to Dad about this. How could any Scottish person say something like this? How could anyone from Scotland not care about beating, or worse, losing to England? Dad had never come across it either. But he reckoned Barry was prob- ably still hurting from the 5-1 obliteration Rangers had taken from us at Pittodrie at the end of January, the biggest mauling we'd ever see them take (before or since). So sore, he'd do anything to scandalise me. I was scandalised all right. And the more I ranted and raved to Fabrice about this, hopelessly trying to get him onside, the more evidence it gave him for the conclusion (that he'd arrived with) that we were all, at the end of the day, just like the English, British/English, all English, all the same.

But that Friday, the Friday of my birthday weekend, was to be my very own Pearl Harbor moment. Rumour spread around the school like wildfire that the same Barry MacGregor had provoked Fabrice in a French tutorial resulting in an incident. By the time the story got to me, Fabrice had decked him and had been kicking him in the head on the ground. I couldn't wait to see him when we got home from school that night.

'What happened with Barry MacGregor?' I launched at him, thundering down the stairs when I heard him coming in.

'Bof!' huffed Fabrice, dismissively, as he walked through to the kitchen. I followed, skipping eagerly around him as he walked.

'What happened, what happened?'

'It was nothing. He insulted me in zee class, in front of everyone.'

'What did you do? Did you hit him?' I asked.

'Like zat,' Fabrice demonstrated a powerful, but controlled jab to the back of the head. It was beautiful. I acted it out myself to get a sense of how it might have felt; Fabrice confirmed I had it right. I stood looking at him, nodding appreciatively for a second.

'But what did he say?' I asked.

'He called me, how you say, a Fenian?' That wasn't a surprise. I'd overheard a conversation between other Rangers fans in PE, who were debating whether he was likely to be a 'Fenian' (it would be some time before we learned that 'Fenian' meant

Irish Freedom fighter and was not synonymous with 'Catholic') on the basis that most French people were Catholic, although there was some doubt about this.

'Zee others in zee class told me this meant "Catholique".' Fabrice paused and stared at me ominously. 'I am not Catholique,' he said emphatically, pointing back at his chest with his left hand, 'I am anarchiste.'

As usual with Fabrice, it was not at all what I had expected. And I was fairly sure that no Rangers fan I knew had ever been punched as a result of offending an anarchist, certainly not at Perth High.

'So I heet heem,' he said with a Gallic shrug, as if to say he had no option.

'But that's what I've been trying to say to you,' I exclaimed, following him through to the dining room both carrying the cutlery and sauces as we began to set the table. 'This is the guy I was telling you about. This is the guy who even said he didn't care if Scotland lost to England, can you believe that? But that's what the Rangers fans are like.'

'Ah non,' asserted Fabrice, interrupting his cutlery setting task for a second. 'Zees eez not about Rangeurs.' He looks me in the eye. 'Zees eez much bigger zan zat. It's about zee réligion.'

I stopped too. I knew it was about religion, but surely it was still about Rangers?

'And when zee réligion attaque me, I must attaque it, to défende myself. If you are anarchiste, you do like zees.'

'Right,' I said tentatively after a pause. I didn't have a clue what he was on about. But I wasn't complaining. The fact that Fabrice was aligned with my cause for whatever reason, the fact that he had punished a Rangers supporter, was good enough for me.

Fabrice went on though. 'You 'ave to look through what zees boy has said. Behind, you find zee church. Rangeurs,

Celtiques, zey are just, how you say, "véhicules" for zee réligious wars.' I nod, still clueless about where Fabrice was going with this, but now I was distracted. I heard Granda and Dad coming through from the lounge. While I was quite happy to listen to Fabrice explaining his agnostic philosophies, especially given the circumstances, I was wary about how my Granda might react to this sort of stuff. I knew he was 'old school' when it came to the church. But there was no stopping Fabrice. 'All wars, all over zee world are like zis: Israeliens against Palastiniens, Indiens against Pakistanais, you see? As anarchistes, we are against zee wars, therefore we are against zee réligion.'

'What!' bellowed Granda, stopped in his tracks a couple of feet from the table, staring at the Frenchman, who in turn slowed the pace at which he was laying the cutlery at the other side of the table, turning his head to stare at Granda. In that instant, the tension in the room soared. It was the 'High Noon' moment that had been threatening since they'd met way back in August. I gulp hard … 'Ye canna say that min!'

'Oh come on,' laments Fabrice, 'you cannot deny eet.' Granda stands behind his seat for a moment, arms folded, his tongue rubbing nervously around his back tooth, a sure sign that Fabrice had already got to him. 'Look at Irelonde, eet's even worse zere zan anywhere else in zee rest of Europe.'

Granda looked so disgusted with what he was hearing, he didn't seem to know where to start.

'Eet's not just zee conflict, but look also 'ow repressed zee English life eez, especially zee Sundays?' argued Fabrice as we all finally sit down to eat. This was really the point he was trying to make on Sundays when he would often wear no more than a T-shirt, his eccentric leather slippers and a pair of very tight, very skimpy black pants. It was Fabrice's very deliberate, very personal assault on the quality of life during weekends in Scotland: there was nothing to do, and there was no point pretending there was by getting dressed.

'Zis ees because of zee English church.'

'Right, you listen tae me min,' barked Granda, as he spread an illiberal dose of mustard along the edge of his plate. 'For a start, we're nae English!' Having had enough of Fabrice's national label problems, I wondered when this was going to happen. But then came the bombshell of the decade …

'We're British!' rasps Granda, slamming the mustard pot down back in the middle of the table to underline his point.

What? Did I hear right? Why … wh …

'No, Granda … ' I peep … He turns to me and looks me square in the eye. I'd dared to speak, the first attempt at adult-to-adult disagreement I'd ever risked with him but I had to, I had to be sure that I'd got it wrong … 'We're Scottish Granda, are we not?'

'Aye 'at's right, but we're British first!' reasserts Granda, his steely gaze cuts through me like a knife. I freeze, only my intensely pounding heart moves. I can't believe it. No one has told me, or maybe even my dad, that my Granda, my own flesh and blood believed this. I turn to Dad, who is conveniently focusing on manoeuvring the next cargo of sprouts and carrots towards his fork. But Granda still stares at me, his unwavering conviction challenging me for mine. He really does believe it, and he clearly believes I should too.

'Zee monarchie is behind zee oppression of zee church 'ere,' interjects Fabrice, itching to get back into his rant. 'In France we are not oppressed, we 'ave killed our monarchs many years ago – you must do zees sooner or later.' I can't follow though, I feel like I've been shot off the planet into a silent, slow, bewildering orbit. What was the point in sorting out people like Barry MacGregor if this is what the likes of my own Granda believes?

'Listen, 'at monarchy sa' us, and you lot, through the war!' shouts Granda, who hasn't even managed to start eating. As I stared confused at him, I realised this also meant that Granda wouldn't have been bothered by what we found at Ibrox back in November.

'Zee war, always zee war ... ' laments Fabrice, 'we must look forwards not back.'

Oh my God ... Maybe Granda had been wooed by that great Rangers side of the 30s; maybe he was one of the 'turncoats' that Geordie banged on about?

Granda now downs his fork and knife with purpose. 'You should be down on yer hands and knees every day min, beggin' forgiveness and thanking us for oor part in liberatin' you lot fae the Germans!' shouts Granda, now pointing at Fabrice as he made his views clear. God almighty. He might as well stand up and sing 'God Save the Queen' right now! How on earth ...

'If zee French were to sank anyone for zee Seconde World War, it is zee Russians, and it was a pity zey did not make eet as far as France,' counterattacks Fabrice, surely now trying to wind up my Granda.

'Och, ye dinna ken fit yer spikin' aboot min,' spits Granda, tossing his paper napkin into his untouched dinner before getting up from his seat, tutting loudly and decamping to the lounge. Dad scurries after him almost immediately to talk him down. Soon, he was back in the kitchen where I was doing the dishes, making emergency sandwiches for the now quite peckish Granda.

'Dad,' I whispered. 'Why was Granda going on about the Queen and being British?' I said angrily, 'Is he a bloody Rangers fan too?'

'No, no, he's not a Rangers fan,' says Dad smirking. 'Look, I'll explain it to you another time. But he's come a' the wey doun fae Kemnay for your birthday and tae pick up yer bike, so let's nae upset him ony mair.'

'OK.' Dad was right. He finished preparing Granda's sandwiches and went back to the lounge. I went off to bed.

The next day, Granda set off in the morning to look at some more second-hand caravanettes before picking up my bike on his way home. He finally arrived back with my bike a little after four in the afternoon. But as luck would have it, the timing could not have been worse.

'Stuart! I've got your bike!' he announced, laying it against the shelving five or six feet away from me. Even in the dark garage, its gleaming, dazzling golden finish dominated every other thing in the room. He stood looking over to me, smiling, expecting me to leap out of the seat and bound over enthusiastically, showing him all its features, bubbling over with gratitude. But at the moment, it, along with everything else, including my compulsion to behave respectfully around Granda, were not registering with me. The radio suspended from a rusty hook in the garage roof is still vibrating with the full force of Parkhead's reaction to the goal Celtic had scored. It has put me into a sort of coma, slouched in an ancient wooden carver with my legs up on the workbench between two vices. A posture, whether linked to something to be grateful about or not, I knew was somehow offensive to him.

'It's 1-0 to Glasgow,' said Fabrice, for some reason standing 'at ease' at the garage door. That was 'Glasgow Celtic', as I'd explained to him a million times. Saying the word 'Glasgow' on its own did not impart the team. But Granda didn't even acknowledge that Fabrice was there, let alone his remark, not that the score would have meant anything to him. And just as Granda's by-now palpable indignation became unbearable behind me, forcing me to muster up the energy to get up and show an interest in my bike, the killer blow came … Celtic were awarded a penalty. I froze. Granda stared me. Fabrice stared at Granda …

McStay strikes, and SCORES! There's no way back for Aberdeen now, 2-0 to Celtic and the title race is blown wide open again!

I closed my eyes and slumped back into my carver. Now it was confirmed. The truth, the harsh, real, naked truth, that I had been facing up to, or trying to all season, was laid bare for all to see. We had lost our edge. We simply could not hack the big-ticket games now. And we were about to throw away the league. Granda tutted loudly, turned and went back into the kitchen, but I couldn't care about anything now. I knew that nothing could sink my birthday to a lower depth.

'Stuart?' called Mum from the kitchen door, just as the final whistle was blown.

'What?' I blurt grumpily.

'That was Shirley Rogers on the phone; they've finally got confirmation about your school trip to Venice. It's on!'

Nothing could sink my birthday to a lower depth now. Apart from this!

Chapter 22

An Incident in San Marco

It's Sunday morning, 14 April 1985, and we've just landed at Glasgow Airport. For the last 24 hours I've been trapped on roads and in the air on my way back from the school trip to Venice. As the plane trundles around the landing strip and then taxis towards the terminal building, a flat, strange-looking van starts zooming towards us. It's the baggage van, and I realise that its driver is the first sign of home life any of us have seen for over a week. The driver knows everything that's happened here over the last 24 hours, he must do. All of us in our plane, on the other hand, know absolutely nothing. Nothing at all, including the result of yesterday's Scottish Cup semi-final, Aberdeen v Dundee United at Tynecastle. This was as weird as it had ever been.

I'd never had to go more than an hour or so after a game ended without finding out the score (give or take the odd instance of complacency like the Airdrie League Cup disaster). I could always phone someone, someone who'd know the score immediately, my dad, Uncle George. Failing that, my mum or grandad or Auntie Helen, who definitely would not know the result, but who were normally quite happy to take instructions to watch the TV or listen to the radio at a certain time and phone back later. Whatever the circumstances, you could always work something out. But none of that had been possible over the past 13 or 14 hours. Firstly, we'd been cooped up in a bus for ten hours on our way to Ljubljana airport in Yugoslavia, then we had no currency to use phones in the airport and the Yugoslav aircrew had just smiled politely when I asked them the score. That makes the driver of the flat van the first living thing I've seen that must know. Even though I know I can't get it from him, just knowing he knows the score absorbs me as we wait and wait and wait to get off the plane. Then, from the corner of my eye, a piercing gaze, training on me from a face walking down the aisle, caused me to freeze like I'd been caught in the act. In a bizarre sort of way I had, although Robert Barber, the Dundee United supporter staring malignantly at me, had no idea. But an incident involving him, following a conversation about the exact same stuff three days ago, had ruined my holiday. An incident that had brought me to hate Robert Barber more than anyone I'd ever met in my life, even more than I hated his team. And that was saying something. It was an encounter that was to raise the stakes of the semi-final result more than I could ever have imagined.

The idea of going away on a school trip had seemed like a great idea way back in October. In particular, the idea of going behind the Iron Curtain had made it particularly appealing for us. My two mates in my Latin class, Heid and Moir, were dead keen too, or so they had seemed before Christmas when I'd got my mum and dad to sign up and pay my deposit. But the main reason for my interest was that I'd overheard Vicki MacInnes discussing it enthusiastically with our teacher, and decided from this that she'd definitely be going too. By Christmas though, the true scale of the disaster I had organised for myself was starting to take shape.

Heid, my new second-year mate, a Hibbee, had pulled out because he was going skiing up in Aviemore. Moir, my old Dons fan mate from Oakbank, was off to Germany with his mum and dad. Maybe not so bad, if Vicki was still going, especially if we were going to be the only second years. But, of course, she wasn't going. It was all confirmed on my birthday in February, we'd paid the full whack for the holiday and it was strictly non-refundable, and I was the only second year going. Unbelievable. And worst of all, when we'd be driving home through the Italian-Slovenian Alps, the Scottish Cup semi-final would be taking place. A win would see Aberdeen make a record-breaking fourth consecutive Scottish Cup Final. No side, not even the Old Firm, had done this, let alone win the Scottish Cup four years on the trot, which of course, we had to do. That, along with the league of course, was the one thing that could compensate for all the League Cup and European Cup failures and the general fall off in quality we'd suffered in the last year.

I was distraught not be able to go to the game, not just because of its historic significance. United, who we had killed last season, were back from the dead. Their sole purpose now, as they stumbled about in third or fourth place in the league, was to damage Aberdeen. All they had done that season was to beat us in two crunch games over the winter, with the same zeal, the same confidence, the same superior quality on the park that only Dundee United had ever been able to produce. So for the semi, I just had to be there, but there was no way back now. And as it happened, the only thing I thought I had going for me on the Venice trip was that someone else who was in exactly the same boat, only from the Dundee United side of the fence. This was Robert Barber, who'd miss the game too. But I didn't even know him, I only knew *of* him.

'Don't worry, Robert's going to Venice, he's a lovely boy,' both my mum and my Latin teacher had reassured me. I'd often heard them speaking highly of him before the trip. He was hard working, well behaved in class and could engage the teachers with his precocious interpersonal skills and surprisingly mature chat. But above all, the passport to respect among the staff at any Scottish secondary, he was super-bright. And pupils that attracted this sort of review from PHS staff were the sort I, as a teacher's son, was expected to become friends with, or least foster a good relationship with, even though they were normally so square that it wasn't true. But, faced as I was with a week on my own, I could have thought of worse characters to have to rely on as emergency mates. As the bus pulled up in front of us outside Ljubljana airport, I'd positioned myself two or three people behind Robert, so I could negotiate a seat next to, or near to him for the six-hour journey to Venice. But before we were even on board, I'd discovered a side of him, or certainly his vocabulary, I reckoned was unknown to my mum and her colleagues when he turned to his two mates, 'Who's that wee fat fucker with us on the plane?' Jesus, this was the last thing I needed reminded of right now.

'Dunno, some wee second year, Mrs Donald's son I think.'

'Ah ... that's him.' He was maybe not familiar with my appearance, but the intonation in his voice definitely revealed that he knew something about me. I had a fairly good idea what it was. But anyway, there was no way I was sitting anywhere near him now. Wee fat fucker? Fuck him. I blank them as I move up the bus to some empty seats nearer the back, and sit on my own. As we get underway, the effect of my solitude started taking its toll and the homesickness bulged at the back of my throat, announcing that some tears were on their way. It would rise and fall, as it had been doing since we left Perth the night before. I had my work cut out to fight the tears off to avoid being heard snivelling and bubbling if I'd any chance of making new friends amongst my older PHS peers. After a couple of hours, things were back under control, and I had discovered that Robert's fan base extended well beyond PHS teachers.

Eavesdropping on him holding court with his back to the steamed-up windows in the middle of the bus, his quite unashamed female entourage tittered adoringly, almost vying with one another to cackle the loudest at his wisecracks. Eventually, everyone is asleep apart from Robert, his immediate harem, and his most loyal lieutenants. About to doze off myself, my ears immediately prick up, as they turn to the subject of football.

'That'll surely be Aberdeen's third title in five or six years, is it not?' remarks Richard, one of two senior officials in his male entourage, his cheeky face visible to me between the seats. A tense silence has everything on ice, while they wait for Robert to pronounce …

'Shut it,' responds Robert, dead-pan, causing yet another round of tittering, this time not only from the girls, but Richard and all the rest of Robert's lackeys too.

'He totally hates Aberdeen, man!' exclaims a third voice I only knew as Paul, who wades in, to feast more shamelessly on Robert's balls than anyone. But the fact that his lackeys continued discussing Aberdeen's league campaign among themselves and Robert drifted into the chat of the girls still awake around him, seemed to confirm maybe he did 'totally hate' Aberdeen. Paul and Richard on the other hand, who I'd worked out by now were Saints fans, did not.

I couldn't believe what I was hearing. It was the sort of stuff that Dad had banged on about all year that I'd been totally dismissing. Dismissing on the basis of my dad's bias. But you should have heard these guys, Richard and Paul. They spoke about the recent Dundee match at Dens Park where we'd destroyed them 4-0 and then the Hibs game away again at Easter Road, 5-0; both games we'd been at, both were on TV and both were towering performances. They sympathised with the 'poor bastards', the Hibs and Dundee fans that had turned up out of blind loyalty to watch their sides ripped apart by Aberdeen, recalling that they'd been there as Saints fans the season before. 'Massacred', 'wasted', 'hammered'. They used all these sorts of words to describe what we'd been doing to teams all season. And now, following another win at Ibrox yesterday, we were four points from reclinching the title. For Richard and Paul it was a foregone conclusion and a reason to taunt Dundee United supporters about it. They were in awe of my team. And just now, no one is saying this for my benefit, to be nice to me, to make me feel better about things. This was independent, neutral, unfettered information, the truth as these two Saints fans saw it, and they'd no idea who I was or what it might mean to me, or that I was even listening. This was what Aberdeen meant to Scottish football, as long as there were no Dons fans around to hear it.

But all this just made me feel even worse. My mind was full of Dad, bounding and leaping out of the garage with his dungarees on, to signal 2-0 through the lounge window, where I sat brooding in front of the TV, wallowing in my pre-school trip misery. I'd even deliberately played down my reaction to the news to underline my sulk to him. All this seemed unthinkable now, how was I able to behave like that? It causes another monster lump at the back of my throat, telling me to steer off the self-pity trip. I couldn't help it though … Dad was so right and I'd become such a spoilt brat, so ungrateful. And now I'm here, on my own trying not to cry, on a bus somewhere in the Slovenian Alps.

After a couple of days, I gradually got used to things. My third-year companions had decided, to my eternal relief, that my nickname would be 'Nae mates'. And that was about as much interaction as I'd get from them, I was on my own all the time. But at least I was being spared the 'fat-boy' labels that I seemed to attract from literally everyone else I knew at that time. I'd been dreading that more than anything else. By Wednesday, after a couple of days of bus journeys to Lake Garda, Padua and then Verona, we were set for the visit to the main attraction, Venice proper. This was really what the school trip was all about. And this was where my hatred of Dundee United would be pushed to new, unthinkable levels.

We'd just got the boat to Piazza San Marco at the end of the Grand Canal, and for the first time on our trip, it was a godsend to have no one to talk to. The canals are the roads, the little brown boats are the taxis, and the bigger white boats are the buses. I even saw a spat between two irate taxi-drivers, queuing up at the canal-side petrol pumps. It was like some enormous experimental theme park, which you could see if you were able replace tarmac with seawater. I was enthralled by it all. And within two or three steps of leaving our river bus I found myself in front of the most enormous stall selling nothing but scarves, pennants and other Italian football memorabilia. I'd arrived in heaven.

I'd never seen a football stall like this. It ran the full length of the 'boat-stop', had what looked like a skirt running along its front made up of football scarves and the back wall inside the stall was a dazzling collage of football pennants of all shapes and sizes. At home, scarf and flag sellers never seemed to have stalls, and you only ever saw them on the way to matches. In fact they normally did no more than commandeer a street corner, and used the naturally occurring fixtures and fittings they'd find there for their makeshift display. Hanging their scarves over the road sign or threading them through fencing and at the very best, a bit of plywood to pin up their range of lapel badges and patches, but even that would be perched against the wall on the ground. Standing next to me, similarly absorbing this quite remarkable shrine to football memorabilia, I sensed another figure. It was Robert. We could only have been standing there for a couple of minutes or so it seemed, but when I turned round to find the others, they'd vanished. We both scampered over towards the Piazza San Marco that we'd yet to set eyes on, and we were greeted with the biggest open public space either of us had seen. We immediately knew we were now lost in Venice. I bet Robert couldn't believe his luck.

Initially he seemed to be pretending that I wasn't there, in spite of the fact that I prattled continuously through the excitement of being lost, and lost with him too. He eventually decided after some hopeless padding around, that we needed some height if we were to find our group. We sat down in a terraced café overlooking the enormous square. Robert broke his silence by bollocking me for trying to sit down with my back to the square, missing the significance of our elevation. He then proceeded to confidently order two coffees ... in Italian. Jesus, he really is brilliant.

'Right, look that way. D'you know what you're looking for now?'

'Yes, I do,' I said. Fair enough, I'd been a bit thick. I started doing a slow, intense scanning movement, pendulum like, backwards and forwards, with the odd meerkat bob, to periscope over to the back of the square where my vision alerts me to something, checking from the corner of my eye that he can see I'm working hard. He just seems to be gazing into the sea of flashing Japanese cohorts, and pockets of other tourists. Twenty minutes or so pass, we see no one, we say nothing. Then, out of the blue, some contact ...

'Yer dad going to the semi on Saturday?' I just knew it. I knew he would know I was an Aberdeen fan. I knew simply by the way he'd spoken about football on the bus. People like us seemed to maintain subconscious dossiers on other known football people and their profiles. Not just who you supported, but how active you were, if you went to games, home and/or away, how you got there, if there was a bus or a dad involved. I keep on scanning and meerkating, but I was keen to matey up to him. Cool.

'Aye. Yours?'

'Aye.'

'You and me'll be in a bus somewhere in the Alps.'

'Yeah!' I blurt enthusiastically. He's clearly decided I'm all right. And he's been thinking about the game too. 'Well, whoever wins, you know who we'll be playing in the Final. It really bugs me that.'

'What d'you mean, like?'

Excellent, he's interested in my line of thought. The other semi, to be played on the same day was Motherwell v Celtic, with a Celtic win written all over it as usual. Maybe he'd never noticed how predictable and how annoying it was that teams like those always just rolled over against the Old Firm ...

'These teams, Motherwell, St Mirren, who else has there been in the semis ... Morton, all that lot. Why do they even turn up for semi-finals against the Old Firm? They just can't handle the Old Firm at Hampden, can they? I mean, they seem capable of beating the Old Firm in the league every now and then, so why on earth ...'

OH. MY. GOD ... I realise mid-sentence that I could just as well be talking about Dundee United. Their track record against the Old Firm in cups was more tragic, more appalling, more laughable than any of these teams ... can't reveal this though, must follow through, oblivious ... 'why on earth, when it comes to the big cup matches against them, do they ... do they, eh ... struggle, I don't know ...'

I was sure he'd have worked out that I'd been running up to a punchline of 'fuck it all up like bunch of poofters' or 'never manage to turn up with any balls'. I look round towards Robert warily, but in the immediate few seconds there's no reaction, other than some chortling and an odd bobbing movement, although I sensed from the corner of my eye that he had fixated his stare on to me. Silence.

'Your team's not like that though, eh?' he said.

I stayed silent, trying my hardest, racking my brains for a way out. But all I could come up with were stats that just underlined my point more and more emphatically ... fifteen bouts against the Old Firm in the cups since Fergie arrived, only losing two or three ... I'd yet to see Aberdeen lose to anyone in Glasgow let alone Hampden ... stop, stop!

'Not like Aberdeen, though,' Robert continued sarcastically. 'You think because you've had lucky cup wins that you're up there with Brazil. That's what you think, isn't it? You Aberdeen people. That is what you really think?'

'No, no ... we don't, we don't think that, that's not what I mean ... I mean, I bet if yous get to the Final this year, you'll definitely manage it this time, yous'll definitely beat Celtic ... it's got to be ...' I splutter, desperately to retrieve the situation, resorting to all-out, shameless ass-kissing.

'*MANAGE* IT!'

I sat motionless as my body hit emergency perspiration mode, staring straight ahead in shock, still not really clear why he's so upset.

'THIS TIME!'

Robert crashes his coffee cup on to his saucer, and springs to his feet, 'TWAT!' he mutters at me as he picks up his ruck-sack and turns off back into the main café area, towards the toilets, I presumed.

I continued to sit, squirming with embarrassment, staring now motionless into the sea of tourists. Five minutes pass ... How could he be so sensitive? Nothing I'd ever heard from a peer or someone at school would have caused me to react like this. Another 10 minutes pass ... I knew he was as dedicated, as committed a United supporter as I would ever meet. He and his dad had even been to see United play away in Europe too ... 15 minutes gone, I hadn't moved an inch and there was no sign of Robert. Maybe he'd done a runner and left me on my own? Surely not. It was 'lump-in-the-back-of-the-throat' time again. I was now at rock bottom.

Sitting alone at my terraced café, I started drifting in and out of stifled sobs, wondering if I'd ever get home, let alone find the group here in Italy. Then out of the blue, I saw a group of third-year girls crossing one of the vennels. Convinced that Robert, absent now for at least 20 minutes, had done a runner, I bolted from my café seat and ran desperately to catch them. They, in turn, ran to hide from me when they saw me coming and when I finally caught up with them they made me walk far enough behind to ensure that no one thought I was with them, while they zipped in and out of shops trying to flirt with Italian men. We eventually found the main group, where I picked up yet another humiliation. Mrs Rogers rollocked me in front of the whole party for getting lost in the first place and then secondly for abandoning Robert on his own at the café. By now, hate had properly set in. For the remaining three days of my holiday, which I spent on my own, all I could think about was revenge. We had to beat United for what I'd been through ... we had to.

After an inexplicable hour and 20 minute wait inside the stationary plane, we're finally released back into Scotland. Walking through the series of interminable corridors, my legs were like jelly as if around the corner I might be confronted with the score on a wall, or somehow see the winning goal ... Within 20 seconds, I'd barged to the front of our group, scanning up the passageways for people, anyone that looked plausible enough to know the score. Everyone we passed were women cleaners ... finally into the baggage hall, a passport controller at a desk, a bloke on his own. 'D'you know who won the semi-final at Tynecastle yesterday?' I ask, begging with my voice that he'd say 'Aberdeen'.

He stares at my passport for what seemed like 30 seconds, looks up at me, pauses ...

'Naeb'dy,' he drawls in strong Glaswegian, as he hands my passport back, 'nil-nil it finished.'

'Really?'

'Aye, really!' he blurts. As I sat down on the edge of the baggage conveyor, I could hear the sound of my entire system powering down a couple of thousand revs. What a relief. I've never been so elated at a draw. It meant a replay on Wednesday, so I'd see the game after all. Then, I see Robert approaching the passport controller, I immediately try to bring a huge smile over my face, to put him through the horror of thinking they'd lost, and I'd just found out. Just as our eyes meet, he refocuses his glance beyond me, he senses I know the score and he certainly doesn't want to hear or even attempt to read it from my face. Before we leave the baggage hall, I watched as Robert reacted passively to the score he got from the passport control guy too, before he eventually sat down himself, head in hands on the other baggage belt, just as relieved as me. A couple of hours later, I was finally back home in Perth.

And four days later came the cruellest blow, the most painful Dundee United twist of my life. We deservedly lost the replay 2-1 to them. Bang went our chance to make history with a fourth Scottish Cup on the trot, bang went the idea that we could sweep United aside when we needed to. It was a new milestone of despair, the worst night of my life. And I knew I had to face him at school. But I was ready for him.

'Enjoy that then young man?' says Robert, before winking patronisingly as he passed me standing in the dinner queue the next day.

'No,' I retort, without looking him in the eye. 'But I bet Celtic did.' He stopped in his tracks and stared expressionless at me, seemingly taken aback that I'd dare bring that up again. Or maybe he was shitting it, totally shitting it. And so he should have been. They'd never beat the Old Firm in the Final. And of course, true to form, I was right. In four weeks' time and for the fourth time in four years, United would bottle it in a final against the Old Firm, losing 2-1 to Celtic.

And following that, a number of years would pass before Robert Barber and I would speak or even acknowledge each other again.

Before all that though, we had somehow to pull ourselves together for our last league game against Celtic in ten days. It was our last chance to avenge the 2-0 defeat we'd suffered at Parkhead on my birthday, and more generally, to punish someone, anyone for the semi-final defeat to Dundee United. It was our last chance to remind them and the rest of the country who was the daddy, who could win the ultimate crunch matches when it mattered. The way it had always been. But above all, it was a match that could see us clinch the title again.

Chapter 23

Two Johnny Hewitts

The ball breaks to Simpson, and a simple pass is on to let Hewitt clean through on goal ...

My thigh muscles tense up, ready to spring me off my seat, because if Hewitt scores we win 2-1, and we win the league. Right there and then. We'll get the trophy presented to us, the first time we'd have won any trophy definitively at home, at Pittodrie. If it does not go in the game finishes 1-1, and we'll win the league anyway. We won't get the post-match celebrations, but Celtic need to recover a deficit of a dozen goals as well as relying on us losing our two remaining games. Not likely. But this split second has the power, the scope to change how I would record the entire season. It would cancel out the grief of our shock European Cup exit so early on in the season, our humiliating defeat to Airdrie in the League Cup, our horrific defeat against Dundee United in the Scottish Cup only ten days ago and prove to the world that we still had it against the other big teams, on the big days. He just *has* to score. We have to score, not least because we've been up to our old tricks again, even today. The game had already been a summary of the whole season.

Simpson's perfectly weighted pass glides towards Hewitt's right foot, it has to happen ...

Of all the Celtic matches that had ever happened here, this was the day for a 4-0 tanking, this was the day to impose ourselves. And what have we done instead? Allowed Celtic to dominate the first half and take a deserved lead, when Roy Aitken scored a penalty with such force it left the whole goal-frame shuddering. It was a sickening replay of Stuart Beedie's volley that put Dundee United up 2-0 at Tynecastle in the Scottish Cup semi-final replay, a shot that looked like it was to put the goal-frame into orbit, let alone shudder. I did not need to be reminded of this, certainly not today. We'd equalised midway through the second half, but it was just not right either. The only thing right about it was that it was Willie Miller who scored. But instead of a net-busting rocket from the edge of the box, it turned out to be one of the most eccentric goals I'd ever seen.

> *Hewitt controls Simpson's pass … ten yards from goal, only Paddy Bonner to beat …*

A free-kick was swung in from the right, just outside Celtic's box, towards Willie who was locked in a mid-air tussle with Tom McAdam, heads cocked, arms all over the place. With a combination of his right shoulder and his 1980s perm, he bounced and bundled the ball past Paddy Bonner (it was just as well it wasn't the 1970s when contact with the ball might have been dampened by big hair, or the 1990s when it might have sped past a tighter crop). Ridiculous. And then worst of all, three minutes ago, things got even more ridiculous. Celtic had a goal chopped off, and judging by the reaction of their players, all of them, it's obvious the referee has made a bad call. 'Yes referee!' bellows Dad, along with the rest of the middle-aged population of the South Stand, exaggerating their clapping in approval of the ref's inexplicable decision. I'd sat, arms folded, shaking my head as I watched them all revelling in the injustice, delighted that we were robbing them of their lead, still taking everything we can get. But now, we are all crouched, halfway out of our seats, rising in anticipation of Hewitt putting this right, blasting the ball home, crushing Celtic fair and square, putting all this nonsense behind us. But there was another enormous problem in that split second. Everyone knew it. The problem was that there were two Johnny Hewitts ...

Hewitt checks his spot, draws back his right leg to shoot ...

My teeth clench as I pray that the Johnny Hewitt we all loved was the one that had the ball right now. He was the one that scored the two crucial goals in the Cup-Winners' Cup campaign of 1983. The one who'd appeared at least once a season, sometimes for a single game, other times for a couple of months, to win matches single-handedly. Please don't be the other one ... the slapstick striker, who'd make us gasp in exasperation when he would play as if his boots were three sizes too big, and arguments would break out between the Johnny Hewitt fundamentalists, holding Hewitt perennially beyond reproach because of his wonder goal against Madrid, and the pragmatists, calling for his head. Please ...

He strikes, Bonner dives ... he must score ... It's past the post.

For Christ's sake! I fall back to my seat, head in the grip of my hands. That was our chance. The final whistle goes: Aberdeen 1 Celtic 1. They all clap and clap and cheer and whistle as the players commence their lap of honour around the edge of the park. How could he miss from there? I half-turn towards Dad, who I find is beaming like never before, but stop myself, sensing it's absolutely the wrong time. But how could they not care how we won the league? I mean, how could we be so happy with scavenging on the dead or the near dead, the Dundees, Dumbartons, Mortons and Hibs or scraping through on dodgy refereeing decisions like today? Ten minutes later, we're still clapping as the players embark on yet another canter around the ground. The more it goes on, the more I realise that only I am still bothered. Only I seemed to be hankering after what we did last year, when we were top of the food chain, predating on everything and anything, winning through power, skill, class. This year was supposed to be all about the league, the cup and Europe and here we were doing our best as usual to wobble, to under-perform on the day the title – the one trophy we surely could not throw away – was there to nail in style. And still we clap, still we cheer. I just wanted to go. An hour later, sitting slouched in the P6 as we drove home, the Strathmore spring sun streaming over me through the endless avenue of A94 trees, Dad was doing his best to put it all in perspective for me, to explain what winning the league at home really meant.

'OK, so we didna win the day. But today we made history min. Naeb'dy's ever clinched the league title against the Old Firm,' he looked across at me for a second, pulling his chin away to underline the significance of this. I knew what this meant to him. That season, just like every other, he'd come up to my room with the fixture list in his hand, his finger over the last Old Firm game at home, and said, 'Wouldn't it be amazin' if we won the league that day min?' He'd then get carried off into his imaginary 'Judge Dad' court where he sat and presided over his very own 'provincial' tribunal, one that could mete out justice to whichever Old Firm team was being received in the Beach End dock. 'The charge, a hunner years o' crimes against the rest of Scottish Fitba,' he'd say. 'I sentence you lot as charged to watchin' the Dons win the league at your expense the day and a further one hunner years of humble pie thereafter. Sheriff Miller, take the accused down please.

Court dismissed!' And then burst out laughing. But right now, he's still trying to buck me up.

'Listen min, think aboot a' your Hibs, Dundee, Saints fan pals, the only teams they've seen win the league at hame are the Old Firm teams.' He adds, 'Celtic or Rangers fans a' o'er the pitch, takin o'er the ground, takin' o'er the toun, hellish min'. He pauses. 'But none o' them hiv seen fit we sa' the day.' Dad tilts his head away to underline his point. Maybe he was right. We had won the league after all. And it was his birthday too.

When I look back on that day now, it is difficult to believe I could have felt like that. Especially now that we know that the Old firm have kept the trophy literally every season since that day. But, at the time, all I had known was our meteoric rise, our domination of everyone and anyone we'd play, at home and in Europe. And I still expected that. But it wasn't coming back. Things would never be as they'd been in the days of Strachan and McGhee. In fact, things would never even be as good as they'd been this season again. But, before any of that would become clear, in just a few days, something happened that made me more confident, more bullish about the future than ever: we signed Jim Bett.

We all rated Jim Bett. Jock Stein had rated Jim Bett, guaranteed in his first Scottish XI every time. That said it all. Not only this, but he said he was only coming back to Scotland if he could play for us. Dad and I raved and lectured everyone we met all summer. But it was far more significant than just another player. As Dad pointed out, this was the result of year-in, year-out success. If today a player could see this, let alone a top one, if anyone could choose Aberdeen over the Old Firm, then the ground was definitely levelling out across Scottish football. And so it seemed. By mid-November 1985, it looked like season 1985/86 would be the most amazing one ever: we had won the League Cup in October, we were top of the

league and clear by four points, demolished Celtic at home
4-1, Frank McDougall scoring all four goals. But, most important of all, we had finally gone the critical distance in the big
one, reaching the quarter-finals of the European Cup for the
first time ever. And then, it all started to go horribly wrong.
All because of a bunch of upstarts. Upstarts on the pitch, and
upstarts in my life at home in Perth.

Chapter 24

Upstarts

'Right Duck, you know what yees have to do the morn,' said Heid, getting up to go home after another routine Friday night chewing the fat at my house in anticipation of tomorrow's games, '… thump those Jambo bastards, and thump them hard!' he bellows towards me, pointing assertively in the general direction of Pittodrie as he gets up. As a Hibs fan, Heid seemed to think it was his duty to make this sort of exaggerated verbal attack on Hearts whenever possible. No one else could express so much ill feeling for a team as inoffensive as Hearts. But, according to Heid, we'd never understand, it was that Edinburgh rivalry thing. Since December though, he'd more reason than normal to be concerned. Hearts had been on a run of form that amazingly had taken them to the top of the league. With Hibs already concerned about relegation, there was a lot more than bravado tonight in his 'instructions'. We weren't worried though. If I was honest with myself, we'd gone off the boil over Christmas, losing a whole host of away games to nonsense like Clydebank, St Mirren and, of course, Dundee United and it was far from clear that we'd recovered our form. But one thing was not in doubt: beating teams like Hearts at home was a foregone conclusion.*

* We hadn't lost to anyone at home for 13 months, it was almost three years since we'd lost at home to a 'joker' team (i.e. outside Celtic and United) and we hadn't lost to Hearts at home in over seven years – so long ago, I couldn't even remember it myself!

'Heid,' I said, smiling with my hands up in the style of a mafia boss expressing generosity, 'who better than the nation's European Cup quarter-finalists to burst the Hearts bubble?' I turn and wink provocatively at Pete, my other new best mate in third year. He was a Dundee United fan, the first Dundee United fan I'd been able to hold down a relationship with, and this sort of remark would normally have tested this to the limit (the United people were absolutely shitting it that we'd make the European Cup semis like they had two years ago – the one thing they had done that we had not). But tonight, instead of a tirade of abuse, Pete just shakes his head and smiles, in keeping with our unusually friendly evening of banter. It was all because for once, league football was not really the focus of the weekend in our minds, although we'd spent the whole time talking about it. I suspected that they were both as buzzed up as me about Saturday's main event – Gengerbaw's house party. As it happened, both the football and this event were to shape my life for the rest of my third year at school and beyond.

'Right, where are we meeting up for the morn's night?' I ask as they approach the door of my room. Gengerbaw's was to be the latest in a series of house parties that third year had produced, and Heid and Pete had already been to a number. I, on the other hand, was yet to make one, on account of the fact that they'd been on nights when we'd been at games in Aberdeen so I'd been too late back. This time though, I was definitely going – I'd told Vicki MacInnes I was going.

'Oh, what's this? Have you been takin' the brave pills Duck?' smirks Heid over his shoulder as we trot downstairs to the front door. I knew this was coming. The truth was that no one bought my Aberdeen trip excuse. Although I'd never admitted it, they all knew that I was shit scared about getting battered. It seemed someone always got a kicking at these things, and as an Aberdeen fan I reckoned I was particularly high risk. I'd even picked up the nickname 'Boo Radley' (the recluse in *To Kill a Mockingbird* that we'd been studying in English) from Sarah Jones (Vicki MacInnes's best pal) on account of the fact that there was 'no evidence' that I ever left my house outside of school. But this time, Vicki would be there, unlike on my disastrous escapade to Venice or the hours and hours of hanging about speculatively near her house with my new cool bike. I just had to go, especially since things had been going from strength to strength at school. I now walked her home every night (pretending I was walking home with Heid and Pete, although this added an extra two miles to my journey), we were writing secret letters to each other through the day at school. Most significant of all, my 15-year-old adolescent body had decided to bless me with the loss of about a stone in weight; I was now as slim as the next third-year boy. No one looked at me and thought 'seal pup' nowadays.*

'That's right Duck, there'll will be loads o' MBS there,' says Pete with an unnerving smile. The MBS, the 'Mainline Baby Squad', were the Perth Saints casuals' 'under-five crew'.† They had attracted the majority of the tastier Caly Road boys with whom we'd joined Perth High, a host of nutters from the other Perth schools and a number of cool hangers-on. I knew all this, and this time I was prepared to face the risks. But there was something in the way Heid and Pete were speaking that was concerning me. There was something else I didn't know. And then it came out.

'D'you no ken what happened last Saturday night?' asked Heid.

'No,' I gulp. Here we go. I could guess what was coming now.

---

* Apart from my mum.
† Whose motto was, 'fight for fun, kick to kill, join today!'

'Two hundred o' your casuals stopped in the High Street, battered fuck out of 15 MBS boys including Raymie P, n' ran the rest o' them right up North Muirton,' says Pete. This was disastrous. It would have been total humiliation for them, Raymie P was their top boy and North Muirton was right on the edge of Perth – they'd have almost been run out of their own town! They'd have been raging. 'Beanie got stabbed and wis up the PRI.' A stabbing? Jesus Christ. It couldn't be worse.

'What was it Dargie said last week?' said Pete looking to Heid. 'All known Aberdeen fans were to be … ' answered Heid. '… battered on sight' they said in unison, chuckling to each other as they walked out the front door. It sounded like a wind up, but Dargie had actually said this to me himself the time before when they'd been routed by our casuals back in November. I didn't go anywhere in Perth other than school for five weeks after that, let alone to a weekend house party. So how could I even consider going to Gengerbaw's house party tomorrow night after the Hearts game?

'We'll just see ye in there Duck!' shouts Pete, as they mosey away, still laughing. I stood, my heart pounding. How could I go to this? But then again, how could I not go? I had to go, I just had to.

Twenty minutes left to play, Aberdeen 0 Hearts 0. Hearts have the ball in midfield, probing, looking for a way through, as I continue to deny the truth staring me in the face. Our lull in form over winter was *not* past, contrary to what we'd kept telling ourselves. If we'd turned the corner, why were we struggling so badly now, against Hearts? The sudden anticipation of the packed maroon and white Beach End immediately causes me to look up as they break again, sweeping from midfield, Robertson to Colquhoun, a clever one-two that creates a half-chance for Clarke, he shoots … Leighton saves well, down to his right, saving our arse for surely the 15th time today.

'Jesus Christ Aberdeen,' I whisper under my breath, falling back to my seat, my head in my hands. It's been like this for the whole match. With every Aberdeen move that broke down and every Hearts move that came ever closer to a goal, we were being forced to accept it. Our form *had* turned the corner, but right now, this Hearts team was simply better than ours. The same Hearts team Pete, Heid and I had derided last night. The Hearts team that Dad had been joking about at half-time, going on about the skip allegedly parked outside Ibrox with 'to Tynecastle' written on the side, for the constant stream of Rangers rejects they always seemed to pick up. Hearts, better than Aberdeen? But we were still favourites for the title. Even if the score stayed at 0-0, we were still only four points behind Hearts with two games in hand. As the match enters the last ten minutes, I check my watch constantly, rocking back in my seat as we continue to escape attack after attack by the skin of our teeth. The truth was that we were praying that Hearts' clear superiority on the pitch came to nothing, that they would go home, back into their also-ran box and never do this sort of thing again, so we could all forget that it ever happened and go on and win the league. Like we were supposed to ... But then the inescapable truth broke through ...

Colquhoun picks up a perfectly timed through ball from Jardine ... he breaks free ... runs half the length of the pitch with only Leighton to beat ... and lashes a shot towards goal, it smashes into the back of the net ... the enormous Hearts support in the Beach End erupts, Old Firmesque, only with even more delight than we'd ever seen. They knew as we did, that this was the stuff of champions elect. I sit numb through the final ten minutes. The whistle goes for full time. A vacant groan rises from the Aberdeen fans. We leave the ground and head up Merkland Road. An empty hubbub accompanies us as we walk. Dad and I have not spoken since half-time. I expect that he, like me, is still in a state of shock. But as usual, he has a different view.

'Weel, 'at wis unlucky,' he remarks.

Unlucky? UNLUCKY? I look in shock at the side of his face as we walk. 'What was unlucky Dad?' I asked. 'What?' I reiterate, shrugging my shoulders. How on earth could he think this? For the first time ever, we had watched our Aberdeen being outclassed, outplayed and out-thought by a nobody. For the first time since the Porto defeat way back in April 1984, we had been beaten by a team who were simply better than us even when we were on form. Dad still says nothing.

'Unlucky that we were at full strength Dad?' I stare at him, imploring him to agree. He knew as well as I did that this was our best team, McDougall back fit, Tommy McQueen back too. 'And Jim Bett?' I add. The great white hope, the towering Jim Bett that we'd banged on about all year as the saviour. The truth was he had never really played either. Still no response from Dad.

'Unlucky that they played us off the park Dad?' I ask objectively, 'I mean what is the point in being in the European Cup quarter-finals if we can't beat joke teams like Hearts?' I sulked 'We don't deserve to be there now!' I grump.

'Listen min, I've seen a lot worse,' Dad finally responds, 'I've seen the Hairts come here and haimmer the Dons 4-0!'

'When?' I probe, looking at him even more disbelievingly. 'Last year? The year before?'

'The 50s,' Dad says.

'The 50s? What on earth has Hearts in the 1950s got to do with today?' I argue back, wary of the now dozens of disapproving grimaces and shaking heads aiming at me from all around my dad. He says nothing. I continue staring at him, now speechless. How was that supposed to help right now?

Right now is about the untouchable shine that this team had just lost. Lost, lost for ever, a shine that had kept Aberdeen miles out of reach of teams like Hearts, the nobodies, the also-rans, that we'd panned into the ground effortlessly for as long as I could remember. A shine that made defeats, real defeats, only possible at the hands of on-form Dundee United, Celtic, Liverpool and Porto and even then, that had happened only a handful of times. Still staring at Dad, I know, whether he responds or not, there is simply not an answer. And just then, at the very moment when the frustration was about to boil over, leaving me with no alternative but to break the spine of the pennant I'd bought before the game under my jacket, something caused me to snap out of it. All of a sudden, a tidal wave of mulleted heads, Burberry scarves and golf brollies came flooding and tripping through us. It was the casuals, running to beat the police obstacles blocking their route to battle with the away fans' buses on the sea front – the same casuals that had routed the Perth Saints MBS last week. I swallowed hard as the madness of my night out started to pray on my fears again.

The fear continued to torment me, advising strongly against going all the way home in the car, while I got changed and while I had my dinner. Mum gave me a run up to Gengerbaw's house and I even got her to drop me at the door.* All I had to do was get into the house and hope that Heid and Pete were there. Just when I thought I was safe, about to ring the doorbell, out of the corner of my eye, a portly mulleted head appeared from behind me.

'Duck!' barked Dargie hatefully, before hauling me through

* I'd originally planned to get dropped a few blocks away to protect my street cred in case anyone saw me getting out of my mum's car right at the door, but the thought of bumping into some MBS outside the party had even greater risks, e.g. punishment for Beanie's stabbing!

the wooden gate into the dark back garden, pinning me up against the wall … Jesus … this is it … I'm dead!

'Dinnay you fuckin' go near her, RIGHT!' he snarled. What? Who the hell was he talking about? Oh my God … has Dargie worked out that I fancy Vicki MacInnes? How on earth? For a split second I am more terrified by the thought that anyone could know this than the onset of a kicking … the only person that had worked it out was Fabrice, way back in November 1984, and I was still fairly sure that that was a fluke … Dargie pushes me further up the wall, now throttling me around the throat.

'Who? Who?' I squeaked.

'You fuckin' well ken fine who!' He'd definitely worked it out … the only way he could have known this was if Fabrice had told him, and he'd been back in France for a year (Dargie was not the sort to have a French pen-pal). But since that moment of revelation with Fabrice, I'd gone out of my way to cover things up, skilfully elaborating new ways to disguise my ever more overwhelming attraction to her. It was impossible that he could know. Surely …

'I thought you lot were warned no tae come here anyway!' Dargie tightens his grasp around my throat, this was surely it … the kicking I'd evaded all my life is finally coming … and then, out of the blue, Sligo, another MBS guy, appeared from the back door. I'd never been so delighted to see a Saints casual in all my life, he was an old friend from years back. I looked at him, hoping he's racing through the same memories of how we'd been like brothers, playing in our sand-pit, me helping him perfect the art of imitating how tigers did poos, among other things … silence … he looked back at me, and then at Dargie.

'Dinney batter um Dargie,' Sligo said to my relief. I could see in the whites of Dargie's eyes that he was still itching to kill me, probably realising like me that if he'd been keeping a tighter dossier on our encounters over the years, he'd have remembered that I was due a hiding. 'Dargie! Jist leave um!'

'Get oot o' my fuckin' sight, ya wee dick!' As soon as I was free from Dargie's grasp, I bolted across the garden, triple-jumping the border, lawn and border again and launched myself through the curtain of conifers, delineating the garden's edge. On landing on the pavement, I continued running at full pelt for five minutes, reverting only to a walking pace when I saw a group of people coming towards me. It had to be … it was Vicki and her pals, who in turn teased me about going in the wrong direction. Of course, there was no way I could explain what had happened or what I was doing. I eventually got home and went to bed, drawing to a close probably the most disastrous day of my life to date. Only to discover the following Monday that it had in fact been even more disastrous than I'd thought: it was Sligo, and not Dargie, who ended up snogging Vicki MacInnes that night. So much for all the our time in the sandpit. Fucking casuals. I hated them all.

That was it. In a single day, I watched my team suffer a hideous humiliation and my third-year romance was over before it even started. And it seemed like this was just the beginning. Every other Monday, I'd get reports from the ever more frequent weekend house parties and discos – that were now too dangerous for me to attend – that Vicki and Sligo were still an item. Every other week, Aberdeen's form continued to falter, out of the European Cup on away goals to Gothenburg in March and then out of the title race in April, leaving us with an unimaginable four weeks of league fixtures that meant nothing. And the one thing we had done, reaching our fourth Scottish Cup Final in five years, was the thing I was dreading more than anything else. That was because we were to play Hearts in the Final. To my horror, every other week, we watched as the new upstarts continued to defy everything, beating everyone home and away, now with a clear lead at the top of table. And so, when the last day of the season came round, we were all set for part one in their amazing Double-winning season. Hearts, champions of Scotland. It seemed like a foregone conclusion.

> *Kidd rises to meet the knocked-on corner, AND SCORES!!*
> *Dundee 1 Hearts 0 — well would you believe it! Is the championship on its way back to Parkhead? Sensational!*

Before I have time to compute the implications of this goal, I find myself mid-air, staring at Pete, who is mid-air too, both of us with our arms stretched out, somehow surprised, overpowered by a surge of jubilation. It was like watching someone score against England, when a wee mad half-cut Jacobite springs out from a dark place in my Scottish psyche, to bludgeon to death any goodwill I might have been experimenting with for the England team. This isn't England though, it's Hearts. But it feels so right, so satisfying, so just. It is only in this moment that I realise just how threatened I'd felt due to Hearts' sensational form over the last six months. And it's clear that my Dundee United pal Pete is in the same boat. But right now, if they lost to Dundee, the league title would go to Celtic … Still staring at each other bug-eyed, we both instinctively know somehow that Celtic as champions was the lesser of two evils. We brace ourselves for the remaining six minutes; you wouldn't bet against an equaliser from them … you couldn't …

> *… two minutes left for Hearts to salvage an equaliser …*
> *Dundee's Albert Kidd picks the ball up … a beautiful one-two*
> *on the edge of the box and he scores a wonderful goal! That's*
> *it! Who would believe it! It's all over now, Dundee 2 Hearts 0!*

Pete and I leap once again into the air, now shrieking and laughing out loud, congratulating each other with a huge hug.

The unthinkable, the impossible had happened. There was no way back for Hearts now. When the final whistle goes, we thundered downstairs and outside. We go into the garage and find Dad on his back under the elevated car, the radio is already off.

'What about that then Dad, eh?' I remark, pretending to express excitement about the thrilling climax, as opposed to the fact that there might be something good about Celtic winning the league. Dad says nothing. I'd suspected as much. And he knows what we're thinking. 'Come on Dad, it wasn't us that lost today? We'd never have flopped like that? It'll soften them up for the Cup Final next week, think about the Dons?'

'Aye,' Dad grunts reluctantly after another pregnant pause. I've had enough of this already. I knew he would think there was something unhealthy about my mood, but I'm not going to hang around for any of his sombre, big-picture bullshit, about fighting the Old Firm and all that guff. Hearts had failed. They just weren't good enough. We'd never have done that.

'Right, see you in a couple of hours, we're away to the Plainies.' Pete and I mount our bikes and set off for the four-a-side game we'd organised earlier. Fuelled by the renewed energy our sensational afternoon had given us, Pete starts singing the Hearts song as we cycled and I join in.

'Hearts, Hearts, glorious Hearts, it's down at Tynecastle we bide!'

But then, standing looking over at us from inside the ten-foot wire fence as we sing loudly, freewheeling our way down Needless Road, was the imposing figure of Andy Scott, my new Rangers fan mate. I immediately stopped singing and came over all flushed, as if I'd been caught red-handed. I had in a way.

'Pete … ' I whisper urgently, hoping he'd pick up on it as

we climb the back stairs from the Needless Road entrance to
the Plainies.

Andy Scott had joined Perth High a couple of months ago,
from the Academy. I knew he was a die-hard Rangers fan, but
we were still getting to know each other, and the Hearts
miracle had served as diplomatic middle ground for us, keeping
us off the controversial stuff that we both knew would lead
to fall outs. So right now, I know we'd some explaining to do.
Pete on the other hand does not.

'Follow the Hearts, and YOU can't go wrong!' Pete belts,
lunging forward in that strange way the Hearts fans did, again
and again, over the word 'you', in this most ironically tragic
line in their club song. I could see as my head became level
with the grass that Andy was more and more pissed off, already
turning to face us, hands now on hips, shaking his head.

'Pete … stop,' I whisper again out of the side of my mouth.
But I can tell Pete isn't getting it, expecting everyone to be
as amused by what had just happened as him.

'See when the first goal went in, me and Duck were up
bouncing about all over the place man!'

'What the fuck were yees daein' that fur?' Andy rages.

'Och, it was just a reaction to the surprise, you know what
I mean?' I add, trying my best to play it down.

'Ya pair o' sick bastards!' Andy shouts, taking out his disgust
at us on the ball. But the more ferociously he rifled it into
the fence as we lace up our football boots, the more hilarious
it all seemed. I catch Pete's eye, as we both can't help snig-
gering under our breath. Andy continues belting the ball at
the fence. Five minutes later Philly Drysdale, Eastiecakes and
Jimmy Fleming, all Dundee United supporters, turned up.
They too were cavorting around, acting out their reactions to
Kidd's goals with as much delight and ridicule as Pete. Andy
clearly had not seen any of this coming and is now even more
irate.

'What are you pricks up to now?' he bellows towards the tangerine clad troupe. They too go silent realising how livid Andy is, but still tittering under their breath.

'Och come on Andy, can you not see the funny side of it too?' I said trying to get him to lighten up.

'What is good about Celtic winning the league?'

Silence, again, as I start some keepy-uppies while we wait for our missing player, Heid. And, of course, as a Hibs fan I knew that for him it would be too good to be true. I saw him appear over the brow of the playing field, freewheeling down the path at full speed, with his legs sticking out. He races towards the fence and leaps from his bike with a few metres to go, allowing it to crash into the fence at speed as if it's some sort of deliberate metaphor for Hearts season.

'Funny as fuck!' he shrieks elatedly beaming from ear to ear as he bounds towards us. I can see Andy's temples pulsing on the side of his head. He turns immediately and marches towards the Needless Road gate. Familiar with what he could be like in this mood, we all give him a wide berth as he walks through us. True to form, he gives Heid's bike an almighty welly on the ground on his way to the steps, leaving us to enjoy Hearts failure for the rest of the afternoon.

That afternoon, from the moment of the first Dundee goal, was the high point of the league season. As we cavorted about, acting out Kidd's goals again and again, it was as much about a huge unexpected sigh of relief for all of us as anything else. Certainly for Hibs who were Hearts' arch rivals. For United fans, I'd imagined that they were simply delighted that Hearts had proved to be nothing other than an even more tragic version of their own team.

For me though, the relief was about something else. Their failure meant that Hearts would not be admitted to Aberdeen's exclusive club, a club for League and Cup Double-winners, for real challengers to the Old Firm, who could win trophies on the big stage, on the big day. This was more than confirmed when we completed Hearts' mugging in the Cup Final the following week, destroying them 3-0. But as the dust settled in the days and weeks after the season's dramatic climax, the truth came home. If I'd felt short-changed last year because we won the league by only drawing with Celtic, then what was there to say about this year? It had been a complete and utter disaster. OK, we won the two cups, but we weren't in it for that. We had suffered our own, slow-burn collapse, throwing away our lead in the league and our best opportunity ever in the European Cup. And that was with Jim Bett.

So once again I faced a summer of hoping, still dreaming that next season we'd be back, and that the magic of 1983 would resurface making us a force in Europe again. But deep down I knew it was over. And we already knew a new force, a new Old Firm force, was stirring. If I'd been impressed that Celtic had the reach to woo Mo Johnston a couple of years ago, then I'd another think coming over the summer of 1986. Rangers had signed Liverpool legend, midfielder Graeme Souness as player-manager, Terry Butcher – England legend and World Cup quarter-finalist – and Chris Woods, England's second goalie. This was to be the Old Firm revolution of the century. This time it would be massive. This time it would bring the end of the road for my hopes and the end of my time as an active Dons fan. But first there came an important resignation. It was the last of the false dawns.

Chapter 25

Good Riddance

'What on earth are you doing?' calls my mum to my shock from the behind the closed dining room door. I apologetically paw the dent that she'd just heard me punch into the front panel of the ancient 1960s radio, hoping for it to spring miraculously back to its normal convex self before she comes through to investigate the damage. She decides to my amazement and relief not to come through. The commentator raves on and on about Ally McCoist's sensational goal that had forced me to violence, scored on the break to make it 2-0 Rangers. As we enter the final five minutes, I stand smouldering in the kitchen, my arms folded, my heart racing. Begg keeps goading me, going on about the goal being possibly offside, continually fuelling the constant, barely controllable urges to punch the radio again and again … 2-0 down, three minutes to go … This Aberdeen team is never coming back from that. And what use would a draw be anyway. The final whistle goes. I manage at the last second to rechannel a final urge to punch the radio again by thrusting it back against the wall, distancing myself from the nagging voice of Davie Begg, still charged, still animated by McCoist's breakaway goal, although it happened five minutes ago.

'Get upstairs to your room … NOW!' gasps Mum as soon as she hears the second thud. I make for my room, as this time she's definitely coming through. 'There'll be no more football for you this year!' she shouts as I pass.

'Good!' I shout back insolently. I mean it. I thump upstairs, enter my room and slam the door before launching myself face down on to my bed, waiting for the inevitable visit from my dad. We hadn't lost to them since I'd been in primary school, almost four years ago. But we knew it was coming. Rangers had been totally transformed under the Souness revolution. And our form had been worse again than at any time I could remember. Even worse than last season. We were in September and everything was already in tatters. But it was all the more painful for me because of that second goal.

Today's result had ruined one of our proudest records, one of the few surviving from our untouchable days – the statistical evidence that proved that Miller, McLeish and Leighton had been, and still were, one of the best defences in European, if not world football. Aberdeen simply never lost by a margin more severe than 0-1 or 1-2.* For my whole life at Perth High, this amazing statistical truth had won me bets for a running total in excess of £20 not to mention rights to several punches in the face (none of which I'd used, of course). I'd even at times managed to turn the rare 1-0 or 2-1 defeats to United or Celtic into moral victories for me, as this statistical truism became legendary in the minds of my United and Celtic pals, often destroying any pleasure they might have got from their narrow wins.† But today for the first time ever, it let me down. This time, not even to Celtic or United; this time, for

* From early September in season 1982/83 Aberdeen had lost 19 of their 20 league defeats either 1-0 or 2-1. Only Celtic had beaten us by a margin of two, and no one had scored three against us in competitive football for almost half a decade. Our defence was, in a word, 'shit-hot'.
† Twelve of the 20 defeats over the glory years came at the hands of Celtic and United, six each.

the first time in my memory, we'd lost like this to Rangers. Dad's footsteps start making their way upstairs, on his way to see me from the garage, having been briefed by Mum no doubt about what I'd done.

'Fit's gan on min?' barks Dad assertively from outside my room. I say 'barks', but I knew from his tone that he is only doing this to give my mum the impression that he meant business. He comes in, closes the door and collapses backwards on to the end of my bed, holding his head in his hands.

'Two-nil to Rangers, it disna get ony worse, dis it?' he commented. 'But listen min, 'at's nae excuse for takin' it oot on the radio in the kitchen?' I lay in silence.

'Mum's so upset that she's saying we shouldna be goin' to ony mair fitba 'is year,' he pleads.

'What's the point Dad?'

He raises his head, turned and looked at me, his jaw gaping making him look a bit gormless. 'Fit d'ye mean, what's the point?'

'Losing to United again, beaten by Celtic in the League Cup, losing to Hearts at home again and now losing to Rangers? Five points off the top of the table? We're almost out of the title race and it's not even winter!' Dad looks away, screwing his eyes up. He knew it was true. 'I mean, it's even worse than last year, if that's possible,' I say out of the side of my mouth with my face buried in my pillow. 'What is the point in going to the football if this is what it is going to be like?' Dad turns slowly and looked at me, with a puzzled, searching look.

'I mean I still want to go like Dad,' I add, putting my hand up to shore up any doubt he might still have, '... but it's just hopeless, isn't it.'

'Aye, ah ken,' he said.

He still stared at me for a second, as if he was trying to read what I was really thinking, before standing up, opening and closing my door firmly and going downstairs. Deep down, I'd quite happily stop going to games, but I was far from being able to speak to him about this. There were other things I could do with my Saturdays. My new mates, Andy, Pete, Heid, none of whom had a football-mad dad to worry about, were going to fewer and fewer games, preferring to muck about in town on Saturdays, or go to places like Stirling or Dundee to muck about there too (under the guise of 'shopping'). But as I lay on my front, kicking from the knee into my bed, left then right, left then right, whether I went to the games or not would not affect the impact of this latest milestone of despair. Losing to Rangers would sting wherever I was. But this result was more than simply a defeat. On Monday morning, I had to face Andy Scott, by now our year-group's loudest Rangers fan, who'd bet me £1 that Rangers would win by a margin of two or more. It was payback time.

'Make way for Her Majesty's Glasgow Rangers!' he bellows hysterically towards me, as he swaggers along the 200-metre long concourse that ran under the main Perth High building. I already have my £1 note in my hand, ready to hand it over. I plan trying to argue that McCoist's goal, the second, all-important goal for my pride and for our bet, was blatantly offside – which, of course, we all knew. But before I'd even decided to open my mouth, he'd snatched the money out of my hand and walked on, without even as much as changing his stride, blanking me, saying nothing, and not looking back. And over the next ten days, more joke results allowed him and the ever-burgeoning ranks of Rangers fans (i.e. half the school), to punish me again and again for my years of boastings: out of the Cup-Winners' Cup in the first round to Swiss minnows Sion, losing 3-0 away (even worse that we destroyed them 11-1 on aggregate four years ago), and then worst of all, we shipped three goals to newly promoted Falkirk, who'd barely scored at all since arriving in the big league. Aberdeen's international class defence was left in tatters. So was I.

And then, on Thursday 5 November 1986, came the bomb-shell of all bombshells.

'Far aboot were you fan you heard the news?' asks John Leys, sitting next to us in the King Street End. Everyone here for the visit of St Mirren is talking about what happened two days before. They all know exactly where they were and what they were doing. And I mean 'exactly'. Some people were in shops along Union Street, others up ladders or visiting relatives in hospital, you'd have thought it was 9/11. And right enough it was no laughing matter. On Thursday 5 November 1986, Alex Ferguson resigned as manager of Aberdeen to take up the Manchester United job. It was the biggest bombshell to hit Aberdeen for donkeys. Or at least since a doodlebug crashed into Aberdeen ice rink during the Second World War, as I'd heard some old comedian come away with in the rows behind us.* I don't think I'd ever heard so much shite talked in all my life. And now, here was Dad about to come away with some more.

'Weel, I wis jist comin' in tae Methven, five miles oot o' Perth.' Here we go again. 'An fan the newscaster finished his sentence wi' "Ferguson awa' tae Man United," I thought my jaw hid smashed a' the wey through the chassis o' the car on to the tarmac! I wis sae shocked that I almost run into the back o' the car in front, and so I hid tae swerve oot into the middle o' the road, endin' up screechin' sideways a' the wey through the village.' Oh really Dad? I thought. I'd now heard his account at least 50 times and it kept getting more dramatic. It was actually all Granda's fault. He just happened to be down

* It was actually a German Heinkel bomber that crashed into the ice rink, not a V-1 bomb.

in Perth on the day the news of Fergie's departure for Man United broke. He'd been sitting in the lounge when Dad came home, and was the first person Dad had a chance to speak to about it. I don't think I ever saw my Granda so amused about anything. So much so, that he inadvertently egged Dad on to even claim that he'd actually caused a pile-up in the village in that particular version. Granda went on and on about it for years, literally years afterwards. It was another eye-opening indication that highlighted just how removed Granda was from what really mattered. This incident for him was entirely about my dad's slapstick, not Aberdeen's fate, Fergie or what was going to happen to us now, good or bad. And Granda's reaction to it had Dad feeling like he'd just discovered a career on the stage. Maybe, it was my dad's way of dealing with the magnitude of what we'd lost.

That Thursday though, when I came home and Granda was having a snooze, I found a different Dad in the kitchen. 'It's finished min!' Dad spat from the far end of the breakfast bar, sitting in front of a cup of coffee, staring out of the window and scratching his throat pensively. 'How could he dee 'is tae us, min? Aifter a'thin?' I stared at his face, he looked so let down, so cheated. He was upset all right. Little did I know at the time but Dad was in the first few hours of a strop with Fergie that would run for the rest of his life.* I'd rarely seen him as upset. It was now my turn to play dad. I had to buck him back up.

'Fuck 'im Dad!' I exclaimed, with some much needed swearing (my mum and sister were out somewhere). 'Fuck 'im!' I reinforce, thrusting out with a pointed finger. 'We don't need Fergie and we've still got our best players Dad? Miller, McLeish, Leighton, Simpson, they're still here, aren't they?'

* It also explains a curious interest he'd come to show in Arsenal throughout the 1990s and 2000s.

Dad swings his head away to look out the window again, in a way that told me that I wasn't on his wavelength. I most certainly was *not* on his wavelength. I saw Fergie's resignation in a totally different light. I was actually excited, enthused at the idea of a fresh start.

'Come on Dad, we'll get someone else. Things couldn't get much worse, could they?'

Dad stares at me, expressionless. He says nothing. He'd eventually snap out of it, I thought. I turned and bounded upstairs, buoyed and convinced that this was a change for good. Three weeks later, Aberdeen appointed the little known figure of Ian Porterfield as manager. For a couple of weeks, following his inaugural match in which we beat Rangers 1-0 at home, everything seemed OK. But soon the downward spiral was back and things were even worse than before.

Chapter 26

Rock Bottom

''At's a fuckin' disgrace, referee!' remonstrates Dad, part of a wall of violent, bitter outrage towards the ref from the whole ground. He has just red-carded Willie Miller. Willie Miller sent off. There were some things that were simply beyond the pale for us, and this one was almost unimaginable. We'd have been less upset if St Mirren had just scored their third goal.

'Yur a blint' fuckin' bastard referee!'

Dad and most of the other old timers sitting next to me are going as mental as I've seen them. As I look all around me, I can hear their desperation, their pain more loudly than ever. They seem to finally know that the game is up but they are still not admitting it. They are still begging the ref to reverse his decision (although not very politely). They are still praying for something to avert yet another clear statement that it was over, and that it was never coming back. They are still pretending that someone could put an end to the continual reinforcement of the fact that we were a shit team, an also-ran, and that an eternity of defeats against Central Belt dross stood before us, just like the one we're watching today. Just like it had for most of their years before the Ferguson era. By now though, I was almost past caring. Or so I was trying to convince myself.

As soon as the red card was displayed, a malignant smile crept over my face. I looked at our manager Porterfield and his odd-shaped head. He looked like a knob and he was a knob. How I despised him now. This was a knob who thought he could win our favour by crowing about his 15-match unbeaten run since taking charge. A run that came to an end with a defeat that knocked us out of the Scottish Cup one week, and another one that effectively killed off our title hopes the very next. That meant the competitive season had ended on my birthday – nothing to play for and it was only February. I'd bet good money I wasn't even born the last time we suffered a season as crap as this. But Porterfield was still crowing about it now, like it was a trophy we'd won, two months after it ended. I bet right now that he was probably planning his next 'Manager's Update' for the programme, licking his lips at the opportunity the sending off would give him to blame the ref for us failing to perform. As Miller eventually leaves the field, and the old guys are still up, firing off at the ref for daring to send Miller off, I noticed that something was up with Timothy. He was one of two friends that Dad and I had been taking to the games that season, sitting next to me on my right (the other one was called Graeme). He'd gone quite pink, and kept darting confused grimaces at the dozens of irate old timers all lambasting the ref around us … I should have known it … He doesn't agree … he doesn't agree. He thinks Miller *should* be sent off.

'Oh come on!' Timothy exclaims, looking round towards one guy right behind him, 'It was clearly a second yellow card!' Oh my God … I do not believe my ears … 'He had to go, it was a definite sending off!' He shouts, loud and clear, with his clean Perth accent (with an inexplicable hint of Berkshire). I catch Graeme's cringing eye, looking over towards me fearfully. This was Willie Miller he was talking about … this was a moment like at a funeral, where you had to say nothing, show your respect (unless you were attacking the ref). Did he not get anything?

'Hey min, Miller could a chopped 'at cunt up wi' an axe and still shouldna been sent aff!' bellows an older Dons fan from three rows behind us. This was exactly what Timothy needed to hear: a perfect, albeit ridiculous metaphor to get it through his thick head that he was being a complete arse. Willie Miller should never, ever be sent off.

'Fa's side are you on?' shout numerous others at him. By now his face was going from pink to crimson. All of a sudden, he stands up and starts pushing his way stroppily along our row to the passageway. He was no doubt getting up to go to the toilets to bubble on his own. As he wrestled his way to the stairwell, Dad stood up concerned about where he was going.

'I hope he gets a smack in the face on his way!' I snarled quietly in Dad's ear.

'Now min!' grumbled Dad at me under his breath as he decides he should make his way to follow Timothy to the toilets.

'Och it would serve him right!' I said. Dad tutted and shook his head, before following the gangling Timothy as he stumbled up the steps, head down trying to mask his hissy fit.

As much as I tried to deny it, I knew I was as devastated as the rest of them about Miller's sending off, but I'm allowing myself to believe it was really Timothy's reaction that was annoying me. This was just another one of the many things he was capable of that really wound me up. I hated how he'd bounce on his toes when we'd score, tamely raise his arms in the air, cheeping, 'Hurray! Hurray!' No one said 'Hurray' at a football match. It made me think of my Primary 7 school pantomime outing to watch Attarah's Band when the sappy kids responded to the repeated appearance of the Pink Panther on the stage. I hated how after Dad would rip into the ref, roaring and remonstrating like an enraged Jurassic carnivore, Timothy would often go quiet, and look disapprovingly across at Dad once his tirade had finished. Graeme had told me that he'd complained to his own dad about his language, even describing him as an 'animal'. Timothy was a square beyond help and a bad faith one at that.

But if I'm really honest with myself, it ran deeper than even this. Timothy and Graeme simply depressed me because they hammered home to me how disgruntled I'd become with football. For them, simply getting to see Aberdeen, Miller and McLeish, Simpson, Weir got them buzzed up. Even to the extent that they could watch us lose 1-0 at home to Hearts or draw 0-0 at home to Hamilton, but still be able to spend the entire car journey home enthusiastically dissecting the tactical merits of playing Angus behind the midfield, Bryan Mitchell's wing-back efforts or Davie Robertson's pace. Meanwhile, I'd sit in silence in the front seat, sometimes snapping at them to shut up, a defeat was a defeat. If I were even more honest with myself, I'd far rather be at home, hanging about in Perth town centre with my new mates. But I still wasn't ready to admit this.

Now that I had mates like Andy Scott and Ally Downie, my 'Boo Radley' days were finally over. Ally was Andy's old mate from the Academy and they were the first mates I had who seemed to be both bright – like my square mates – but also had an edge. They were interested in music and seemed to be well enough connected to the nutters of Perth to protect me from any anti-Aberdeen retribution I might otherwise face. But there were things we'd started doing that were even better. Andy or Ally, who both looked older than me, would buy Merrydown and Martini and we'd get pished up the South Inch or up the Resy, arse around there or go to someone's house if no parents were around. The problem was that I'd only been able to do this with them on a couple of occasions. This was because now that Dad had a new Cavalier 1.8 GLS, the best car we'd ever had, we were watching more football

than ever. No away ground posed a distance too insurmount-
able, even on Wednesday nights, for Dad and his new wheels.
I'd almost expected we'd be driving to the continent next
season for the first away game in the UEFA Cup.*

But, much as I thought about it, I still couldn't bring myself
to tell Dad that I didn't want to go to all the games. I couldn't
get past the guilt of stopping Dad from going since I reckoned he wouldn't go on his own. But right now, waiting for
Timothy and Dad to reappear, I'd reached rock bottom. And,
as I looked round at the moment when Timothy's square face,
wearing its gormless, exaggerated smile again (clearly not having
been smacked as I'd hoped), came bounding back down the
steps followed by Dad, the thought of more enthusiastic
wittering for the rest of the game told me it was time. Tonight,
on the way down the road, I should speak to Dad. Tonight
was the night. I'll tell him that in two weeks the boys and me
were going to Edinburgh, so I wouldn't be going to the
Clydebank game. That's what I'd do ... and then a gasp of
anticipation, a glimmer of hope on the pitch ...

The whole ground simultaneously breaks out of its indifferent hubbub, rising in unison as Peter Weir flashes up the
left wing, just like he used to ... he hits the byline, crosses
perfectly, while the ball is mid-air my imagination runs ahead,
visualising a thumping header that hits the top corner ...
1-1 ... then we'll maybe get some news from Ibrox that
Motherwell have scored twice and now lead 2-1, we go on
and score two late screamers ourselves, our form changes, we
topple Rangers to go top in a couple of weeks, we beat Rangers
here in May and win the league! In the event, Irvine rises to

* Our standards were maybe below par, but there was never any doubt
about qualifying for Europe. It was as guaranteed as a victory playing
Dundee at Dens Park. Many seasons would come and go before this would
be in the balance.

head, it flies two yards over the bar ... I slump back into my seat. It was never coming back. That was it. I'd decided. I was speaking to Dad in the car about the Clydebank game. Definitely.

'Dad?' I said, clearing my throat breaking the unusual silence of our journey home.

'Aye?'

'You know the Saturday of the Clydebank game?' I pronounce, pretending to casually look out of the window.

'Aye.'

'Well ...'

'At's right, Clydebank in two wiks, I'd forgotten aboot 'at,' interrupts Dad. 'Are you two up for the Clydebank match?' asks Dad, looking to the back seat in his mirror.

'Yes please Mr Donald!' chirps up Timothy obsequiously. My God! I couldn't believe it. How had this happened? As I sat stunned, something was telling me that this didn't work either. I mean, how could I go to Edinburgh with Andy and Ally now? I ran my hands up around my ears as I realised there was no way I could go to Edinburgh. Not with Timothy at Pittodrie in my shoes ... with my dad. My head started to shake involuntarily in disbelief at my predicament.

'You a'right min?' asks Dad, picking up on the palpable anguish coming from me in the passenger seat.

'Yeah, yeah, fine,' I confirm. I was anything but. The force of habit of a lifetime of football with Dad, the loyalty I felt to him was still too strong. I wondered if I would ever be free of it. Staring at Timothy in the wing mirror all the way home, I tried desperately to find a way to make his excruciatingly annoying face help me to just get over it. So what if Timothy and Graeme went with Dad to games? So what if I wasn't there? But much as I tried, I just couldn't bring myself to do it. I realised I was trapped.

And so it was. We all went to the Clydebank game. We all went to the Motherwell game away and the Hearts game away. Our pointless season would climax with the visit of Rangers in May, which turned out to be the worst football match experience in my life (still to date), which saw them win the league, at Pittodrie. Over the summer though, my new mate Ally would start paving the way for me to leave it all behind, once and for all.

Chapter 27

Woolies

'Come on Duck, you know it makes sense,' says Ally, almost knocking over an old lady as we passed by the pick 'n' mix counter, in his insistence to seal my commitment to the Woolworths job. As we started our walk home through town in the August evening sunshine, I knew this was coming. He'd been working there over the summer and on Saturdays for over a year now and had organised the interview for me. As far as he was concerned, there was only one answer. But I just couldn't commit to it like that.

'I mean, what is there to think about?' snaps Ally again, now incapable of containing his frustration, tutting and shaking his head, my silence irritating him more and more. I knew why he was so bothered. He'd spent the whole of yesterday evening, and most of the summer, selling me the job and I had been making the right noises.

It all sounded fantastic. It had a massive stockroom the length of a football pitch with a labyrinth of passageways and stock bins. Apparently, you could disappear into it for hours, to prepare ambushes the other Saturday kids or just skive if you couldn't be arsed. The sales floor was predominantly staffed by middle-aged women to whom Ally had successfully sold himself as an adorable sort of nephew character. This meant that they were quite happy to take guidance from him about things like the cash desk rota. As a result, Ally had managed to make sure that he never went on a till, ensuring that the younger kids got 'as much till experience as possible' so Ally could 'supervise'. 'Awright Ally,' they'd dotingly agree. 'He's an awfy bright boy that Ally,' I'd heard them comment on the numerous occasions over the summer when I'd hung around the middle cash desk, the centre of Woolies shop-floor control, waiting for Ally to finish work. They didn't know the half of it.

More important than anything, there was the money you could earn. According to Ally, an eight-hour shift on Saturdays plus a four-hour stint on double time on a Sunday could earn you an amazing £32, meaning you could make more over the weekend than our mate Andy, who was on a Youth Training Scheme (YTS), could earn through the entire week (£28). This was a stat that Ally would regularly bring up, to Andy's disgust, especially since Ally was a full-time student otherwise. But what was missing for Ally was a partner in crime. Someone who could be relied upon to coordinate the till rotas, someone prepared to skive for hours, with whom to organise the stockroom ambushes and other pranks, someone with whom to build a wise-guy empire. And that was me, so he had decided. And to be fair to him, so had I last night, when it all seemed so attractive. But that was last night and right now, in the cold light of day, there was some-thing else I'd somehow managed to overlook – football and Dad.

'Look, let me speak to my dad about it first, right?'

'What?' rasps Ally stopped in his tracks momentarily. 'You're not thinking about going back to the games again?' rages Ally. I stop too, frowning back at him. I couldn't believe it.

'Where did this come from? I mean you've spent the whole summer whingeing about how hellish it is.' He hadn't under-stood a thing. Maybe I *had* spent the whole summer talking about it, maybe I had spent hours going over the fact that our

form had been worse than ever, that we'd finished the season
with a whimper, well behind Rangers who won the league.
But surely he realised that this didn't necessarily mean you
didn't want to go back?

'And what about all that stuff the Rangers fans did to your
ground you've been bleating on about?'

'Bleating?' I baulk. How could he use a word like that to
describe that day, the day Rangers won the league at Pittodrie
back in May. In other words, the worst day, the most awful
day, the most hideous day of my life.

'Who on earth would want to go back for more of that?'
Still standing in the middle of the pavement causing pedes-
trian traffic jams, our silent stand-off continued, although now
I'm shaking my head slowly, realising, not for the first time,
that this was the problem with non-football guys like Ally.
They just didn't get it.

If ever there was a reason to keep going to football, if
ever there was a cause never to stop going, it was to avenge
what happened that day. The ever-present memories flood
back through my mind. The moment the shocking news from
Parkhead, that Celtic had just gone down 2-1 to Falkirk,
spread like wildfire around the South Stand, the King Street
End, the Main Stand, revealing to my horror just how many
Rangers fans had sneaked into our parts of the ground that
day. News that confirmed that, if the score stayed at 1-1 in
Aberdeen, Rangers would be champions in minutes. In that
moment, it felt like a home game for them ... in my ground!
My house! But this was only the start. As they grew in confidence and the final whistle neared, they all gradually stand
up, start shaking hands, leaning over us in the rows behind
to hug each other, as if we, the resident, we the indigenous
Dons fans were simply not there. And then as a result, when
for the first time in history Dad decided we'd leave early, it
just got worse and worse. Squeezing past the revellers, some

of them in the rows above and below us feel confident to sing us off, 'Cheer-io, cheer-io,' right into our faces, waving their arms inches above our heads. One of those guys even skelped my head in a drunken lunge which caused me to throw caution to the wind, daring in that moment to stare angrily, provocatively, at an Old Firm supporter for the first time in my life.

'Stuart!' shouted Dad anxiously from behind me. I stood my ground. I was up for it. And just when my high noon moment was about to come to something, the final whistle went and all hell broke loose. We stood rooted to the spot as they burst on to our pitch. My hands automatically rose to cover my face as they mounted and tore down our Beach End goal, they hacked into and ripped up our turf, our special, our sacred turf, and ripped out our red South Stand seats at the far end, to then stand brandishing them at us like trophies. How I turned to Dad, how we'd looked at each other, speechless, helpless, his face more crumpled, more defeated, sadder than I'd ever known it. And then, as if to applaud this act, as if to approve of it, Souness and the players reappeared, carried shoulder high in among the fans on the pitch, trampling over our now felled goalposts, smiling, cheering, singing, joining in the destruction of our home. And no one did anything. No casuals, no police, nobody.

'Come on, you've been saying it all summer, you know you can't compete with the Old Firm now,' he cocked his head and made a 'have to be pragmatic, mate' sort of face.

'Look we did it before, we'll do it again!' I blurt back at him, pointing assertively into his chest. Ally sighs and looks away, sensing this was not the line of argument to take.

'Come on Duck, you need to get your life back on track, get away from all this grief. Look at what it's doing to you.'

I tut loudly and turn away from him to start back, walking up the road.

'What about your mates, and your Granda too?' Ally adds. 'He's gettin' on nowadays mate.'

I sigh long and hard again. This was true. I'd fallen out with my grandad badly back in May, a couple of weeks after Rangers had desecrated our ground, and still hadn't spoken to him yet. But no wonder. He had teamed up with our two Rangers fan mates, Peg Bain and Andy Scott, when I'd been having a go at them for doing a Loyalist march up our drive to wind me up, pacing on the spot, rattling their tongues off the roofs of their mouths before singing the full three verses of 'God Save the Queen' at me through the lounge window. We spent much of our time arguing about this, but I didn't need my Granda involved, certainly not on the side of our new number one enemy. When he started giving me the 'Queen and country' lines, Peg and Andy were falling over themselves trying to shake hands with him, I fell out with all of them there and then, barred the Rangers fans from our house and told my mum to banish my Granda too. As a result, for the past two months, we'd stopped talking.

'Can't go on mate. Can't do it,' says Ally, reinforcing his point. It was worse than that though. There were things I'd done I hadn't told anyone about. In a peak of rage one night, I'd destroyed every single Rangers programme I had, even my dad's ancient ones from the 1960s. As I walked, I knew he was right. This was ridiculous. I needed out and Woolies would be the perfect escape route. I just needed to check one other thing.

'Is there a radio anywhere in Woolies?'

'Of course there is!' said Ally immediately. 'Several in fact. And mate …' adds Ally with a cheeky glint in his eye, '… you know what else there is in Woolies … talent!' That was true, and there were already a couple of extremely good-looking girls I'd noticed earlier that day, right enough. 'You'll no get that at the football.' That was true also. That was it. I'd decided. I wouldn't wait to speak to Dad, in case I lost my nerve again. I was ready.

'Right,' I sigh. 'Let's do it.'

We pick up our pace and march for the rest of the way to my house, Ally now silent, concerned not to interfere with my focus. We arrive at the house and walk through to the kitchen. Ally lifts the phone off the wall, hands me the receiver and dials Woolies' number. I eventually get a hold of John Bain, the manager, and confirm I'm taking the job.

'Well done mate, you know it makes sense,' Ally says as I replaced the receiver calmly. I smile back, relieved finally to have made a decision one way or another. Now all I had to do was face Dad. No sooner was the phone down than I heard the front door open and close before he paused to check his mail in the hall. We listen in silence to the rustling paper, as one, then two then three envelopes are fingered open with even tears. I glance once at Ally when the footsteps pick up, indicating that he is making his way through to the kitchen.

'Look fit came the day!' says an extremely upbeat Dad, holding up two heavy cardboard booklets in his right hand as he strides through the dining room. I could feel the blood draining from my face as Dad continued beaming at me, his broad smile now filling the room, amplified by the mid-afternoon sunshine streaming in through the window. Jesus. He'd bought season tickets! As a surprise! All I can do is stare in horror at the booklets in his hand.

'Will ye be happy gan back tae the Main Stand min?' utters Dad. 'Fan he wis a little loon he didna like the Main Stand,' says Dad chortling towards Ally, who did a strained grin back and a single drawn out nod. 'He made me tak him to the Beach End, d'ye mine 'at min?' he asks.

I stood with my arms folded and swallowed hard, unable to answer.

'Fit's wrang?' says Dad, realising something's up.

'Dad,' I stop. How do I tell him? '... Em, I've just got a job in Woolies. Today. Working on Saturdays like ...'

'Oh right?' Dad said looking at me, trying to play down his shock.

'But Dad, you never said ... '

'At's OK, 'at's OK,' he says, his hands dampening towards the ground reassuringly, but looking at me vacantly. 'Look, nae problem. Em ... I'll spik tae Geordie ... Aye, he'll come, aye, 'at's fine.'

He stared at the ground for a couple of seconds, picked up the season tickets, turned and went through to the study, leaving me and Ally with just the boiling kettle breaking our silence.

'You did well son,' says Ally with a cheeky wink.

'Just go mate.' Ally too stood for a second, before realising he had to go. Dad continued shuffling papers around in his study and I eventually went upstairs to my room, realising he wasn't coming back through. As I sat down on the ground with a lump in my throat, my programme collection in a pile by the bed stared back at me. They'd sat there the whole summer, so I could lose myself programme by programme in the nostalgia, the buzz, the hope of the great days. Right now, there was one poking out of the side that I recognised just from the nose and moustache of Andy Watson, one of Dad's favourites. I pull it out to reveal Neil Simpson and Neale Cooper, slightly out of focus either side of Watson, all in red. It was the programme of the game Dad had tried to joke about when he'd brought in the season tickets. The day we first went to the Beach End because I was bored of the Main Stand. I remembered his beaming face, that glow of real hope, the famous Johnny Hewitt overhead kick to beat Celtic 1-0 in the Scottish Cup. That was the day it all really started, way back in February 1982. The victory that took us on the cup run and the watershed 4-1 Final against Rangers that led to our

Cup-Winners' Cup and Super Cup victories. It's never coming back, and now neither were we.

As I sat that fateful evening, staring wistfully at Andy Watson's profile on the front cover of my programme, my life away from football was about to begin. Within a couple of weeks, I would start getting used to organising my Saturdays around the stockroom radio at 4.30 (when I wasn't being ambushed). Geordie would gratefully take up Dad's offer of the season ticket. A number of years later, when the Dons as a real force were finally petering out and my life took me outside the reach of Radio Scotland, the stockroom radio would be replaced with teletext and internet cafes. And by the end of the 1990s when our form hit new depths, I'd get the scores wherever I was through 'goal texts' direct to my mobile phone (I stopped this in 2002 when a 7-0 rogering at Parkhead cost me almost a quid for the pleasure). But some things did not change. If truth be told, there's a big part of me that is still locked away in my bedroom that night, staring at that programme, still waiting, still expecting to get teleported back to that day, 13 February 1982, to watch my Aberdeen rise up, hammer the Old Firm all over the country, win the league, win it again and dominate the game at home and beyond.